Beginning Object-Oriented Programming with VB 2005

From Novice to Professional

Daniel R. Clark

Apress®

Beginning Object-Oriented Programming with VB 2005: From Novice to Professional

Copyright © 2006 by Daniel R. Clark

ISBN (pbk): 1-59059-576-9

Printed and bound in the United States of America 9 8 7 6 5 4 3 2 1

Lead Editor: Jonathan Hassell
Technical Reviewer: Jon Box
Editorial Board: Steve Anglin, Dan Appleman, Ewan Buckingham, Gary Cornell, Tony Davis, Jason Gilmore, Jonathan Hassell, Chris Mills, Dominic Shakeshaft, Jim Sumser
Project Manager: Beth Christmas
Copy Edit Manager: Nicole LeClerc
Copy Editors: Marilyn Smith and Ami Knox
Assistant Production Director: Kari Brooks-Copony
Production Editor: Janet Vail
Compositor: Kinetic Publishing Services, LLC
Proofreader: Christy Wagner
Indexer: Rebecca Plunkett
Artist: Kinetic Publishing Services, LLC
Cover Designer: Kurt Krames
Manufacturing Director: Tom Debolski

Distributed to the book trade worldwide by Springer-Verlag New York, Inc., 233 Spring Street, 6th Floor, New York, NY 10013. Phone 1-800-SPRINGER, fax 201-348-4505, e-mail orders-ny@springer-sbm.com, or visit http://www.springeronline.com.

For information on translations, please contact Apress directly at 2560 Ninth Street, Suite 219, Berkeley, CA 94710. Phone 510-549-5930, fax 510-549-5939, e-mail info@apress.com, or visit http://www.apress.com.

The source code for this book is available to readers at http://www.apress.com in the Source Code section.

Contents at a Glance

PART 4 ■■■ Appendixes

Contents

PART 1 ■■■ Object-Oriented Programming and Design Fundamentals

PART 2 ■ ■ ■ Object-Oriented Programming with Visual Basic

PART 3 ■■■ Developing Applications with Visual Basic

PART 4 ■ ■ ■ **Appendixes**

About the Author

DAN CLARK is a senior IT consultant specializing in .NET and SQL Server technologies. He is a Microsoft Certified Solution Developer and Microsoft Certified Database Administrator. For the past decade, he has been developing applications and training others how to develop applications using Microsoft technologies. Dan is a regular speaker at various developer conferences and user group meetings. He finds particular satisfaction in turning new developers on to the thrill of developing and designing object-oriented applications.

About the Technical Reviewer

As a Microsoft Regional Director and Chief Architect at ProTech Systems Group in Memphis, **JON BOX** serves as a .NET evangelist focused on delivering solutions and assisting developers to utilize .NET. Jon's current work emphasizes developing mobility solutions with Microsoft technologies, empowering software development with Visual Studio Team System, and building web sites with ASP.NET 2.0 and DotNetNuke. Being a presenter and a Microsoft MVP, Jon has given presentations at TechEd and MEDC, hosted MSDN web casts, spoken at various .NET user groups around the country, and serves on the INETA Speakers Bureau. Jon writes for the *.NET Developer's Journal*, coauthored *Building Solutions with the Microsoft .NET Compact Framework* with Dan Fox, and has a variety of mobility whitepapers on MSDN. Jon also is the cofounder and coleader of the Memphis .NET Users Group (www.memphisdot.net). You can see his current musings on technology at http://jonbox.dotnetdevelopersjournal.com.

Introduction

It has been my experience as a Visual Basic trainer that most people do not have trouble picking up the syntax of the language. What perplexes and frustrates many people are the higher-level concepts of object-oriented programming methodology and design. To compound the problem, most introductory programming books and training classes skim over these concepts or, worse, do not cover them at all. It is my hope that this book fills this void. My goal in writing this book is twofold. First, to provide you with the information needed to understand the fundamentals of programming with Visual Basic. Second and more importantly, to present you with the information required to master the higher-level concepts of object-oriented programming methodology and design.

This book provides you with the information needed to understand how you go about architecting an object-oriented programming solution aimed at solving a business problem. As you work your way through the book, first you will learn how to analyze the business requirements. Next, you will model the objects and relationships involved in the solution design. Finally, you will implement the solution using Visual Basic .NET. Along the way, you will learn the fundamentals of software design, the Unified Modeling Language (UML), object-oriented programming, Visual Basic (VB), and the .NET Framework.

Because this is an introductory book, it is meant to be a starting point for your study of the topics presented. As such, this book is *not* designed to make you an expert in object-oriented programming and UML; nor be an exhaustive discussion of VB and the .NET Framework; nor be an in-depth study of Visual Studio. It takes considerable time and effort to become proficient in any one of these areas. It is my hope that by reading this book, your first experiences in object-oriented programming will be enjoyable, comprehensible, and instill a desire for further study.

Target Audience

The target audience for this book is the beginning VB programmer who wants to gain a foundation in object-oriented programming along with the VB language basics. Programmers transitioning from a procedural-oriented programming model to an object-oriented model will also benefit from this book. In addition, there are many pre-.NET VB programmers who do not have a firm grasp of object-oriented programming. Now is the time to become acquainted with the fundamentals of object-oriented programming before transitioning to the current version of VB and the .NET Framework. Because the experience level of a "beginner" can vary immensely, I have included a primer in Appendix A, which discusses some basic programming tenets. I would suggest you review these concepts if you are new to programming.

Organization of the Book

This book is organized into three parts:

Part 1 delves into object-oriented programming methodology and design—concepts that transcend a particular programming language. The concepts presented are important to the success of an object-oriented programming solution regardless of the implementation language chosen. At the conclusion of this part, a case study walks you through modeling a "real-world" application.

Part 2 looks at how object-oriented programming is implemented in Visual Basic. You will look at creating class structures, creating hierarchies, and implementing interfaces. This part also introduces object interaction and collaboration. You will see how the object-oriented programming topics discussed in Part 1 are transformed into Visual Basic coding constructs.

Part 3 returns to the case study introduced and modeled at the end of Part 1. Using the knowledge gained in Part 2, you will transform the design into a fully functional VB application. This includes designing a graphical user interface, implementing the business logic, and integrating with a relational database to store data. Along the way you will be exposed to the .NET Framework classes used to work with data, and see how to create a Windows-based user interface, a Web-based user interface, and a Web service-based programmatic interface.

Activities and Software Requirements

One of the most important aspects of learning is doing. You cannot learn to ride a bike without jumping on a bike, and you cannot learn to program without "cranking out" code. Any successful training program needs to include both a theory component and a hands-on component. I have included both components throughout this book. It is my hope that you will take these activities seriously and work through them thoroughly and even repeatedly. Contrary to some students' perception that these activities are "exercises in typing," this is where the theory becomes concrete and true simulation of the concepts occurs. I also encourage you to play during the activities. Do not be afraid to alter some of the code just to see what happens. Some of the best learning experiences occur when students "color outside the lines."

You can download the starter files referred to in this book from the Apress Web site at www.apress.com. The UML modeling activities in Part 1 are for someone using Objecteering's UML Modeler. I chose this program because of its simple user interface and the fact it can be downloaded for free at www.objecteering.com. You do not need a CASE tool to complete these activities; a paper and pencil will work just fine. You can also use another CASE tool such as Visio to complete the activities. The activities in Part 2 require Visual Studio 2005 with Visual Basic installed. I encourage you to install the help files and make ample use of them while completing the activities. The activities in Part 3 require Microsoft SQL Server 2000 or 2005 with the Pubs and Northwind databases installed. Appendix C includes instructions on downloading and installing the sample databases. You can find a trial edition of both Visual Studio 2005 and SQL Server 2005 at www.msdn.microsoft.com.

■**Note** The web addresses mentioned are subject to change without notice. Check the Apress site (www.apress.com) for any updates.

PART 1

Object-Oriented Programming and Design Fundamentals

■ ■ ■

CHAPTER 1

Overview of Object-Oriented Programming

To set the stage for your study of object-oriented programming and Visual Basic, this chapter will briefly look at the history of object-oriented programming and the characteristics of an object-oriented programming language. You will look at why object-oriented programming has become so important in the development of industrial-strength distributed software systems. You will also examine how Visual Basic has evolved into one of the leading business application programming languages.

After reading this chapter, you will be familiar with the following:

- What object-oriented programming is

- Why object-oriented programming has become so important in the development of industrial-strength applications

- The characteristics that make a programming language object-oriented

- The history and evolution of Visual Basic

What Is OOP?

Object-oriented programming (OOP) is an approach to software development in which the structure of the software is based on *objects* interacting with each other to accomplish a task. This interaction takes the form of messages passing back and forth between the objects. In response to a message, an object can perform an action, or *method*.

If you look at how you accomplish tasks in the world around you, you can see that you interact in an object-oriented world. If you want to go to the store, for example, you interact with a car object. A car object consists of other objects that interact with each other to accomplish the task of getting you to the store. You put the key in the ignition object and turn it. This, in turn, sends a message (through an electrical signal) to the starter object, which interacts with the engine object to start the car. As a driver, you are isolated from the logic of how the objects of the system work together to start the car. You just initiate the sequence of events by executing the start method of the ignition object with the key. You then wait for a response (message) of success or failure.

Similarly, users of software programs are isolated from the logic needed to accomplish a task. For example, when you print a page in your word processor, you initiate the action by clicking a print button. You are isolated from the internal processing that needs to occur; you just wait for a response telling you if it printed. Internally, the button object interacts with a printer object, which interacts with the printer to accomplish the task of printing the page.

OOP concepts started surfacing in the mid-1960s with a programming language called Simula and further evolved in the 1970s with advent of Smalltalk. Although software developers did not overwhelmingly embrace these early advances in OOP languages, object-oriented methodologies continued to evolve. A resurgence of interest in object-oriented methodologies occurred in the mid-1980s. Specifically, OOP languages such as C++ and Eifle became popular with mainstream computer programmers. OOP continued to grow in popularity in the 1990s, most notably with the advent of Java and the huge following it attracted. And in 2002, in conjunction with the release of the .NET Framework, Microsoft introduced a new OOP language, C# (pronounced *C-sharp*) and revamped Visual Basic so that it is truly an OOP language.

Why Use OOP?

Why has OOP developed into such a widely used paradigm for solving business problems today? During the 1970s and 1980s, procedural-oriented programming languages such as C, Pascal, and Fortran were widely used to develop business-oriented software systems. Procedural languages organize the program in a linear fashion—they run from top to bottom. In other words, the program is a series of steps that run one after another. This type of programming worked fine for small programs that consisted of a few hundred code lines, but as programs became larger, they became hard to manage and debug.

In an attempt to manage the ever-increasing size of the programs, structured programming was introduced to break down the code into manageable segments called *functions* or *procedures*. This was an improvement, but as programs performed more complex business functionality and interacted with other systems, the shortcomings of structural programming methodology began to surface:

- Programs became harder to maintain.

- Existing functionality was hard to alter without adversely affecting all of the system's functionality.

- New programs were essentially built from scratch. Consequently, there was little return on the investment of previous efforts.

- Programming was not conducive to team development. Programmers needed to know every aspect of how a program worked and could not isolate their efforts on one aspect of a system.

- It was hard to translate business models into programming models.

- It worked well in isolation but did not integrate well with other systems.

In addition to these shortcomings, some evolutions of computing systems caused further strain on the structural program approach:

- Nonprogrammers demanded and were given direct access to programs through the incorporation of graphical user interfaces and their desktop computers.

- Users demanded a more-intuitive, less-structured approach to interacting with programs.

- Computer systems evolved into a distributed model where the business logic, user interface, and backend database were loosely coupled and accessed over the Internet and intranets.

As a result, many business software developers turned to object-oriented methodologies and programming languages to solve these problems. The benefits included the following:

- A more intuitive transition from business analysis models to software implementation models

- The ability to maintain and implement changes in the programs more efficiently and rapidly

- The ability to more effectively create software systems using a team process, allowing specialists to work on parts of the system

- The ability to reuse code components in other programs and purchase components written by third-party developers to increase the functionality of programs with little effort

- Better integration with loosely coupled distributed computing systems

- Improved integration with modern operating systems

- The ability to create a more intuitive graphical user interface for the users

The Characteristics of OOP

In this section, you are going to look at the some fundamental concepts and terms common to all OOP languages. Do not worry about how these concepts get implemented in any particular programming language; that will come later. My goal is to merely familiarize you with the concepts and relate them to your everyday experiences in such a way that they make more sense later when you look at OOP design and implementation.

Objects

As I noted earlier, we live in an object-oriented world. You are an object. You interact with other objects. To write this book I am interacting with a computer object. When I woke up this morning, I was responding to a message sent out by an alarm clock object. In fact, you are an object with data such as height and hair color. You also have methods that you perform or are performed on you—for example, eating and walking.

So what are objects? In OOP terms, an *object* is a structure for incorporating data and the procedures for working with that data. For example, if you were interested in tracking data associated with products in inventory, you would create a product object that is responsible for maintaining and working with the data pertaining to the products. If you wanted to have printing capabilities in your application, you would work with a printer object that is responsible for the data and methods used to interact with your printers.

Abstraction

When you interact with objects in the world, you are often concerned with only a subset of their properties. Without this ability to abstract or filter out the extraneous properties of objects, you would find it hard to process the plethora of information bombarding you and concentrate on the task at hand.

As a result of *abstraction*, when two different people interact with the same object, they often deal with a different subset of attributes. When I drive my car, for example, I need to know the speed of the car and the direction it is going. Because the car is an automatic, I do not need to know the RPMs of the engine, so I filter this information out. On the other hand, this information would be critical to a racecar driver, who would not filter it out.

When constructing objects in OOP applications, it is important to incorporate this concept of abstraction. If you were building a shipping application, you would construct a product object with attributes such as size and weight. The color of the item would be extraneous information and filtered out. On the other hand, when constructing an order-entry application, the color could be important and would be included as an attribute of the product object.

Encapsulation

Another important feature of OOP is *encapsulation*. Encapsulation is the process in which no direct access is granted to the data; instead, it is hidden. If you want to gain access to the data, you must interact with the object responsible for the data. In the previous inventory example, if you wanted to view or update information on the products, you would need to work through the product object. To read the data, you would send the product object a message. The product object would then read the value and send back a message telling you what the value is. The product object defines what operations can be performed on the product data. If you send a message to modify the data and the product object determines it is a valid request, it will perform the operation for you and send a message back with the result.

You experience encapsulation in your daily life all the time. Think about a human resources department. The human resources staff members encapsulate (hide) the information about employees. They determine how this data can be used and manipulated. Any request for the employee data or request to update the data must be routed through them. Another example is network security. Any request for the security information or a change to a security policy must be made through a network security administrator. The security data is encapsulated from the users of the network.

By encapsulating data, you make the data of your system more secure and reliable. You know how the data is being accessed and what operations are being performed on the data. This makes program maintenance much easier and also greatly simplifies the debugging process. You can also modify the methods used to work on the data, and if you do not alter how the method is requested and the type of response sent back, then you do not need to alter the other objects using the method. Think about when you send a letter in the mail. You make a request to the post office to deliver the letter. How the post office accomplishes this is not exposed to you. If it changes the route it uses to mail the letter, it does not affect how you initiate the sending of the letter. You do not need to know the post office's internal procedures used to deliver the letter.

Polymorphism

Polymorphism is the ability of two different objects to respond to the same request message in their own unique way. For example, I could train my dog to respond to the command "bark" and my bird to respond to the command "chirp." On the other hand, I could train them to both respond to the command "speak." Through polymorphism, I know that the dog will respond with a bark and the bird will respond with a chirp.

How does this relate to OOP? You can create objects that respond to the same message in their own unique implementations. For example, you could send a print message to a printer object that would print the text on a printer, and you could send the same message to a screen object that would print the text to a window on your computer screen.

Another good example of polymorphism is the use of words in the English language. Words have many different meanings, but through the context of the sentence, you can deduce which meaning is intended. You know that someone who says, "Give me a break!" is not asking you to break his leg!

In OOP, you implement this type of polymorphism through a process called *overloading*. You can implement different methods of an object that have the same name. The object can then tell which method to implement depending on the context (in other words, the number and type of arguments passed) of the message. For example, you could create two methods of an inventory object to look up the price of a product. Both of these methods would be named getPrice. Another object could call this method and pass either the name of the product or the product ID. The inventory object could tell which getPrice method to run by whether a string value or an integer value was passed with the request.

Inheritance

Most objects are classified according to hierarchies. For example, you can classify all dogs together as having certain common characteristics, such as having four legs and fur. Their breeds further classify them into subgroups with common attributes, such as size and demeanor. You also classify objects according to their function. For example, there are commercial vehicles and recreational vehicles. There are trucks and passenger cars. You classify cars according to their make and model. To make sense of the world, you need to use object hierarchies and classifications.

You use *inheritance* in OOP to classify the objects in your programs according to common characteristics and function. This makes working with the objects easier and more intuitive. It also makes programming easier, because it enables you to combine general characteristics into a parent object and inherit these characteristics in the child objects. For example, you can define an employee object that defines all the general characteristics of employees in your company. You can then define a manager object that inherits the characteristics of the employee object but also adds characteristics unique to managers in your company. The manager object will automatically reflect any changes in the implementation of the employee object.

Aggregation

Aggregation is when an object consists of a composite of other objects that work together. For example, your lawn mower object is a composite of the wheel objects, the engine object, the blade object, and so on. In fact, the engine object is a composite of many other objects. There are many examples of aggregation in the world around us. The ability to use aggregation in OOP is a powerful feature that enables you to accurately model and implement business processes in your programs.

The History of Visual Basic

By most accounts, you can trace the origins of Visual Basic to Alan Cooper, an independent software vendor. In the late 1980s, Cooper was developing a shell construction kit called Tripod. What made Tripod unique was it incorporated a visual design tool that enabled developers to design their Windows interfaces by dragging and dropping controls onto it. Using a visual design tool hid a lot of the complexity of the Windows Application Programming Interface (API) from the developer. The other innovation associated with Tripod was the extensible model it offered programmers. Programmers could develop custom controls and incorporate them into the Tripod development environment. Up to this point, development tools were, for the most part, closed environments that could not be customized.

Microsoft paid Cooper for the development of Tripod and renamed it Ruby. Although Microsoft never released Ruby as a shell construction kit, it incorporated its form engine with the QuickBasic programming language and developed Thunder, one of the first rapid application development (RAD) tools for Windows programs. Thunder was renamed to Visual Basic, and Visual Basic 1.0 was introduced in the spring of 1991.

Visual Basic 1.0 became popular with business application developers because of its ease of use and its ability to rapidly develop prototype applications. Although Visual Basic 1.0 was an innovation in the design of Windows applications, it did not have built-in support for database interactivity. Microsoft realized this was a severe limitation and introduced native support for data access in the form of Data Access Objects (DAO) in Visual Basic 3.0. After the inclusion of native data support, the popularity of Visual Basic swelled. It transitioned from being a prototyping tool to being a tool used to develop industrial-strength business applications.

Microsoft has always been committed to developing the Visual Basic language and the Visual Basic integrated development environment (IDE). In fact, by many accounts, Bill Gates himself has taken an active interest in the development and growth of Visual Basic. At one point, the design team did not allow controls to be created and added to the Toolbox. When Bill Gates saw the product demo, he insisted that this extensibility be incorporated into the product. This extensibility brought on the growth of the custom control industry.

Third-party vendors began to market controls that made programming an application even easier for Visual Basic developers. For example, one vendor marketed a Resize control that encapsulated the code needed to resize a form and the controls the form contained. A developer could purchase this tool and add it to the Toolbox in the Visual Basic IDE. The developer could then simply drag the resize control onto the form, and the form and the controls it contained would resize proportionally.

By version 6.0, Visual Basic had evolved into a robust and industrial-strength programming language with an extremely large and dedicated developer base. Nevertheless, as strong as Visual Basic had become as a programming language, many programmers felt it had one major shortcoming. They considered Visual Basic to be an *object-like* programming language— not a true object-oriented programming language. Although Visual Basic 4.0 gave developers the ability to create classes and to package the classes in reusable components, Visual Basic did not incorporate basic OOP features such as inheritance and method overloading. Without these features, developers were severely limited in their ability to construct complex distributed software systems. Microsoft recognized these shortcomings and changed Visual Basic into a true OOP language with the release of Visual Basic .NET 1.0.

Since the .NET Framework's initial release in 2002, Microsoft has continued to improve and innovate it, along with the core languages built on top of the framework: C# and Visual Basic. Microsoft is also committed to providing .NET developers with the tools necessary to have a highly productive and intuitive programming experience.

With the release of Visual Basic 2005 and Visual Studio 2005, Microsoft has greatly enhanced both the language and the design-time developing experience for Visual Basic developers. As you work your way through this book, I think you will come to appreciate the power and productivity that Visual Studio and the Visual Basic language provides.

Summary

In this chapter, you were introduced to OOP and got a brief history of Visual Basic. Now that you have an understanding of what constitutes an OOP language and why OOP languages are so important to enterprise-level application development, your next step is to become familiar with how OOP applications are designed.

Successful applications must be carefully planned and developed before any meaningful coding takes place. The next chapter is the first in a series of three aimed at introducing you to some of the techniques used when designing object-oriented applications. You will look at the process of deciding which objects need to be included in an application and which attributes of these objects are important to the functionality of that application.

■ ■ ■

CHAPTER 2

Designing OOP Solutions: Identifying the Class Structure

Most software projects you will become involved with as a business software developer will be a team effort. As a programmer on the team, you will be asked to transform the design documents into the actual application code. Additionally, because the design of object-oriented programs is a recursive process, designers depend on the feedback of the software developers to refine and modify the program design. As you gain experience in developing object-oriented software systems, you may even be asked to sit in on the design sessions and contribute to the design process. Therefore, as a software developer, you should be familiar with the purpose and the structure of the various design documents, as well as have some knowledge of how these documents are developed.

This chapter introduces you to some of the common documents used to design the static aspects of the system. (You'll learn how the dynamic aspects of the system are modeled in the next chapter.) To help you understand these documents, this chapter includes some hands-on activities, based on a limited case study. You'll find similar activities corresponding to the topics of discussion in most of the chapters in this book.

After reading this chapter, you will be familiar with the following:

- The goals of software design

- The fundamentals of the Unified Modeling Language

- The purpose of a software requirement specification

- How use case diagrams model the services the system will provide

- How class diagrams model the classes of objects that need to be developed

Goals of Software Design

A well-organized approach to system design is essential when developing modern enterprise-level object-oriented programs. The design phase is one of the most important in the software development cycle. You can trace many of the problems associated with failed software projects to poor upfront design and inadequate communication between the system's developers and the system's consumers. Unfortunately, many programmers and program managers do not like getting involved in the design aspects of the system. They view any time not spent cranking out code as unproductive.

To make matters worse, with the advent of "Internet time," consumers expect increasingly shorter development cycles. So, to meet unrealistic timelines and project scope, developers tend to forgo or cut short the system design phase of development. This is truly counterproductive to the system's success. Investing time in the design process will achieve the following:

- Provide an opportunity to review the current business process and fix any inefficiencies or flaws uncovered

- Educate the customers as to how the software development process occurs and incorporate them as partners in this process

- Create realistic project scopes and timelines for completion

- Provide a basis for determining the software testing requirements

- Reduce the cost and time required to implement the software solution

A good analogy to software design is the process of building a home. You would not expect the builder to start working on the house without detailed plans (blueprints) supplied by an architect. You would also expect the architect to talk to you about the home's design before creating the blueprints. It is the architect's job to consult with you about the design and functionality you want in the house and convert your requests to the plans that the builder uses to build the home. A good architect will also educate you as to what features are reasonable for your budget and projected timeline.

Understanding the Unified Modeling Language

To successfully design object-oriented software, you need to follow a proven design methodology. One of the most common design methodologies used in OOP today is the Unified Modeling Language (UML).

UML was developed in the early 1980s as a response to the need for a standard, systematic way of modeling the design of object-oriented software. It consists of a series of textual and graphical models of the proposed solution. These models define the system scope, components of the system, user interaction with the system, and how the system components interact with each other to implement the system functionality.

The following are some common models used in UML:

- **Software requirement specification (SRS):** A textual description of the overall responsibilities and scope of the system.

- **Use case:** A textual/graphical description of how the system will behave from the users' perspective. Users can be humans or other systems.

- **Class diagram:** A visual blueprint of the objects that will be used to construct the system.

- **Sequence diagram:** A model of the sequence of object interaction as the program executes. Emphasis is placed on the order of the interactions and how they proceed over time.

- **Collaboration diagram:** A view of how objects are organized to work together as the program executes. Emphasis is placed on the communications that occur between the objects.

- **Activity diagram:** A visual representation of the flow of execution of a process or operation.

In this chapter, you'll look at the development of the SRS, use cases, and class diagrams. The next chapter covers the sequence, collaboration, and activity diagrams.

Developing an SRS

The purpose of the SRS is to do the following:

- Define the functional requirements of the system

- Identify the boundaries of the system

- Identify the users of the system

- Describe the interactions between the system and the external users

- Establish a common language between the client and the program team for describing the system

- Provide the basis for modeling use cases

To produce the SRS, you interview the business owners and the end users of the system. The goals of these interviews are to clearly document the business processes involved and establish the system's scope. The outcome of this process is a formal document (the SRS) detailing the functional requirements of the system. A formal document helps to ensure agreement between the customers and the software developers. The SRS also provides a basis for resolving any disagreements over "perceived" system scope as development proceeds.

As an example, suppose that the owners of a small commuter airline want customers to be able to view flight information and reserve tickets for flights using a web registration system. After interviewing the business managers and the ticketing agents, the software designers draft an SRS document that lists the system's functional requirements. The following are some of these requirements:

- Nonregistered web users can browse to the web site to view flight information, but they cannot book flights.

- New customers wanting to book flights must complete a registration form providing their name, address, company name, phone number, fax number, and e-mail address.

- A customer is classified as either a corporate customer or a retail customer.

- Customers can search for flights based on destination and departure times.

- Customers can book flights indicating the flight number and the number of seats requested.

- The system sends customers a confirmation via e-mail when the flight is booked.

- Corporate customers receive frequent flier miles when their employees book flights. Frequent-flier miles are used to discount future purchases.

- Ticket reservations can be canceled up to one week in advance for an 80-percent refund.

- Ticketing agents can view and update flight information.

In this partial SRS document, you can see that several succinct statements define the system scope. They describe the functionality of the system as viewed by the system's users and identify the external entities that will use it. It is important to note that the SRS does *not* contain references to the technical requirements of the system.

Once the SRS is developed, the functional requirements it contains are transformed into a series of use case diagrams.

Introducing Use Cases

Use cases describe how external entities will use the system. These external entities can be either humans or other systems and are referred to as *actors* in UML terminology. The description emphasizes the users' view of the system and the interaction between the users and the system. Use cases help to further define system scope and boundaries. They are usually in the form of a diagram, along with a textual description of the interaction taking place. Figure 2-1 shows a generic diagram that consists of two actors represented by stick figures, the system represented by a rectangle, and use cases depicted by ovals inside the system boundaries.

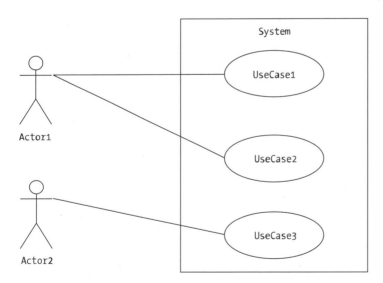

Figure 2-1. *Generic use case diagram with two actors and three use cases*

Use cases are developed from the SRS document. The actor is any outside entity that interacts with the system. An actor could be a human user (for instance, a rental agent), another software system (for instance, a software billing system), or an interface device (for instance, a temperature probe). Each interaction that occurs between an actor and the system is modeled as a use case.

The sample use case shown in Figure 2-2 was developed for the flight booking application introduced in the previous section. It shows the use case diagram for the requirement "Customers can search for flights based on destination and departure times."

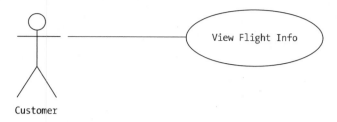

Figure 2-2. *View Flight Info use case diagram*

Along with the graphical depiction, many designers and software developers find it helpful to provide a textual description of the use case. The textual description should be succinct and focused on *what* is happening and not on *how* it is occurring. Sometimes, any preconditions or postconditions associated with the use case are also identified. The following text further describes the use case diagram shown in Figure 2-2:

- **Description:** A customer views the flight information page. The customer enters flight search information. After submitting the search request, the customer views a list of flights matching the search criteria.

- **Preconditions:** None.

- **Postconditions:** The customer has the opportunity to log in and proceed to the flight booking page.

As another example, take a look at the Reserve Seat use case shown in Figure 2-3.

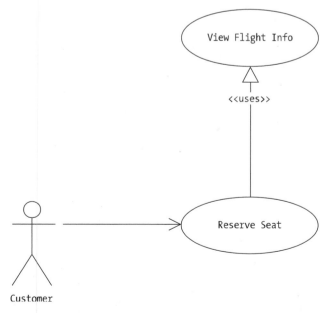

Figure 2-3. *Reserve Seat use case diagram*

The following text further describes the use case diagram shown in Figure 2-3:

- **Description:** The customer enters the flight number and indicates the seats being requested. After the customer submits the request, confirmation information is displayed.

- **Preconditions:** The customer has looked up the flight information. The customer has logged in and is viewing the flight booking screen.

- **Postconditions:** The customer is sent a confirmation e-mail outlining the flight details and the cancellation policy.

As you can see from Figure 2-3, certain relationships can exist between use cases. The Reserve Seat use case includes the View Flight Info use case. This relationship is useful because you can use the View Flight Info use case independently of the Reserve Flight use case. This is called *inclusion*. You cannot use the Reserve Seat use case independently of the View Flight Info use case, however. This is important information that will affect how you model the solution.

Another way that use cases relate to each other is through *extension*. You might have a general use case that is the base for other use cases. The base use case is extended by other use cases. For example, you might have a Register Customer use case that describes the core process of registering customers. You could then develop Register Corporate Customer and Register Retail Customer use cases that extend the base use case. The difference between extension and inclusion is that in extension, the base use case being extended is not used on its own. Figure 2-4 demonstrates how you model extension in a use case diagram.

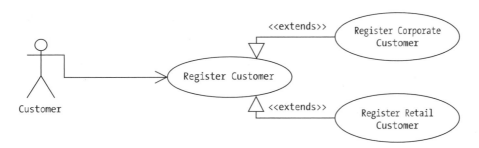

Figure 2-4. *Extending use cases*

A common mistake when developing use cases is to include actions initiated by the system itself. The emphasis of the use case is on the interaction between external entities and the system. Another common mistake is to include a description of the technical requirements of the system. Remember that use cases do not focus on how the system will perform the functions, but rather on what functions need to be incorporated in the system from the users' standpoint.

After you have developed the use cases of the system, you can begin to identify the internal system objects that will carry out the system's functional requirements. You do this through the use of a class diagram.

Activity 2-1. Creating a Use Case Diagram

After completing this activity, you should be familiar with the following:

- Producing a use case diagram to define a system's scope

- Using a UML modeling tool to create and document a use case diagram

Examining the SRS

The software user group you belong to has decided to pool its resources and create a lending library. Lending items include books, movies, and video games. Your task is to develop the application that will keep track of the loan item inventory and the lending of items to the group members. After interviewing the group's members and officers, you have developed an SRS document that includes the following functional requirements:

- Only members of the user group can borrow items.

- Books can be borrowed for four weeks.

- Movies and games can be borrowed for one week.

- Items can be renewed if no one is waiting to borrow them.

- Members can borrow up to a maximum of four items at the same time.

- A reminder is e-mailed to members when an item becomes overdue.

- A fine is charged for overdue items.

- Members with outstanding overdue items or fines cannot borrow new items.

- A secretary is in charge of maintaining item inventory and purchasing items to add to the inventory.

- A librarian has been appointed to track lending and send overdue notices.

- The librarian is also responsible for collecting fines and updating fine information.

The next step is to analyze the SRS to identify the actors and use cases.

1. By examining the SRS document, identify which of the following will be among the principal actors interacting with the system.

    A. Member

    B. Librarian

    C. Book

    D. Treasurer

    E. Inventory

    F. E-mail

    G. Secretary

2. Once you have identified the principal actors, the next step is to identify the use cases for the actors. Identify the actor associated with the following use cases:

A. Request Item

B. Catalog Item

C. Lend Item

D. Process Fine

See the end of the chapter for Activity 2-1 answers.

Creating a Use Case Diagram

Although it is possible to create the UML diagrams by hand or on a whiteboard, most programmers will eventually turn to a diagramming tool or a computer-aided software engineering (CASE) tool. CASE tools help you construct professional-quality diagrams and enable team members to easily share and augment the diagrams. Many CASE tools are on the market, including Microsoft Visio. Before choosing a CASE tool, you should thoroughly evaluate if it meets your needs and is flexible enough. A lot of the advanced features associated with "high-end" CASE tools are difficult to work with, and you spend more time figuring out how the CASE tool works than you do documenting your design.

A good CASE tool to learn on is UML Modeler from Objecteering. It enables you to create UML diagrams without adding a lot of advanced features associated with the higher-end CASE tools. Best of all, you can download a free personal version from Objecteering's web site (www.objecteering.com). UML Modeler is part of the Objecteering/ UML Personal Edition software. After downloading and installing UML Modeler, you can complete the following steps (if you do not want to use a CASE tool, you can create the sample use diagram by hand):

1. Start UML Modeler. Choose File ➤ New. Change the project name to UMLAct2_1 and click OK.

2. Locate the Properties Editor along the left side of the screen (see Figure 2-5). On the left side of the Properties Editor, click the Create a Use Case Diagram button.

Figure 2-5. *UML Modeler Properties Editor*

3. You will be presented with a design surface in the main editor window. Along the left side of the window are shapes used in creating use case diagrams. Click the Create an Actor button (see Figure 2-6). Draw the Actor shape on the design surface. Change the name of the Actor shape to **Member**.

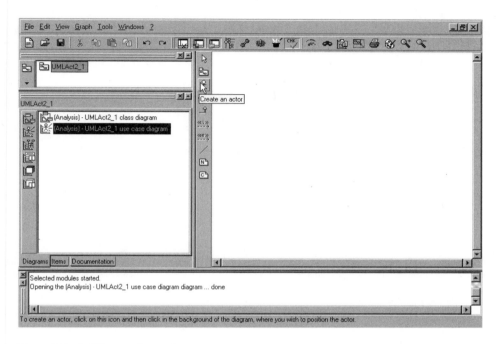

Figure 2-6. *Adding an Actor shape*

4. Right-click the Member shape on the design surface and choose Modify. You will be presented with the Actor dialog box. On the Notes tab, click the Add button. The Note dialog box appears. Under the Type drop-down list, choose Description. In the Contents text box, enter **A dues-paying member of the software users group.** After entering the description, as shown in Figure 2-7, click OK. Click OK again to close the Actor dialog box.

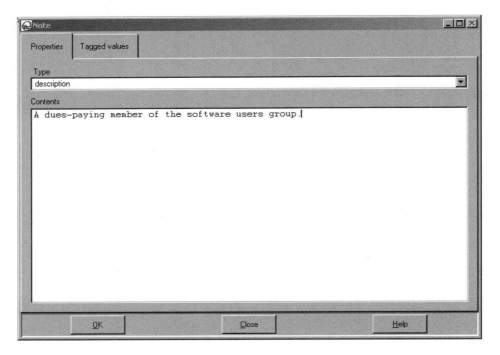

Figure 2-7. *Adding a description for an actor*

5. Repeat steps 3 and 4 to add a Secretary user and a Librarian actor.

6. From the Shapes toolbox, choose the Use Case shape and draw a Use Case shape on the design surface. Right-click the Use Case shape on the design surface and choose Modify. (This can be tricky; make sure you click the oval shape and not the rectangle shape.) You will be presented with a Use Case dialog box. Change the name of the use case to **Request Item**. On the Notes tab, add the following description: **A Member views a list of items, chooses an item from the list, and submits a request for the item.** After entering the description, click OK. Click OK again to close the Use Case dialog box.

7. Repeat step 6 for two more use cases. Include a **Catalog Item** use case that will occur when the Secretary adds new items to the library inventory database. Add a **Lend Item** use case that will occur when the Librarian processes a request for an item. These will be added to the system rectangle created where you added the first use case.

8. From the Shapes toolbox, choose the Communication Link shape and draw a Communication Link shape on the design surface. Attach end 1 to the Member shape and end 2 to the Request Item shape.

9. Repeat step 8 to create a Communication Link shape between the Librarian and the Lend Item shapes. Also create a Communication Link shape between the Secretary and the Catalog Item shapes.

10. From the Shapes toolbox, choose the Extension Relationship shape and draw an Extension Relationship shape on the design surface. Attach end 1 of the Extends arrow to the Lend Item use case, and attach end 2 of the arrow to the Request Item use case.

11. Your completed diagram should look similar to the one shown in Figure 2-8. Choose File ➤ Save and then exit UML Modeler.

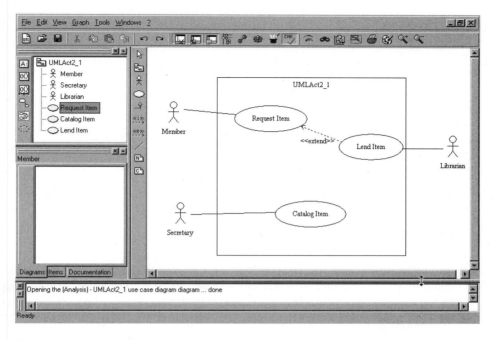

Figure 2-8. *Completed use case diagram*

Understanding Class Diagrams

The concepts of classes and objects are fundamental to OOP. An *object* is a structure for incorporating data and the procedures for working with the data. These objects implement the functionality of an object-oriented program. Think of a *class* as a blueprint for the object. A class defines the structure and the methods that objects based on the class type will contain.

Designers identify a potential list of classes that they will need to develop from the SRS and the use case diagrams. One way you identify the classes is by looking at the noun phrases in the SRS document and the use case descriptions. If you look at the documentation developed thus far for the airline booking application, you can begin to identify the classes that will make up the system. For example, you can develop a Customer class to work with the customer data and a Flight class to work with the flight data.

A class is responsible for managing data. When defining the class structure, you must determine what data the class is responsible for maintaining. The class attributes define this information. For example, the Flight class will have attributes for identifying the flight number, departure time and date, flight duration, destination, capacity, and seats available. The class structure must also define any operations that will be performed on the data. An example of an operation the Flight class is responsible for is updating the seats available when a seat is reserved.

A *class diagram* can help you visualize the attributes and operations of a class. Figure 2-9 is an example of the class diagram for the Flight class used in the flight booking system example. A rectangle divided into three sections represents the class. The top section of the rectangle shows the name of the class, the middle section lists the attributes of the class, and the bottom section lists the operations performed by the class.

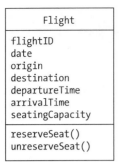

Figure 2-9. *Flight class diagram*

Modeling Object Relationships

In OOP, when the program executes, the various objects work together to accomplish the programming tasks. For example, in the flight booking application, in order to reserve a seat on the flight, a Reservation object must interact with the Flight object. A relationship exists between the two objects, and this relationship must be modeled in the class structure of the program. The relationships among the classes that make up the program are modeled in the class diagram. Analyzing the verb phrases in the SRS often reveals these relationships (this is discussed in more detail in Chapter 3). The following sections examine some of the common relationships that can occur between classes and how the class diagram represents them.

Association

When one class refers to or uses another class, the classes form an *association*. You draw a line between the two classes to represent the association and add a label to indicate the name of the association. For example, a Seat is associated with a Flight in the flight booking application, as shown in Figure 2-10.

Figure 2-10. *Class associations*

Sometimes, a single instance of one class associates with multiple instances of another class. This is indicated on the line connecting the two classes. For example, when a customer makes a reservation, there is an association between the Customer class and the Reservation class. A single instance of the Customer class may be associated with multiple instances of the Reservation class. An asterisk placed near the Reservation class indicates this multiplicity, as shown in Figure 2-11.

Figure 2-11. *Indicating multiplicity in a class diagram*

In some cases, an instance of a class may be associated with multiple instances of the same class. For example, an instance of the Pilot class represents the pilot, while another instance of the Pilot class represents the co-pilot. The pilot manages the co-pilot. This scenario is referred to as a *self-association* and is modeled by drawing the association line from the class back to itself, as shown in Figure 2-12.

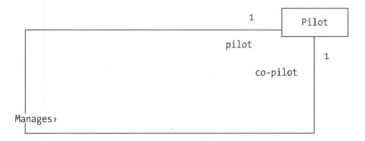

Figure 2-12. *A self-associating class*

Inheritance

When multiple classes share some of the same operations and attributes, a base class can encapsulate the commonality. The child class then *inherits* from the base class. This relationship is represented in the class diagram by a solid line with an open arrowhead pointing to the base class. For example, a CorporateCustomer class and a RetailCustomer class could inherit common attributes and operations from a base Customer class, as shown in Figure 2-13.

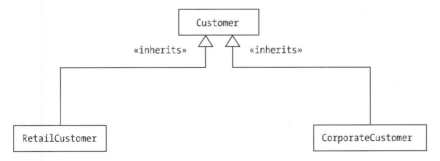

Figure 2-13. *Documenting inheritance*

Aggregation

When a class is formed by a composition of other classes, those classes are classified as an *aggregation*. In a class diagram, an aggregation is represented with a solid line connecting the classes in a hierarchical structure. Placing a diamond on the line next to a class in the diagram indicates the top level of the hierarchy. For example, an inventory application designed to track plane parts for the plane maintenance department could contain a `Plane` class that is a composite of various part classes, as shown in Figure 2-14.

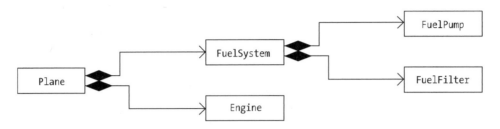

Figure 2-14. *Depicting aggregations*

Association Classes

As the classes and the associations for a program are developed, you may find that an attribute cannot be assigned to any one class, but is a result of an association between classes. For example, a parts inventory application may have a `Part` class and a `Supplier` class. A part can have more than one supplier, and the supplier supplies more than one part. So, where should the `price` attribute be located? It does not fit nicely as an attribute for either class, and it should not be duplicated in both classes. The solution is to develop an *association class* that manages the data that is a product of the association. In this case, you would develop a `PartPrice` class. The relationship is modeled with a dashed line drawn between the association and the association class, as shown in Figure 2-15.

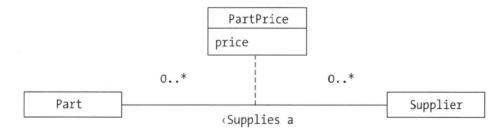

Figure 2-15. *An association class*

Figure 2-16 shows the evolving class diagram for the flight booking application. It includes the classes, attributes, and relationships that have been identified for the system. The operations associated with the classes will be developed in Chapter 3.

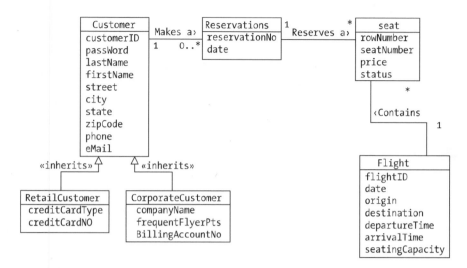

Figure 2-16. *Flight booking class diagram*

Activity 2-2. Creating a Class Diagram

After completing this activity, you should be familiar with the following:

- Determining the classes that need to be constructed by examining the use case and the system scope documentation

- Using a UML modeling tool to create a class diagram

Identifying Classes and Attributes

Examine the following scenario developed for a use case from the user group library application:

> *After viewing the list of available loan items, members request an item to check out on loan. The librarian enters the member number and retrieves information about outstanding loans and any unpaid fines. If the member has fewer than four outstanding loans and does not have any outstanding fines, the loan is processed. The librarian retrieves information about the loan item to determine if it is currently on loan. If the item is available, it is checked out to the member.*

1. By identifying the nouns and noun phrases in the use case scenario, you can get an idea of what classes you must include in the system to perform the tasks. Which of the following items would make good candidate classes for the system?

   A. Member

   B. Item

   C. Librarian

   D. Number

   E. Fine

   F. Checkout

   G. Loan

2. At this point, you can start identifying attributes associated with the classes being developed. A Loan class will be developed to encapsulate data associated with an item out on loan. Which of the following would be possible attributes for the Loan class?

   A. MemberNumber

   B. MemberPhone

   C. ItemNumber

   D. ReturnDate

   E. ItemCost

   F. ItemType

See the end of the chapter for Activity 2-2 answers.

Creating a Class Diagram

To create a class diagram using UML Modeler, follow these steps (you can also create it by hand):

1. Start UML Modeler and choose File ➤ Open. Then select the UMLAct2_1 project and click OK.

2. You should be presented with the use case diagram developed in Activity 2-1. In the main explorer window located in the upper-left corner of the screen, select the UMLAct2_1 node. Double-click the UMLAct2_1 class diagram node in the Properties Editor. The main window will display an editor for creating the class diagram, as shown in Figure 2-17.

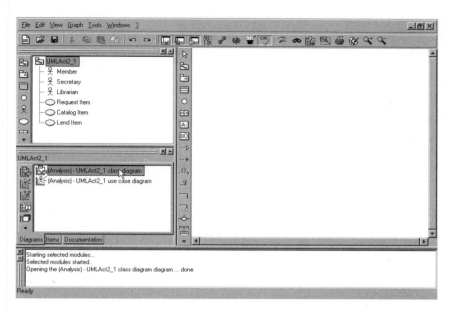

Figure 2-17. *Creating a class diagram in UML Modeler*

3. Along the left side of the editor window is a toolbox containing the shapes used in creating class diagrams. Click the Create a Class button (see Figure 2-18). Draw the Class shape on the design surface.

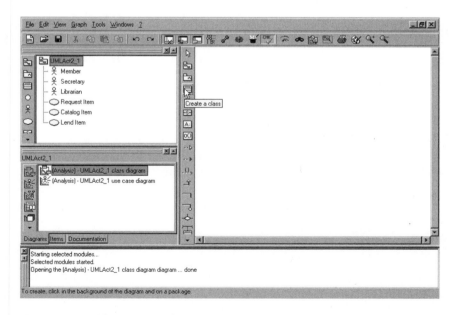

Figure 2-18. *Adding a Class shape*

4. Deselect the class by clicking on the design surface, right-click the Class shape on the design surface, and choose Modify. You will be presented with a Class dialog box.

5. Change the name of the Class shape to cMember. On the Notes tab, enter the following description: **Used to encapsulate and process member data info.** After entering the description, click OK. Click OK again to close the Class dialog box.

6. Repeat the procedures in steps 3 through 5 to add the following classes to the diagram:

   - cLoan: Encapsulates and manages the details of an item currently on loan

   - cItem: Encapsulates and manages data associated with items that are available for loan

   - cBook: A specialization of an Item

   - cMovie: A specialization of an Item

7. From the Shapes toolbox, click and drag an Association Link shape onto the design surface. Attach end 1 to cMember and end 2 to cLoan.

8. Right-click the Association Link shape and click Modify. You are presented with a Binary Association dialog box. On the dialog box's Properties tab, change the In the Association or the Aggregation text box entry to "Makes a." Change the Quantity drop-down list of the end pointing to the cMember class to 1, and change the end pointing to the cLoan class to 0..4. This indicates that a cMember class may be associated with up to four instances of a cLoan class (see Figure 2-19). Click OK to close the Binary Association dialog box.

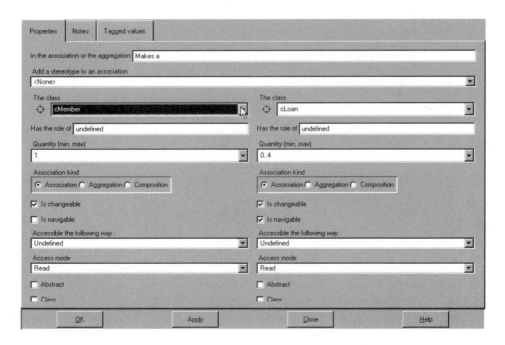

Figure 2-19. *The Properties tab of the Binary Association dialog box*

9. Repeat steps 7 and 8 to create a "Contains a" Association Link shape between the cLoan class and the cItem class. This should be a one-to-one association (choose 1 for the Quantity).

10. From the Shapes toolbox, choose the Generalization Relationship shape and draw a Generalization Relationship shape on the design surface. Attach the tail (end 1) of the Generalization arrow to the cBook class, and attach the head (end 2) of the arrow to the cItem class. This indicates inheritance and shows that a cBook class is a specialization of the cItem class.

11. Repeat step 10 to show the relationship between the cMovie class and the cItem class.

12. Along the left side of the class diagram editor window, click the Attribute button. In the class diagram, click the cMember class to add an attribute. Deselect the class by clicking on the design surface, right-click the attribute, and select Modify. Change the name to MemberNumber, change the Class drop-down list to Integer, and click OK.

13. Repeat step 12 to add a FirstName string type, LastName string type, and EMail string type attributes to the cMember class.

14. Your completed diagram should be similar to the one shown in Figure 2-20. Save the file (File ➤ Save).

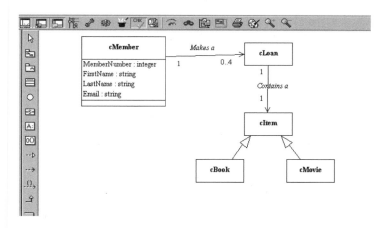

Figure 2-20. *Completed use case diagram*

Summary

In this chapter, you were introduced to the goals of the object-oriented design process and UML. You learned about some of the design documents and diagrams produced using UML. These include the SRS, which defines the scope of the system; use case diagrams, which define the system boundaries and identify the external entities that will use the system; and class diagrams, which model the structure of the classes that will be developed to implement the system.

You saw how modeling the class structure of your applications includes identifying the necessary classes, identifying the attributes of these classes, and establishing the structural relationships required among the classes. In the next chapter, you will continue your study of object-oriented design. In particular, you will look at modeling how the objects in your applications will collaborate to carry out the functionality of the application.

Activity Answers

Activity 2-1 Answers

1. **A, B, G.** The actors are Member, Librarian, and Secretary.

2. **A. Member, B. Secretary, C. Librarian, D. Librarian.** The Request Item use case goes with Member, the Catalog Item use case goes with Secretary, the Lend Item use case goes with Librarian, and the Process Fine use case goes with Librarian.

Activity 2-2 Answers

1. **A, B, C, E, G.** The candidate classes are Member, Item, Librarian, Fine, and Loan.

2. **A, C, D.** The attributes associated with the Loan class are MemberNumber, ItemNumber, and ReturnDate.

■ ■ ■

CHAPTER 3

Designing OOP Solutions: Modeling the Object Interaction

The previous chapter focused on modeling the static (organizational) aspects of an OOP solution. It introduced and discussed the methodologies of the UML. You also looked at the purpose and structure of use case diagrams and class diagrams. This chapter continues the discussion of UML modeling techniques and focuses on modeling the dynamic (behavioral) aspects of an OOP solution. The focus in this chapter is on how the objects in the system must interact with each other and what activities must occur to implement the solution.

After reading this chapter, you should be familiar with the following:

- The purpose of scenarios and how they extend the use case models

- How sequence diagrams model the time-dependent interaction of the objects in the system

- How collaboration diagrams model the contextual interaction of the objects in the system

- How activity diagrams map the flow of activities during application processing

- The importance of graphical user interface design and how it fits into the object-oriented design process

Understanding Scenarios

Scenarios help determine the dynamic interactions that will take place between the objects (class instances) of the system. A scenario is a textual description of the internal processing needed to implement the functionality documented by a use case. Remember that a use case describes the functionality of the system from the viewpoint of the system's external users. A scenario details the execution of the use case. In other words, its purpose is to describe the steps that must be carried out internally by the objects making up the system.

Figure 3-1 shows a Process Movie Rental use case for a video rental application. The following text describes the use case:

- **Preconditions:** The customer makes a request to rent a movie from the rental clerk. The customer has a membership in the video club and supplies the rental clerk with her membership card and personal identification number (PIN). The customer's membership is verified. The customer information is displayed, and the customer's account is verified to be in good standing.

- **Description:** The movie is confirmed to be in stock. Rental information is recorded, and the customer is informed of the due date.

- **Postconditions:** None.

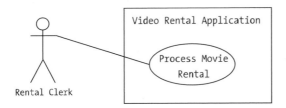

Figure 3-1. *Process Movie Rental use case*

The following scenario describes the internal processing of the Process Movie Rental use case:

1. The movie is verified to be in stock.

2. The number of available copies in stock is decremented.

3. The due date is determined.

4. The rental information is recorded. This information includes the movie title, copy number, current date, and due date.

5. The customer is informed of the rental information.

This scenario describes the best possible execution of the use case. Because exceptions can occur, a single use case can spawn multiple scenarios. For example, another scenario created for the Process Movie Rental use case could describe what happens when a movie is not in stock.

After you map out the various scenarios for a use case, you can create interaction diagrams to determine which classes of objects will be involved in carrying out the functionality of the scenarios. The interaction diagram also reveals what operations will be required of these classes of objects. Interaction diagrams come in two flavors: sequence diagrams and collaboration diagrams.

Introducing Sequence Diagrams

A *sequence diagram* models how the classes of objects interact with each other over time as the system runs. The sequence diagram is a visual, two-dimensional model of the interaction taking place and is based on a scenario. Figure 3-2 shows a generic sequence diagram.

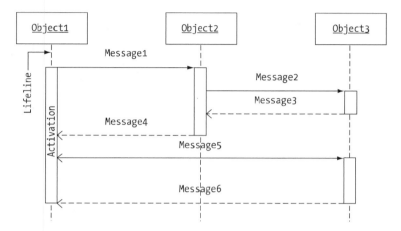

Figure 3-2. *Generic sequence diagram*

As Figure 3-2 demonstrates, the flow of messages from object to object is represented horizontally. The time flow of the interactions taking place is depicted vertically, starting from the top and progressing downward. Objects are next to each other, and a dashed line extends from each of them downward. This dashed line represents the *lifeline* of the object. Rectangles on the lifeline represent *activations* of the object. The height of the rectangle represents the duration of the object's activation.

In OOP, objects interact by passing messages to each other. An arrow starting at the initiating object and ending at the receiving object depicts the interaction. A dashed arrow drawn back to the initiating object represents a return message. The messages depicted in the sequence diagram will form the basis of the methods of the classes of the system. Figure 3-3 shows a sample sequence diagram for the Process Movie Rental scenario presented in the previous section.

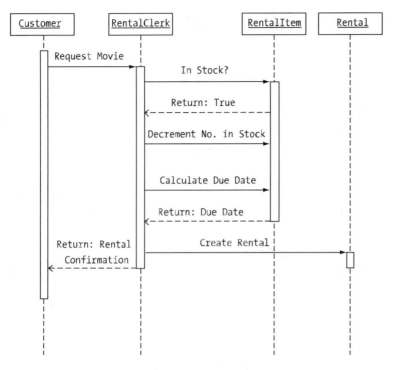

Figure 3-3. *Process Movie Rental sequence diagram*

As you analyze the sequence diagram, you gain an understanding of the classes of objects that will be involved in carrying out the program processing and what methods you will need to create and attach to those classes. You should also model the classes and methods depicted in the sequence diagram in the class diagram. These design documents must be continually cross-referenced and revised when needed.

The sequence diagram in Figure 3-3 reveals that there will be four objects involved in carrying out the Process Movie Rental scenario:

- The Customer object is an instance of the Customer class and is responsible for encapsulating and maintaining the information pertaining to a customer.

- The RentalClerk object is an instance of the RentalClerk class and is responsible for managing the processing involved in renting a movie.

- The RentalItem object is an instance of the RentalItem class and is responsible for encapsulating and maintaining the information pertaining to a video available for rent.

- The Rental object is an instance of the Rental class and is responsible for encapsulating and maintaining the information pertaining to a video currently being rented.

Message Types

By analyzing the sequence diagram, you can determine what messages must be passed between the objects involved in the processing. In OOP, messages are passed *synchronously* or *asynchronously*.

When messages are passed synchronously, the sending object suspends processing and waits for a response before continuing. A line drawn with a solid arrowhead in the sequence diagram represents synchronous messaging.

When an object sends an asynchronous message, the object continues processing and is not expecting an immediate response from the receiving object. A line drawn with a half arrowhead in the sequence diagram represents asynchronous messaging.

An object may also send a message to transfer control to another object. This is referred to as a *simple* or *flat* message and is depicted by an open arrowhead in the sequence diagram. A dashed arrow usually depicts a response message.

Figure 3-4 shows these different types of messages.

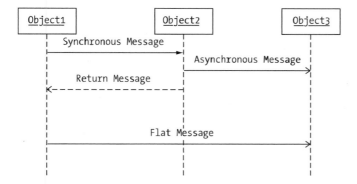

Figure 3-4. *Diagramming various message types*

By studying the sequence diagram for the Process Movie Rental scenario shown in Figure 3-3, you can see the types of messages that must be passed. For example, the RentalClerk object initiates a synchronous message with the RentalItem object, requesting information about whether a copy of the movie is in stock. The RentalItem object then sends a response back to the RentalClerk object, indicating a copy is in stock.

Recursive Messages

In OOP, it is not uncommon for an object to have an operation that invokes another object instance of itself. This is referred to as *recursion*. A message arrow that loops back toward the calling object represents recursion in the sequence diagram. The end of the arrow points to a smaller activation rectangle, representing a second object activation drawn on top of the original activation rectangle (see Figure 3-5). For example, an Account object calculates compound interest for overdue payments. To calculate the interest over several compound periods, it needs to invoke itself several times.

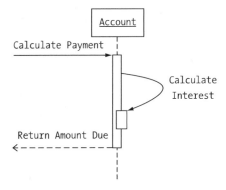

Figure 3-5. *Diagramming a recursive message*

Message Iteration

Sometimes, a message call is repeated until a condition is met. For example, when totaling rental charges, an Add method is called repeatedly until all rentals charged to the customer have been added to the total. In programming terminology, this is an *iteration*. A rectangle drawn around the iterating messages represents an iteration in a sequence diagram. The binding condition of the iteration is depicted in the upper-left corner of the rectangle. Figure 3-6 shows an example of an iteration depicted in a sequence diagram.

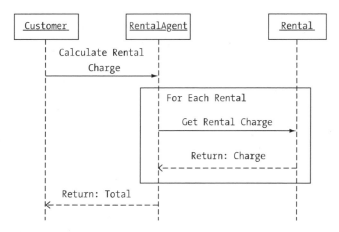

Figure 3-6. *Depicting an iterative message*

Message Constraints

Message calls between objects may have a conditional constraint attached to them. For example, customers must be in good standing in order to be allowed to rent a movie. You place the condition of the constraint within brackets ([ ]) in the sequence. The message will be sent only if the condition evaluates to true (see Figure 3-7).

Figure 3-7. *Identifying conditional constraints*

Message Branching

When conditional constraints are tied to message calling, you often run into a branching situation where, depending on the condition, different messages may be invoked. Figure 3-8 represents a conditional constraint when requesting a movie rental. If the status of the rental item is in stock, a message is sent to the Rental object to create a rental. If the status of the rental item is out of stock, a message is sent to the Reservation object to create a reservation.

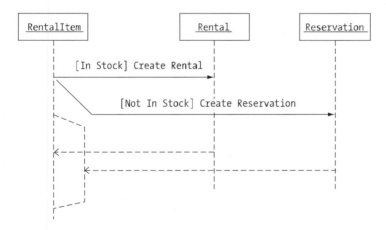

Figure 3-8. *Branching messages in a sequence diagram*

When you diagram the return from a branching call, you split the lifeline of the calling object. You then draw one return message on each line. This avoids the confusion that would occur if they both returned to the same lifeline, which could be erroneously interpreted as both returns occurring one after the other, in sequence.

When branching occurs in a sequence diagram, the diagram is actually modeling different scenarios of the same use case. Including different scenarios in the same sequence diagram can become confusing. It is often a much better idea to model each scenario with its own separate sequence diagram.

Activity 3-1. Creating a Sequence Diagram

After completing this activity, you should be familiar with the following:

- Producing a sequence diagram to model object interaction

- Using a UML modeling tool to create a sequence diagram

- Adding methods to the class diagram

Examining the Scenario

The following scenario was created for a use case in the user group library application introduced in Activity 2-1. It describes the processing involved when a member borrows an item from the library:

When a member makes a request to borrow an item, the librarian checks the member's records to make sure no outstanding fines exist. Once the member passes these checks, the item is checked to see if it is available. Once the item availability has been confirmed, a loan is created recording the item number, member number, checkout date, and return date.

1. By examining the noun phrases in the scenario, you can identify which objects will be involved in carrying out the processing. The objects identified should also have a corresponding class depicted in the class diagram that has been previously created. From the scenario depicted, identify five objects that will carry out the processing.

2. After the objects have been identified and cross-referenced with the class diagram, the next step is to identify the messaging that must occur between these objects to carry out the task. You can look at the verb phrases in the scenario to help identify these messages. For example, the phase *request to borrow item* indicates a message interaction between the Member object and the Librarian object. What are the other interactions depicted in the scenario?

See the end of the chapter for Activity 3-1 answers.

Creating a Sequence Diagram

Follow these steps to create a sequence diagram using UML Modeler:

1. Start UML Modeler. Choose File ➤ New. Change the project name to UMLAct3_1 and click OK.

2. On the left side of the Properties Editor, click the Create a Sequence Diagram button (see Figure 3-9).

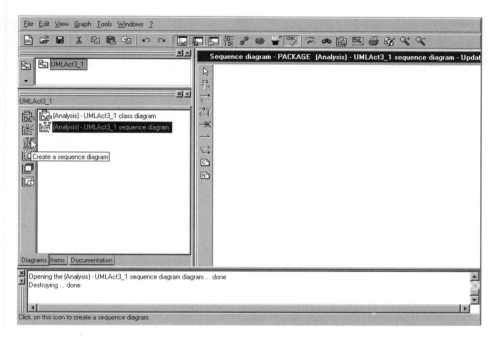

Figure 3-9. *Adding a sequence diagram*

3. You will be presented with a design surface in the main editor window. Along the left side of the window is a shapes toolbox containing shapes used in creating sequence diagrams. Click the Create an Instance button (see Figure 3-10). Draw the Instance shape (object) on the design surface. Change the name of the object to Member.

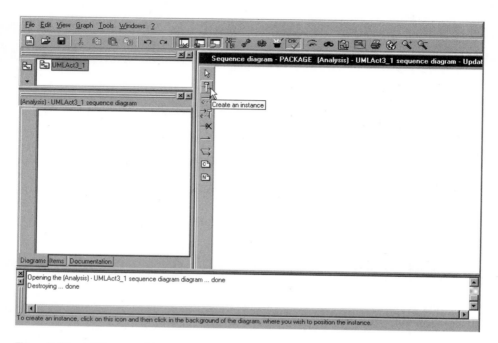

Figure 3-10. *Adding an object instance to the sequence diagram*

4. Repeat the procedures in step 3 to add Librarian, LoanHistory, Item, and Loan objects to the diagram. You should lay them out left to right across the page (see Figure 3-11).

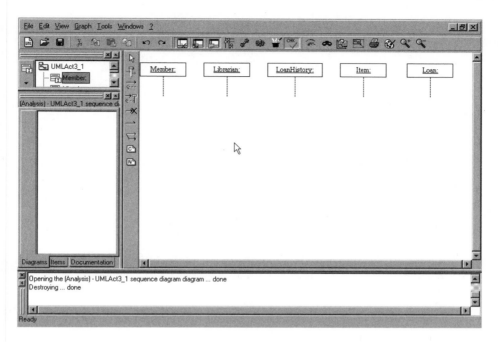

Figure 3-11. *Object layout in the sequence diagram*

5. From the Shapes toolbox, click the Create a Sequence Message button. Draw a Message shape between the Member object and the Librarian object. Attach the tail (end 1) of the arrow to the Member object's lifeline and the head of the arrow (end 2) to the Librarian object's lifeline. Click the message arrow to select it. It will turn blue. Next, right-click the message arrow and choose Modify. Change the name of the message to **request item**. Right-click the return arrow (the dashed line) and choose Modify. Change the name to **return loan info**. Click OK to close the window.

6. Repeat step 5 to create a message from the Librarian object to the LoanHistory object. Attach the tail (end 1) of the arrow to the Librarian object's lifeline after the "request item" message but before the "return loan info" message. Attach the head of the arrow (end 2) to the LoanHistory object's lifeline. Name the calling message (the solid line) **check history**. Name the return message (the dashed line) **return history info** (see Figure 3-12).

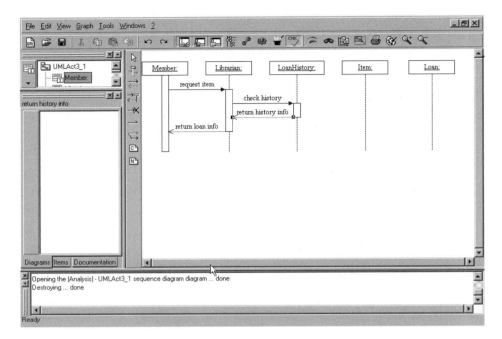

Figure 3-12. *Message layout in the sequence diagram*

7. Repeat step 5 to create a message from the Librarian object to the Item object. Attach the tail (end 1) of the arrow to the Librarian object's lifeline after the "return history info" message but before the "return loan info" message. Attach the head of the arrow (end 2) to the Item object's lifeline. Name the calling message **check availability**. Name the return message **return availability info**.

8. Repeat step 5 once more to create a message from the Librarian object to the Item object. Attach the tail (end 1) of the arrow to the Librarian object's lifeline after the "return availability info" message but before the "return loan info" message. Attach the head of the arrow (end 2) to the Item object's lifeline. Name the calling message **update status**. Name the return message **return update confirmation**.

9. From the Shapes toolbox, click the Create a Creation Message button. Draw a Message shape between the Librarian object and the Loan object. Attach the tail (end 1) of the arrow to the Librarian object's lifeline after the "return update confirmation" message but before the "return loan info" message. Attach the head of the arrow (end 2) to the Loan object's lifeline. Change the name of the message from CreateAction to **create loan object**.

10. Your completed diagram should be similar to the one shown in Figure 3-13. Save the file.

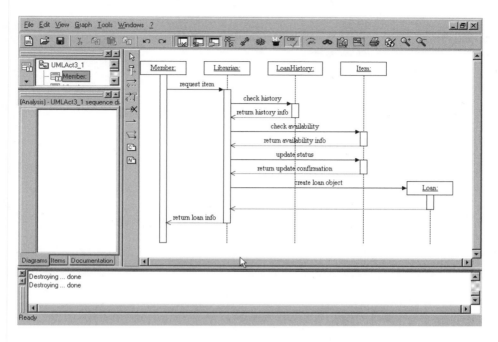

Figure 3-13. *Completed sequence diagram*

Adding Methods to the Class Diagram

After you have developed the sequence diagram, you begin to gain an understanding of the methods that must be included in the various classes of the application. You achieve the message interaction depicted in the sequence diagram by a method call from the initiating object (client) to the receiving object (server). The method being called is defined in the class that the server object is instantiated as. For example, the "request item" message in the sequence diagram indicates that the Librarian class needs a method that processes this message call.

Follow these steps to add the methods:

1. In the main explorer window located in the upper-left corner of the screen, select the UMLAct3_1 node. Double-click the UMLAct3_1 class diagram node in the Properties Editor. The main window will display an editor for creating the class diagram.

2. Draw a class shape on the designer surface and rename it Librarian.

3. Along the left side of the class diagram editor window, click the Create Operation button. In the class diagram, click the Librarian class to add an operation. Right-click the operation and select Modify. You will be presented with the Operation dialog box, shown in Figure 3-14. Change the name to RequestLoanItem.

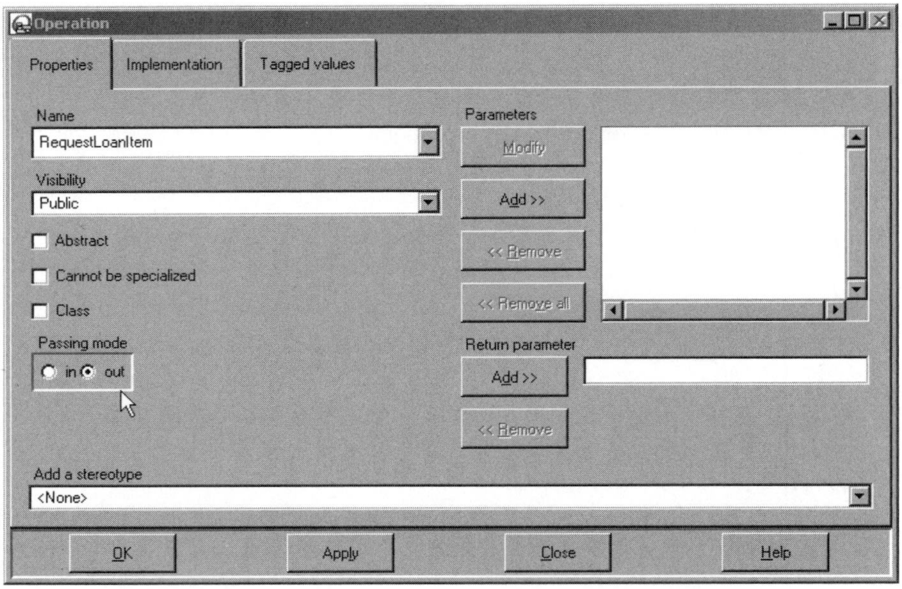

Figure 3-14. *Operation dialog box*

4. The parameters represent information passed in when the method is called. Add a parameter by clicking the Add button in the Parameters section of the Operation dialog box. You will be presented with the Parameter dialog box, as shown in Figure 3-15. Change the name of the parameter to `ItemNumber`, and under the Class drop-down list, choose Integer. Click OK to close the Parameter dialog box.

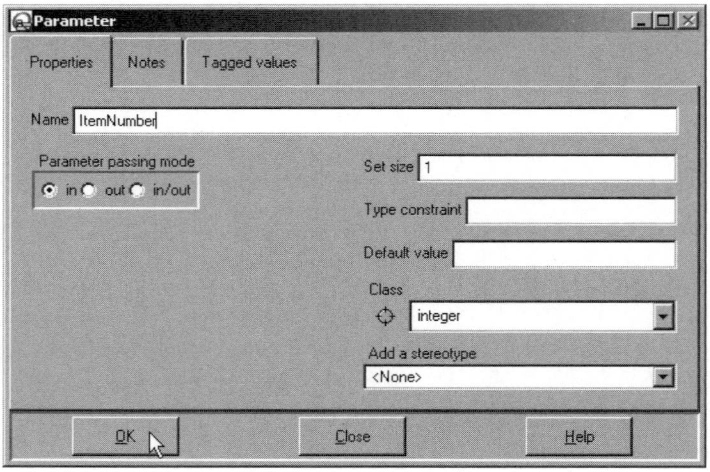

Figure 3-15. *Parameter dialog box*

5. The return parameter represents information passed back to the client object. Add a return parameter by clicking the Add button in the Return Parameter section of the Operation dialog box. You will be presented with the Return Parameter dialog box, as shown in Figure 3-16. Under the Class drop-down list, choose Integer, which will represent the loan number that will be returned to the Member object. Click OK to close the Return Parameter dialog box. Click OK to close the Operation dialog box.

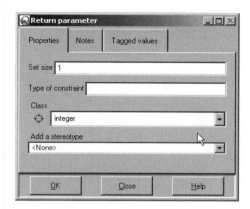

Figure 3-16. *Return Parameter dialog box*

6. Repeat steps 2 through 5 to add an Item class with a CheckAvailability method that receives an integer representing the item number and returns a Boolean indicating if the item is in stock.

7. In the main explorer window, expand the Item node and expand the CheckAvailability node. Information about the operation and parameters is displayed (see Figure 3-17).

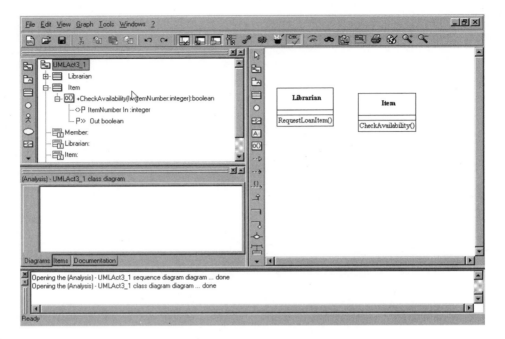

Figure 3-17. *Expanded nodes in the main explorer window*

8. Save the project and exit UML Modeler.

Using Collaboration Diagrams

Although sequence diagrams are useful for revealing the object interaction necessary to implement the functionality of the system, they are not the only UML diagram used for this purpose. A second type of activity diagram, the *collaboration diagram*, is also helpful when modeling object interaction.

While collaboration diagrams convey essentially the same information as sequential diagrams, they are laid out slightly differently. In the collaboration diagram, the time-sequencing order of interaction is de-emphasized, and the context and organization of the interacting objects are emphasized. Rectangles represent objects, and association lines similar to those seen in the class diagram connect them. You draw arrows next to the association lines from the initiating object to the receiving object to represent the messages being passed between the objects. Just as in the sequence diagrams, the shape of the arrowhead indicates whether the message is synchronous or asynchronous. Because there is no timeline in the diagram, numbers represent the sequence of the messaging. Figure 3-18 shows a generic example of a collaboration diagram.

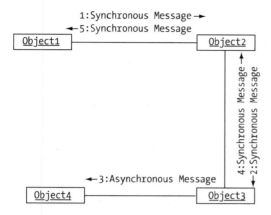

Figure 3-18. *Generic collaboration diagram*

Like the sequence diagrams, the collaboration diagrams are created from the use case scenarios. The sequence diagrams and the corresponding collaboration diagrams should be cross-checked with each other for consistency. Figure 3-19 shows a collaboration diagram for the Process Movie Rental scenario developed earlier in this chapter.

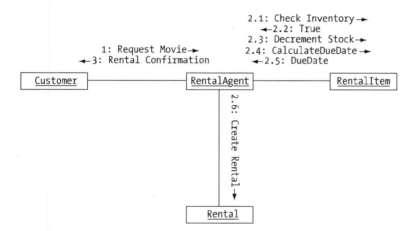

Figure 3-19. *Process Movie Rental collaboration diagram*

Nesting Messages

The numbering of the messages in Figure 3-19 represents the use of *nesting*. Messages grouped together to accomplish a task use a nested numbering system. This makes it easier to revise the set of procedures grouped together without affecting the numbering of the rest of the messages. For example, you need to add a message call that checks to make sure the rental item has not been reserved. You could easily revise Figure 3-19 to include this message call; you would need to alter only the nested numbering of message 2.

Iteration, Constraints, and Branching

Some of the advanced features you can model with sequence diagrams are iteration, conditional constraints, and branching. Figure 3-6 demonstrated how you depict an iteration in a sequence diagram. Figure 3-20 demonstrates how this same iteration would be depicted with a collaboration diagram.

Figure 3-20. *Depicting an iteration in a collaboration diagram*

The asterisk after the message number indicates it will be sent multiple times. You place the binding condition of the iteration in parentheses following the asterisk. The stacking of the object rectangles indicates that multiple object instances occur in the iteration.

Figure 3-21 shows part of a collaboration diagram that depicts conditional constraints and branching. This diagram is equivalent to the sequence diagram shown earlier in Figure 3-8. Notice that the conditional constraints appear in brackets and the branches have the same sequence numbers.

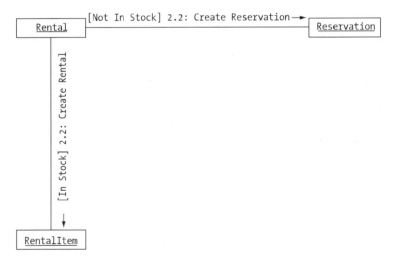

Figure 3-21. *Conditional constraints in a collaboration diagram*

Although the interaction diagrams are valuable for modeling the interaction among the different objects involved in carrying out the functionality of the system, a third type of diagram often further documents the dynamic interactions of the system. Instead of focusing on the objects involved in the system processing, an *activity diagram* focuses on the different activities that need to occur during the processing.

Understanding Activity Diagrams

An activity diagram illustrates the flow of activities that need to occur during an operation or process. You can construct the activity diagram to view the workflow at various levels of focus:

- A high, system-level focus represents each use case as an activity and diagrams the workflow among the different use cases.

- A mid-level focus diagrams the workflow occurring within a particular use case.

- A low-level focus diagrams the workflow that occurs within a particular operation of one of the classes of the system.

The activity diagram consists of the starting point of the process represented by a solid circle and transition arrows representing the flow or transition from one activity to the next. Rounded rectangles represent the activities, and a bull's-eye circle represents the ending point of the process. For example, Figure 3-22 shows a generic activity diagram that represents a process that starts with activity A, proceeds to activity B, and concludes.

Figure 3-22. *Generic activity diagram*

Decision Points and Guard Conditions

Often, one activity will conditionally follow another. For example, in order to rent a video, a PIN verifies membership. An activity diagram represents conditionality by a *decision point* (represented by a diamond) with the *guard condition* (the condition that must be met to proceed) in brackets next to the flow line (see Figure 3-23).

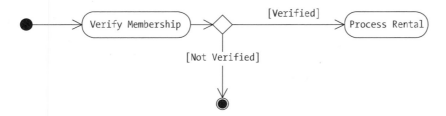

Figure 3-23. *Indicating decision points and guard conditions*

Parallel Processing

In some cases, two or more activities can run in parallel instead of sequentially. A solid, bold line drawn perpendicularly to the transition arrow represents the splitting of the paths. After the split, a second solid, bold line represents the merge. Figure 3-24 shows an activity diagram for the processing of a movie return. The order in which the Increment Inventory and the Remove Rental activities occur does not matter. The parallel paths in the diagram represent this parallel processing.

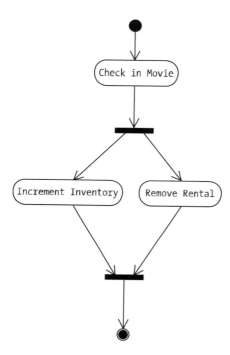

Figure 3-24. *Parallel processing depicted in an activity diagram*

Activity Ownership

The activity diagram's purpose is to model the control flow from activity to activity as the program processes. The diagrams shown thus far do not indicate which objects have responsibility for these activities. To signify object ownership of the activities, you segment the activity diagram into a series of vertical columns called *swim lanes*. The object role at the top of the swim lane is responsible for the activities in that lane. Figure 3-25 shows an activity diagram for processing a movie rental, with swim lanes included.

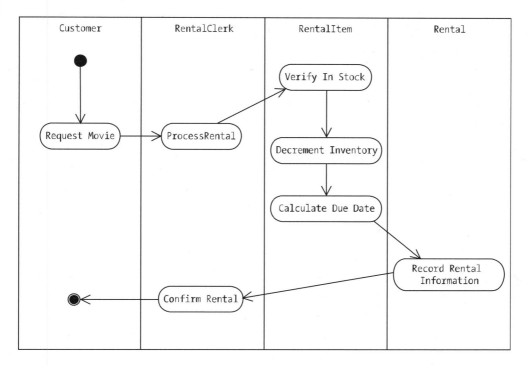

Figure 3-25. *Swim lanes in an activity diagram*

Activity 3-2. Creating an Activity Diagram

After completing this activity, you should be familiar with the following:

- Using an activity diagram to model control flow as the program completes an activity

- Using a UML modeling tool to create an activity class diagram

Identifying Objects and Activities

Examine the following scenario developed for a use case from the user group library application:

After viewing the list of available loan items, members request an item to check out on loan. The librarian enters the member number and retrieves information about out-standing loans and any unpaid fines. If the member has fewer than four outstanding loans and does not have any outstanding fines, the loan is processed. The librarian retrieves information on the loan item to determine if it is currently on loan. If the item is available, it is checked out to the member.

By identifying the nouns and noun phrases in the use case scenario, you can get an idea of what objects will perform the tasks in carrying out the activities. Remember, these objects are instances of the classes identified in the class diagram. The following objects will be involved in carrying out the activities: Member, Librarian, LoanHistory, Item, and Loan.

1. The verb phrases help identify the activities carried out by the objects. These activities should correspond to the methods of the classes in the system. Match the following activities to the appropriate objects:

    A. Request Movie

    B. Process Rental

    C. Check Availability

    D. Check Member's Loan Status

    E. Update Item Status

    F. Calculate Due Date

    G. Record Rental Info

    H. Confirm Rental

See the end of the chapter for Activity 3-2 answers.

Creating an Activity Diagram

Follow these steps to create an activity diagram:

1. Start UML Modeler. Choose File ➤ Open. Choose the UMLAct3_1 project and click OK.

2. You should be presented with the use case and sequence diagrams developed in Activity 3-1. In the main explorer window, in the upper-left corner of the screen, select the UMLAct3_1 node. On the toolbar at the left of the main explorer window, click the Associate an Activity Graph button. This will add an ActivityGraph node to the main explorer window (see Figure 3-26).

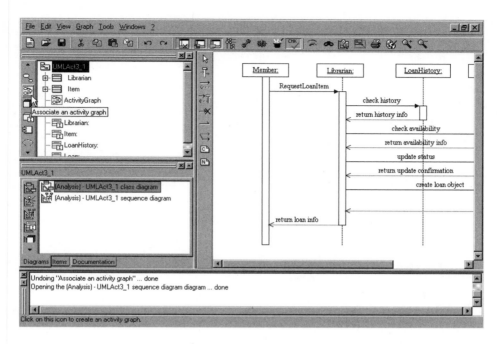

Figure 3-26. *Adding an activity graph*

3. Click the `ActivityGraph` node in the main explorer window. The Properties Editor will display a Create an Activity Diagram button in its toolbar on the left side of the window. Click this button to add an activity diagram to the project. You will see an activity diagram designer in the main editor window. The toolbar at the left of the designer window contains shapes used in creating activity diagrams (see Figure 3-27).

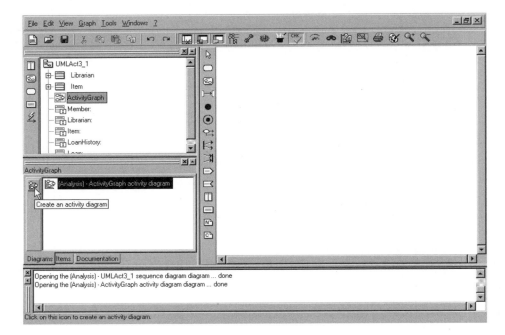

Figure 3-27. *Activity diagram designer*

4. Click the Create a Partition button in the designer toolbar and add a partition to the diagram. Change the name of the partition to Member.

5. Repeat the procedures in step 4 to add partitions for the Librarian, LoanHistory, Item, and Loan objects.

6. From the Shapes toolbar, click the Initial State shape and add it to the Member partition. Below the Initial State in the Member partition, add an Action State shape. Rename the Action State to **Request Item**. Add a transition shape (arrow) from the Initial State to the Request Item action state. Your diagram should be similar to Figure 3-28.

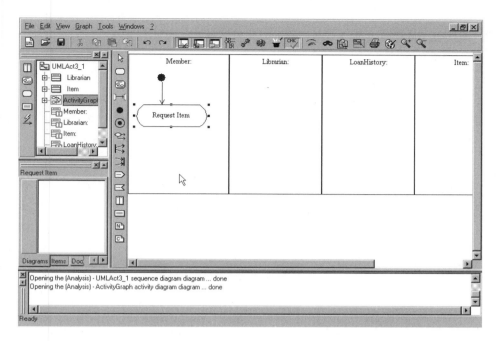

Figure 3-28. *Creating the activity diagram*

7. Under the `Librarian` partition, add a Process Loan action state and a Transition shape from the Request Item action to the Process Loan action state.

8. Under the `LoanHistory` partition, add a Check Member Status action state and a Transition shape from the Process Loan action to the Check Member Status action state.

9. From the Shapes toolbar, click the Conditional Branch shape and add it to the `LoanHistory` partition below the Check Member Status action state. Add a Transition from the Check Member Status action state to the Conditional Branch. From the Conditional Branch, add a Transition to a Deny Loan action state under the `Librarian` partition. Right-click the Transition shape and choose Modify. Enter a guard condition of **fail**. Also add a transition to a Check Item Status action state under the `Item` partition with a guard condition of **pass**. Your diagram should be similar to Figure 3-29.

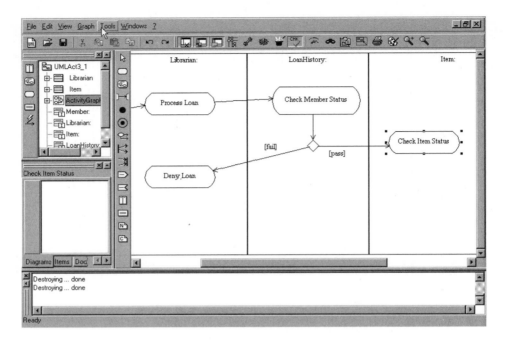

Figure 3-29. *A branching condition*

10. Repeat step 9 to create a Conditional Branch from the Check Item Status action. If the item is in stock, add a Transition to an Update Item Status action state under the Item partition. If the item is out of stock, add a Transition to the Deny Loan action state under the Librarian partition.

11. From the Update Item Status action state, add a Transition shape to a Record Loan Info action state under the Loan partition.

12. From the Record Loan Info action state, add a Transition shape to a Confirm Loan action state under the Librarian partition.

13. From the Shapes toolbar, click the Final State shape and add it to the bottom of the Member partition. Add a Transition shape from Deny Loan to the Final action state. Add another Transition shape from the Confirm Loan action state to the Final action state.

14. Your completed diagram should be similar to the one shown in Figure 3-30. Save the project and exit UML Modeler.

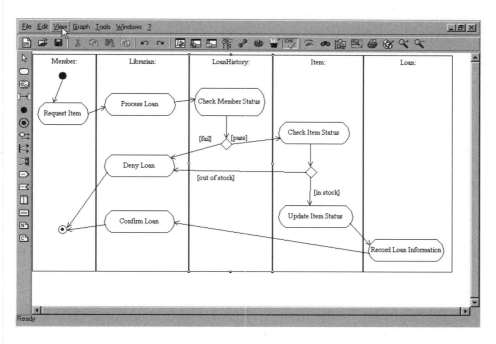

Figure 3-30. *Completed activity diagram*

Exploring GUI Design

Thus far, the discussions of object-oriented analysis and design have focused on modeling the functional design and the internal processing of the application. Successful modern software applications rely on a rich set of graphical user interfaces (GUIs) to expose this functionality to the users of the application.

In modern software systems, one of the most important aspects of an application is how well it interacts with the users. Gone are the days when users would interact with the application by typing cryptic commands at the DOS prompt. Modern operating systems employ GUIs, which are, for the most part, intuitive to use. Users have also grown used to the polished interfaces of the commercial office-productivity applications. Users have come to expect the same ease of use and intuitiveness built into applications developed in-house.

The design of the user interface should not be done haphazardly; rather, it should be planned in conjunction with the business logic design. The success of most applications is judged by the response of the users toward the application. If users are not comfortable when interacting with the application and the application does not improve the productivity of the user, it is doomed to failure. To the user, the application is the interface. It does not matter how pristine and clever the business logic code may be; if the user interface is poorly designed and implemented, the application will not be acceptable to the users. It is often hard for developers to remember that it is the user who drives the software development.

Although UML was not specifically designed for GUI design, many software architects and programmers have employed some of the UML diagrams to help when modeling the user interface of the application.

GUI Activity Diagrams

The first step in developing a user interface design is to perform a task analysis to discover how users will need to interact with the system. The task analysis is based on the use cases and scenarios that have been modeled previously. You can then develop activity diagrams to model how the interaction between the user and the system will take place. Figure 3-31 shows an activity diagram modeling the activities the user goes through to record rental information.

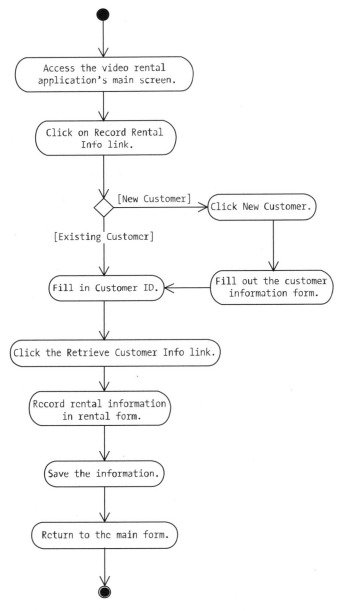

Figure 3-31. *GUI modeling with an activity diagram*

Interface Prototyping

After you have identified and prioritized the necessary tasks, you can develop a prototype sketch of the various screens that will make up the user interface. Figure 3-32 shows a prototype sketch of the Customer Info screen.

```
 ┌──────────────────────────────────────────────────┐
 │ Customer Info Screen                               │
 ├──────────────────────────────────────────────┐    │
 │ ┌─────────┬─────────────┬─────────┐           │    │
 │ │Customer │ Credit Card │ Address │           │    │
 │ ┴─────────┴─────────────┴─────────┴───────────┤    │
 │                                               │    │
 │   ID:[          ]        PIN:[          ]     │    │
 │                                               │    │
 │   Last Name:        First Name:      MI:      │    │
 │   [         ]       [          ]     [   ]    │    │
 │                                               │    │
 │                                               │    │
 └───────────────────────────────────────────────┘   │
 │  ┌─────────┐   ┌─────────┐   ┌─────────┐           │
 │  │  Edit   │   │  Save   │   │  Close  │           │
 │  └─────────┘   └─────────┘   └─────────┘           │
 └────────────────────────────────────────────────────┘
```

Figure 3-32. *GUI prototype sketch*

Interface Flow Diagrams

Once you have prototyped the various screens, you can use interface flow diagrams to model the relationships and flow patterns among the screens that make up the user interface. Figure 3-33 shows a partial interface flow diagram for the video rental application.

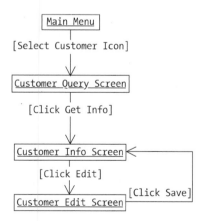

Figure 3-33. *Interface flow diagramming*

GUI Class Diagrams

In many OOP languages, the forms and the controls (text boxes, buttons, and so on) that make up the interfaces are objects based on system classes. You can use class diagrams to model the forms and the objects they contain. Figure 3-34 shows the aggregation between the Customer Info screen and its composite controls.

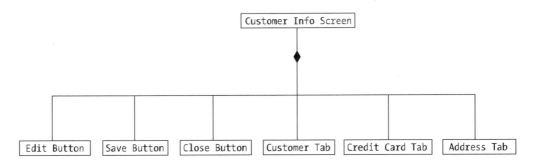

Figure 3-34. *A GUI class diagram*

Application Prototyping

Once you have roughed out the screen layout and the design of the user interface, you can develop a simple prototype. The prototype should contain skeleton code that simulates the functionality of the system. At this point, you should not put a great effort into integrating the user interface front end with the business functionality of the application. The idea is to let the users interact with a working prototype to obtain feedback on the design, allowing the users to suggest any design changes and improvements needed in the application's user interface.

The processes of refining and testing the user interface will be iterative and will most likely continue through several cycles. Once the user interface design and the internal functional design of the application have been completed and prototyped, the next step in the application development cycle is to start coding the application.

Summary

This chapter introduced scenarios, sequence diagrams, collaboration diagrams, and activity diagrams. You saw how to use these diagrams for modeling object interaction. Additionally, you learned how some of the UML diagrams might be used to help model the user interface of the application.

The goal of this and the previous chapters was to introduce you to some of the common modeling diagrams and concepts involved in software design and UML. In Chapter 4, you will take the concepts developed thus far and use them to implement a solution design for a sample case study.

Activity Answers

Activity 3-1 Answers

1. **Member, Librarian, Item, Loan, LoanHistory.** These five objects are involved in the processing depicted in the scenario.

2. The other messaging interactions depicted in the scenario are as follows:

   - The Librarian object checks the lending history of the member with the LoanHistory object.

   - The Librarian object checks the availability of the item through the Item object.

   - The Librarian object updates the availability of the item through the Item object.

   - The Librarian creates a Loan object containing loan information.

   - The Librarian returns loan information to the Member object.

Activity 3-2 Answers

1. **A. Member, B. Librarian, C. Item, D. LoanHistory, E. Item, F. Loan, G. Loan, H. Librarian.** The Member object is responsible for the Request Movie activity. The Librarian object is responsible for the Process Rental and Confirm Rental activities. The LoanHistory object is responsible for the Check Member's Loan Status activity. The Item object is responsible for the Check Availability and Update Item Status activities. The Loan object is responsible for the Calculate Due Date and Record Rental Info activities.

■ ■ ■

CHAPTER 4

Designing OOP Solutions: A Case Study

Designing solutions for an application is not an easy endeavor. Becoming an accomplished designer takes time and a conscious effort, which explains why many developers avoid it like the plague. You can study all the theories and know all the buzzwords, but the only way to truly develop your modeling skills is to roll up your sleeves, get your hands dirty, and start modeling. In this chapter, you will go through the process of modeling an office-supply ordering system. Although this is not a terribly complex application, it will serve to help solidify the modeling concepts covered in the previous chapters. By analyzing the case study, you will also gain a better understanding of how a model is developed and how the pieces fit together.

After reading this chapter, you should be familiar with the following:

- How to model an OOP solution using UML tools

- Some common OOP design pitfalls to avoid

Developing an OOP Solution

In the case-study scenario, your company currently has no standard way for departments to order office supplies. Each department separately implements its own ordering process. As a result, it is next to impossible to track company-wide spending on supplies, which impacts the ability to forecast budgeting and identify abuses. Another problem with the current system is that it does not allow for a single contact person who could negotiate better deals with the various vendors.

As a result, you have been asked to help develop a company-wide office-supply ordering (OSO) application. To model this system you will complete the following steps:

- Create an SRS.

- Develop the use cases.

- Diagram the use cases.

- Model the classes.

- Model the user interface design.

Creating the System Requirement Specification

After interviewing the various clients of the proposed system, you develop the SRS. Remember from Chapter 2 that the SRS scopes the system requirements, defines the system boundaries, and identifies the users of the system.

You have identified the following system users:

- **Purchaser:** Initiates a request for supplies

- **Department manager:** Tracks and approves supply requests from department purchasers

- **Supply vendor processing application:** Receives XML order files generated by the system

- **Purchase manager:** Updates supply catalog, tracks supply requests, and checks in delivered items

You have identified the following system requirements:

- Users must log in to the system by supplying a username and password.

- Purchasers will view a list of supplies that are available to be ordered.

- Purchasers will be able to filter the list of supplies by category.

- Purchasers can request multiple supplies in a single purchase request.

- A department manager can request general supplies for the department.

- Department managers must approve or deny supply requests for their department at the end of each week.

- If department managers deny a request, they must supply a short explanation outlining the reason for the denial.

- Department managers must track spending within their departments and ensure there are sufficient funds for approved supply requests.

- A purchase manager maintains the supply catalog and ensures it is accurate and up to date.

- A purchase manager checks in the supplies when they are received and organizes the supplies for distribution.

- Supply requests that have been requested but not approved are marked with a status of pending.

- Supply requests that have been approved are marked with a status of approved and an order is generated.

- Once an order is generated, an XML document containing the order details is placed in an order queue. Once the order has been placed in the queue, it is marked with a status of placed.

- A separate supply vendor processing application will retrieve the order XML files from the queue, parse the documents, and distribute the line items to the appropriate vendor queues. The vendor will retrieve the order XML documents from the queue.

- When all the items of an order are checked in, the order is marked with a status of fulfilled and the purchaser is informed that the order is ready for pickup.

Developing the Use Cases

After generating the SRS and getting the appropriate system users to sign off on it, the next task is to develop the use cases, which will define how the system will function from the users' perspective. The first step in developing the use cases is to define the actors. Remember from Chapter 2 that the actors represent the external entities (human or other systems) that will interact with the system. From the SRS, you can identify the following actors that will interact with the system:

- Purchaser

- Department Manager

- Purchase Manager

- Supply Vendor Processing Application

Now that you have identified the actors, the next step is to identify the various use cases with which the actors will be involved. By examining the requirement statements made in the SRS, you can identify the various use cases. For example, the statement "Users must log in to the system by supplying a username and password" indicates the need for a Login use case. Table 4-1 identifies the use cases for the OSO application.

Table 4-1. *Use Cases for the OSO Application*

Name	Actor(s)	Description
Login	Purchaser, Department Manager, Purchase Manager	Users see a login screen. They then enter their username and password. They either click Log In or Cancel. After login, they see a screen containing product information.
View Supply Catalog	Purchaser, Department Manager, Purchaser Manager	Users see a catalog table that contains a list of supplies. The table contains information such as the supply name, category, description, and cost. Users can filter supplies by category.
Purchase Request	Purchaser, Department Manager	Purchasers select items in the table and click a button to add them to their cart. A separate table shows the items in their cart, the number of each item requested and the cost, as well as the total cost of the request.

(Continued)

Table 4-1. (*Continued*)

Name	Actor(s)	Description
Department Purchase Request	Department Manager	Department managers select items in the table and click a button to add them to their cart. A separate table shows the items in their cart, the number of each item requested and the cost, as well as the total cost of the request.
Request Review	Department Manager	Department managers see a screen that lists all pending supply requests for members of their department. They review the requests and mark them as approved or denied. If they deny the request, they enter a brief explanation.
Track Spending	Department Manager	Department managers see a screen that lists the monthly spending of department members as well as the running total of the department.
Maintain Catalog	Purchase Manager	The purchase manager has the ability to update product information, add products, or mark products as discontinued. The administrator can also update category information, add categories, and mark categories as discontinued.
Item Check In	Purchase Manager	The purchase manager sees a screen for entering the order number. The purchase manager then sees the line items listed for the order. The items that have been received are marked. When all the items for an order are received, it is marked as fulfilled.
Order Placement	Supply Vendor Processing Application	The supply vendor processing application checks the queue for outgoing order XML files. Files are retrieved, parsed, and sent to the appropriate vendor queue.

Diagramming the Use Cases

Now that you have identified the various use cases and actors, you are ready to construct a visual design of the use cases using a UML modeling program. Figure 4-1 shows a preliminary use case model developed with Objecteering's UML Modeler, which was introduced in Chapter 2.

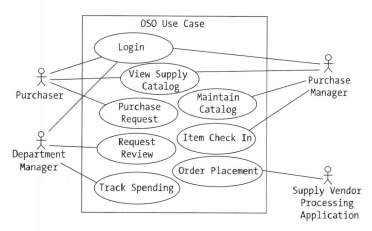

Figure 4-1. *Preliminary OSO use case diagram*

After you have diagrammed the use cases, you now look for any relationships that may exist between the use cases. Two relationships that may exist are the includes relationship and the extends relationship. Remember from the discussions in Chapter 2 that when a use case includes another use case, the use case being included needs to run as a precondition. For example, the Login use case of the OSO application needs to be included in the View Supply Catalog use case. The reason you make Login a separate use case is that the Login use case can be reused by one or more other use cases. In the OSO application, the Login use case will also be included with the Track Spending use case. Figure 4-2 depicts this includes relationship.

■**Note** In some modeling tools, the includes relationship may be indicated in the use case diagram by the uses keyword.

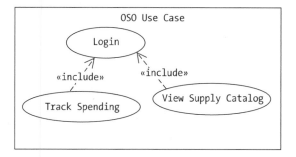

Figure 4-2. *Including the Login use case*

The extends relationship exists between two use cases when, depending on a condition, a use case will extend the behavior of the initial use case. In the OSO application, when a manager is making a purchase request, she can indicate that she will be requesting a purchase for the department. In this case, the Department Purchase Request use case becomes an extension of the Purchase Request use case. Figure 4-3 diagrams this extension.

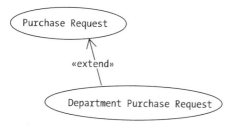

Figure 4-3. *Extending the Purchase Request use case*

After analyzing the system requirements and use cases, you can make the system development more manageable by breaking up the application and developing it in phases. For example you can develop the Purchase Request portion of the application first. Next, you can develop the Request Review portion, and then the Item Check In portion. The rest of this chapter focuses on the Purchase Request portion of the application. Employees and department managers will use this part of the application to make purchase requests. Figure 4-4 shows the use case diagram for this phase.

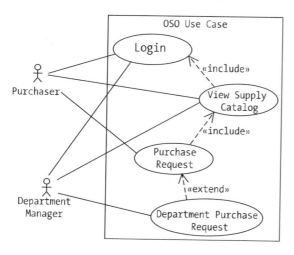

Figure 4-4. *Purchase Request use case diagram*

Developing the Class Model

Developing the class model involves several tasks. You begin by identifying the classes, and then add attributes, associations, and behaviors.

Identifying the Classes

After you have identified the various use cases, you can start identifying the classes the system needs to include to carry out the functionality described in the use cases. To identify the classes, you drill down into each use case and define a series of steps needed to carry it out. It is also helpful to identify the noun phrases in the use case descriptions. The noun phrases are often good indicators of the classes that will be needed.

For example, the following steps describe the View Supply Catalog use case:

1. User has logged in and been assigned a user status level. (This is the precondition.)

2. Users are presented with a catalog table that contains a list of supplies. The table contains information such as the supply name, category, description, and cost.

3. Users can filter supplies by category.

4. Users are given the choice of logging out or making a purchase request. (This is the postcondition.)

From this description, you can identify a class that will be responsible for retrieving product information from the database and filtering the products being displayed. The name of this class will be the `ProductCatalog` class.

Examining the noun phrases in the use case descriptions dealing with making purchase requests reveals the candidate classes for the OSO application, as listed in Table 4-2.

Table 4-2. *OSO Candidate Classes Used to Make Purchase Requests*

Use Case	Candidate Classes
Login	User, username, password, success, failure
View Supply Catalog	User, catalog table, supplies, information, supply name, category, description, cost
Purchase Request	Purchaser, items, cart, number, item requested, cost, total cost
Department Purchase Request	Department manager, items, cart, number, item requested, cost, total cost, department purchase request

Now that you have identified the candidate classes, you need to eliminate the classes that indicate redundancy. For example, a reference to items and line items would represent the same abstraction. You can also eliminate classes that represent attributes rather than objects. Username, password, and cost are examples of noun phrases that represent attributes. Some classes are vague or generalizations of other classes. User is actually a generalization of purchaser and manager. Classes may also actually refer to the same object abstraction but indicate a different state of the object. For example, the supply request and order represent the same abstraction before and after approval. You should also filter out classes that represent implementation constructs such as list and table. For example, a cart is really a collection of order items for a particular order.

Using these elimination criteria, you can whittle down the class list to the following candidate classes:

- Employee

- DepartmentManager

- Order

- OrderItem

- ProductCatalog

- Product

You can also include classes that represent the actors that will interact with the system. These are special classes called *actor classes* and are included in the class diagram to model the interface between the system and the actor. For example, you could designate a Purchaser(UI) actor class that represents the GUI that a Purchaser (Employee or DepartmentManager) would interact with to make a purchase request. Because these classes are not actually part of the system, the internal implementations of these classes are encapsulated, and they are treated as black boxes to the system.

You can now start formulating the class diagram for the Purchase Request portion of the OSO application. Figure 4-5 shows the preliminary class diagram for the OSO application.

Figure 4-5. *Preliminary OSO class diagram*

Adding Attributes to the Classes

The next stage in the development of the class model is to identify the level of abstraction the classes must implement. You determine what state information is relevant to the OSO application. This required state information will be implemented through the attributes of the class. Analyzing the system requirements for the Employee class reveals the need for a login name, password, department, and whether the user is a manager. You also need an identifier such as an employee ID to uniquely identify various employees. An interview with managers revealed the need to include the first and last names of the employee so that they can track spending by name. Table 4-3 summarizes the attributes that will be included in the OSO classes.

Table 4-3. *OSO Class Attributes*

Class	Attribute	Type
Employee	EmployeeID	Integer
	LoginName	String
	Password	String
	Department	String
	FirstName	String
	LastName	String
DepartmentManager	EmployeeID	Integer
	LoginName	String
	Password	String
	Department	String
	FirstName	String
	LastName	String
Order	OrderNumber	Long
	OrderDate	Date
	Status	String
OrderItem	ProductNumber	String
	Quantity	Short
	UnitPrice	Decimal
Product	ProductNumber	String
	ProductName	String
	Description	String
	UnitPrice	Decimal
	VendorCode	String
ProductCatalog	None	

Figure 4-6 shows the OSO class diagram with the class attributes. I have left out the attributes for the DepartmentManager class. The DepartmentManager class will probably inherit the attributes listed for the Employee class.

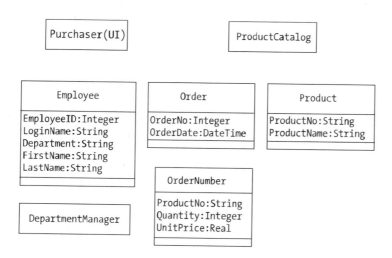

Figure 4-6. *OSO Purchase Request component class diagram with attributes added*

Identifying Class Associations

The next stage in the development process is to model the class associations that will exist in the OSO application. If you study the use cases and SRS, you can gain an understanding of what types of associations you need to incorporate into the class structural design.

Note You may find that you need to further refine the SRS to expose the class associations.

For example, an employee will be associated with an order. By examining the multiplicity of the association, you discover that an employee can have multiple orders, but an order can be associated with only one employee. Figure 4-7 models this association.

Figure 4-7. *Depicting the association between the Employee class and the Order class*

As you start to identify the class attributes, you will notice that the Employee class and the DepartmentManager class have many of the same attributes. This makes sense, because a manager is also an employee. For the purpose of this application, a manager represents an employee with specialized behavior. This specialization is represented by an inheritance relationship, as shown in Figure 4-8.

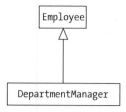

Figure 4-8. *The DepartmentManager class inheriting from the Employee class*

The following statements sum up the associations in the OSO class structure:

- An Order is an aggregation of OrderItem objects.

- An Employee can have multiple Order objects.

- An Order is associated with one Employee.

- The ProductCatalog is associated with multiple Product objects.

- A Product is associated with the ProductCatalog.

- An OrderItem is associated with one Product.

- A Product may be associated with multiple OrderItem objects.

- A DepartmentManager is an Employee with specialized behavior.

Figure 4-9 shows these various associations (excluding the class attributes for clarity).

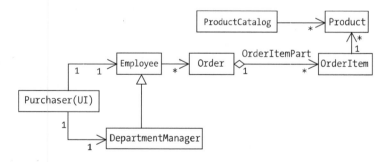

Figure 4-9. *The OSO Purchase Request component class diagram with associations added*

Modeling the Class Behaviors

Now that you have sketched out the preliminary structure of the classes, you are ready to model how these classes will interact and collaborate. The first step in this process is to drill down into the use case descriptions and create a more detailed scenario of how the use case will be carried out. The following scenario describes one possible sequence for carrying out the Login use case.

1. The user is presented with a login dialog box.

2. The user enters a login name and a password.

3. The user submits the information.

4. The name and password are checked and verified.

5. The user is presented with a supply request screen.

Although this scenario depicts the most common processing involved with the Login use case, you may need other scenarios to describe anticipated alternate outcomes. The following scenario describes an alternate processing of the Login use case:

1. The user is presented with a login dialog box.

2. The user enters a login name and a password.

3. The user submits the information.

4. The name and password are checked but cannot be verified.

5. The user is informed of the incorrect login information.

6. The user is presented with a login dialog box again.

7. The user either tries again or cancels the login request.

At this point, it may help to create a visual representation of the scenarios outlined for the use case. Remember from Chapter 3 that activity diagrams are often used to visualize use case processing. Figure 4-10 shows an activity diagram constructed for the Login use case scenarios.

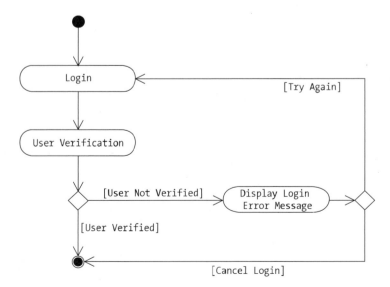

Figure 4-10. *An activity diagram depicting the Login use case scenarios*

After analyzing the process involved in the use case scenarios, you can now turn your attention to assigning the necessary behaviors to the classes of the system. To help identify the class behaviors and interactions that need to occur, you construct an interaction diagram. As discussed in Chapter 3, interaction diagrams can take the form of either a sequence diagram or a collaboration diagram. Sequence diagrams focus on the order of the object interactions taking place, and collaboration diagrams focus on the links occurring between the objects. Figure 4-11 shows a sequence diagram for the Login use case scenarios. The Purchaser(UI) class calls the Login method that has been assigned to the Employee class. The message returns information that will indicate whether the login has been verified.

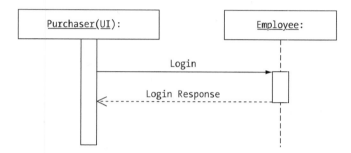

Figure 4-11. *A sequence diagram depicting the Login use case scenarios*

Next, let's analyze the View Supply Catalog use case. The following scenario describes the use case:

1. User logged in and has been verified.

2. User views a catalog table that contains product information, including the supply name, category, description, and price.

3. User chooses to filter the table by category, selects a category, and refreshes the table.

From this scenario, you can see that you need a method of the ProductCatalog class that will return a listing of product categories. The Purchaser class will invoke this method. Another method the ProductCatalog class needs is one that will return a product list filtered by category. The sequence diagram in Figure 4-12 shows the interaction that occurs between the Purchaser(UI) class and the ProductCatalog class.

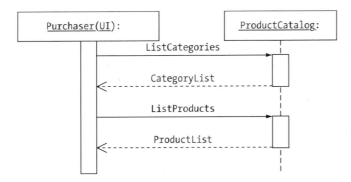

Figure 4-12. *A sequence diagram depicting the View Supply Catalog scenario*

The following scenario was developed for the Purchase Request use case:

1. A purchaser has logged in and has been verified as an employee.

2. The purchaser selects items from the product catalog and adds them to the order request (shopping cart), indicating the number of each item requested.

3. After completing the item selections for the order, the purchaser submits the order.

4. Order request information is updated, and an order ID is generated and returned to the purchaser.

From the scenario, you can identify an AddItem method of the Order class that needs to be created. This method will accept a product ID and a quantity and then return the subtotal of the order. The Order class will need to call a method of the OrderItem class, which will create an instance of an order item. You also need a SubmitOrder method of the Order class that will submit the request and the return order ID of the generated order. Figure 4-13 shows the associated sequence diagram for this scenario.

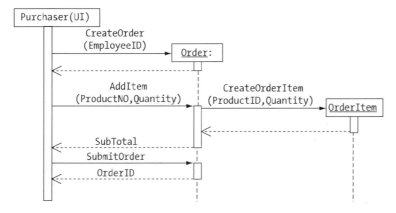

Figure 4-13. *A sequence diagram depicting the Purchase Request scenario*

Some other scenarios that need to be included are deleting an item from the shopping cart, changing the quantity of an item in the cart, and canceling the order process. You will also need to include similar scenarios and create similar methods for the Department Purchase Request use case. After analyzing the scenarios and interactions that need to take place, you can develop a class diagram for the Purchase Request portion of the application, as shown in Figure 4-14.

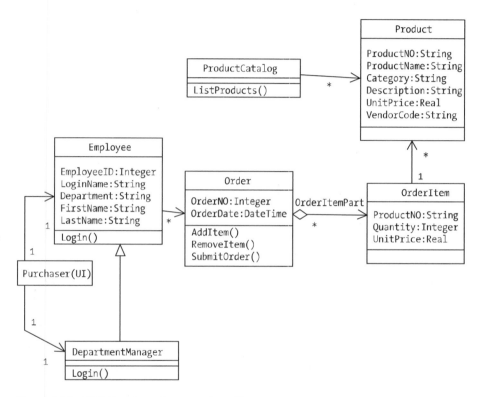

Figure 4-14. *OSO Purchase Request class diagram*

Developing the User Interface Model Design

At this point in the application design process, you do not want to commit to a particular GUI implementation (in other words, a technology-specific one). It is helpful, however, to model some of the common elements and functionality required of a GUI for the application. This will help you create a prototype user interface that you can use to verify the business logic design that has been developed. The users will be able to interact with the prototype and provide feedback and verification of the logical design.

The first prototype screen that you need to implement is the one for logging in. You can construct an activity diagram to help define the activities the user needs to perform when logging in to the system, as shown in Figure 4-15.

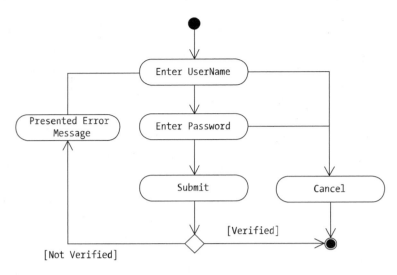

Figure 4-15. *An activity diagram depicting user login activities*

Analyzing the activity diagram reveals that you can implement the login screen as a fairly generic interface. This screen should allow the user to enter a username and password. It should include a way to indicate that the user is logging in as either an employee or a manager. The final requirement is to include a way for the user to abort the login process. Figure 4-16 shows a prototype of the login screen.

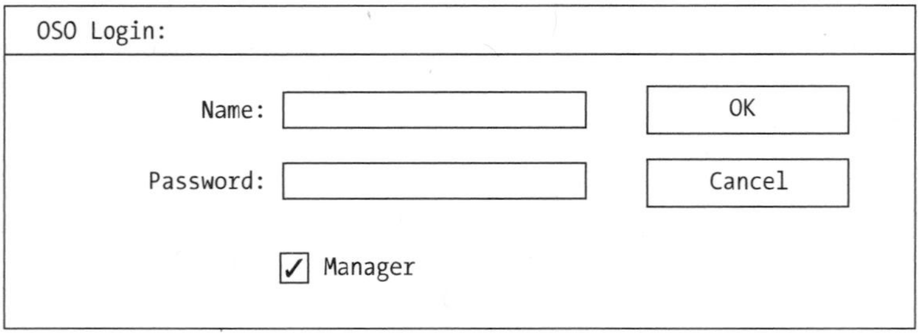

```
OSO Login:

        Name:  [                    ]        [     OK     ]

    Password:  [                    ]        [   Cancel   ]

              [✓] Manager
```

Figure 4-16. *Login screen prototype*

The next screen you need to consider is the product catalog screen. Figure 4-17 depicts the activity diagram for viewing and filtering the products.

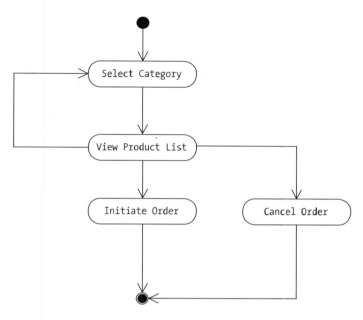

Figure 4-17. *An activity diagram depicting activities for viewing products*

The activity diagram reveals that the screen needs to show a table or list of products and product information. Users must be able to filter the products by category, which can be initiated by selecting a category from a category list. Users also need to be able to initiate an order request or exit the application. Figure 4-18 shows a prototype screen that can be used to view the products.

```
┌──────────────────────────────────────────────────────────────┐
│ OSO Product Catalog                                          │
│                                                              │
│                                                              │
│     Category:  ┌──────────────────────┐ ┌──┐                 │
│                └──────────────────────┘ │▼ │                 │
│                                         └──┘                 │
│     ┌───────────┬───────────┬──────────────────────────┐     │
│     │  Product  │   Price   │      Description          │     │
│     ├───────────┼───────────┼──────────────────────────┤     │
│     │           │           │                          │     │
│     ├───────────┼───────────┼──────────────────────────┤     │
│     │           │           │                          │     │
│     ├───────────┼───────────┼──────────────────────────┤     │
│     │           │           │                          │     │
│     ├───────────┼───────────┼──────────────────────────┤     │
│     │           │           │                          │     │
│     ├───────────┼───────────┼──────────────────────────┤     │
│     │           │           │                          │     │
│     └───────────┴───────────┴──────────────────────────┘     │
│                                                              │
│     ┌─────────────────┐  ┌─────────────────┐  ┌─────────┐    │
│     │  Add to Order   │  │  Cancel Order   │  │  Exit   │    │
│     └─────────────────┘  └─────────────────┘  └─────────┘    │
│                                                              │
└──────────────────────────────────────────────────────────────┘
```

Figure 4-18. *View products screen prototype*

The final screen that needs to be prototyped for this part of the application is the shopping cart interface. This will facilitate the adding and removing items from an order request. It also needs to allow the user to submit the order or abort an order request. Figure 4-19 shows a prototype of the order request screen.

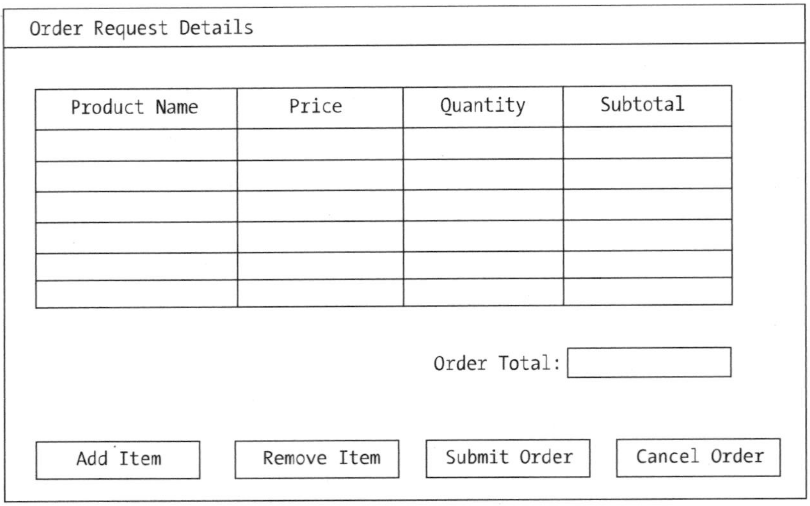

Figure 4-19. *Order request screen prototype*

That completes the preliminary design for this phase of the OSO application. You applied what you learned in Chapters 2 and 3 to model the design. Next, let's review some common mistakes to avoid during this process.

Avoiding Some Common OOP Design Pitfalls

When you start to model your own OOP designs, you want to be sure to follow good practice. The following are some of the common traps that you should avoid:

Confusing modeling with documenting: The main value in modeling is not the diagrams produced, but rather the process you go through to produce the diagrams.

Not involving the users in the process: It is worth emphasizing that users are the consumers of your product. They are the ones who define the business processes and functional requirements of the system.

Trying to model the whole solution at one time: When developing complex systems, break up the system design and development into manageable components. Plan to produce the software in phases. This will provide for faster modeling, developing, testing, and release cycles.

Striving to create a perfect model: No model will be perfect from the start. Successful modelers understand that the modeling process is iterative, and models are continuously updated and revised throughout the application development cycle.

Thinking there is only one true modeling methodology: Just as there are many different equally viable OOP languages, there are many equally valid modeling methodologies for developing software. Choose the one that works best for you and the project at hand.

Reinventing the wheel: Look for patterns and reusability. If you analyze many of the business processes that applications attempt to solve, a consistent set of modeling patterns emerge. Create a repository where you can leverage these existing patterns from project to project and from programmer to programmer.

Letting the data model drive the business logic model: It is generally a bad idea to develop the data model (database structure) first and then build the business logic design on top of it. The solution designer should first ask what business problem needs to be solved and then build a data model to solve the problem.

Confusing the problem domain model with the implementation model: You should develop two distinct but complementary models when designing applications. A *domain model* design describes the scope of the project and the processing involved in implementing the business solutions. This includes what objects will be involved, their properties and behaviors, and how they interact and relate to each other. The domain model should be implementation-agnostic. You should be able to use the same domain model as a basis for several different architecturally specific implementations. In other words, you should be able to take the same domain model and implement it using a Visual Basic rich-client, two-tier architecture or a C# (or Java, for that matter) n-tier distributed web application.

Summary

Now that you have analyzed the domain model of an OOP application, you are ready to transform the design into an actual implementation. The next part of this book will introduce you to the Visual Basic language. You will look at the .NET Framework and see how Visual Basic applications are built on top of the framework. You will be introduced to working in the Visual Studio IDE and become familiar with the syntax of the Visual Basic language. The next section will also demonstrate the process of implementing OOP constructs such as class structures, object instantiation, inheritance, and polymorphism in the Visual Basic .NET language. You will revisit the case study introduced in this chapter in Chapter 10, at which time you will look at transforming the application design into actual implementation code.

PART 2

Object-Oriented Programming with Visual Basic

CHAPTER 5

■■■

Introducing Visual Basic and the .NET Framework

Business application programming has evolved from a two-tier, tightly coupled model into a multitiered, loosely coupled model, often involving data transfer over the Internet or a corporate intranet. In an effort to allow programmers to be more productive and deal with the complexities of this type of model, Microsoft developed the .NET Framework. To effectively program in Visual Basic (VB), you need to understand this underlying framework upon which it is built.

After reading this chapter, you should be familiar with the following:

- The .NET Framework

- Features of the Common Language Runtime

- How the just-in-time compiler works

- The .NET Framework base class library

- Namespaces and assemblies

- The features of the Visual Studio integrated development environment

Introducing the .NET Framework

The .NET Framework is a collection of fundamental classes designed to provide the common services needed to run applications. Let's look at the goals of the .NET Framework and then review its components.

Goals of the .NET Framework

Microsoft designed the .NET Framework with certain goals in mind. The following sections examine these goals and how the .NET Framework achieves them.

Support of Industry Standards

Microsoft wanted the .NET Framework to be based on industry standards and practices. As a result, the framework relies heavily on industry standards such as the Extensible Markup Language (XML) and Simple Object Access Protocol (SOAP). Microsoft has also submitted a Common Language Infrastructure (CLI) Working Document to the European Computer Manufacturers Association (ECMA), which oversees many of the common standards in the computer industry.

The CLI is a set of specifications needed to create compilers that conform to the .NET Framework. Third-party vendors can use these specifications to create .NET-compliant language compilers; for example, Interactive Software Engineering (ISE) has created a .NET compiler for Eifle. Third-party vendors can also create a Common Language Runtime (CLR) that will allow .NET-compliant languages to run on different platforms. For example, a CLR could be developed that gives VB applications the ability to run on the Linux platform.

Extensibility

To create a highly productive environment in which to program, Microsoft realized the .NET Framework had to be extensible. As a result, Microsoft has exposed the framework class hierarchy to developers. Through inheritance and interfaces, you can easily access and extend the functionality of these classes. For example, you could create a button control class that not only inherits its base functionality from the button class exposed by the .NET Framework, but that also extends the base functionality in a unique way required by your application.

Microsoft has also made it a lot easier to work with the underlying operating system. By repackaging and implementing the Windows operating system application programming interface (API) functions in a class-based hierarchy, Microsoft has made it more intuitive and easier for OOP programmers to work with the functionality exposed by the underlying operating system.

Unified Programming Models

Another important goal Microsoft incorporated into the .NET Framework was cross-language independence and integration. To achieve this goal, all languages that support the Common Language Specification (CLS) compile into the same intermediate language, support the same set of basic data types, and expose the same set of code-accessibility methods. As a result, not only can classes developed in the different CLS-compliant languages communicate seamlessly with one another, but you can also implement OOP constructs across languages. For example, you could develop a class written in VB that inherits from a class written using C#. Microsoft has developed five languages that support the .NET Framework. Along with VB, the languages are C#, managed C++, JScript, and J#. In addition to these languages, many third-party vendors have developed versions of other popular languages designed to run under the .NET Framework, such as Perl and SmallTalk.

Easier Deployment

Microsoft needed a way to simplify application deployment. Before the development of the .NET Framework, when components were deployed, component information had to be recorded in the system registry. Many of these components, especially system components, were used by several different client applications. When a client application made a call to the component, the registry was searched to determine the metadata needed to work with the component. If a newer version of the component was deployed, it replaced the registry information of the old component. Often, the new components were incompatible with the old version and caused existing clients to fail. You have probably experienced this problem after installing a service pack that ended up causing more problems than it fixed!

The .NET Framework combats this problem by storing the metadata for working with the component in a *manifest*, which is packaged in the assembly containing the component code. An *assembly* is a package containing the code, resources, and metadata needed to run an application. By default, an assembly is marked as private and placed in the same directory as the client assembly. This ensures that the component assembly is not inadvertently replaced or modified and also allows for a simpler deployment because there is no need to work with the registry. If a component needs to be shared, its assembly is deployed to a special directory referred to as the Global Assembly Cache (GAC). The manifest of the assembly contains versioning information, so newer versions of the component can be deployed side by side with the older versions in the GAC. By default, client assemblies continue to request and use the versions of the components they were intended to use. Older client assemblies will no longer fail when newer versions of the component are installed.

Improved Memory Management

A common problem of programs developed for the Windows platform has been memory management. Often, these programs have caused *memory leaks*. A memory leak occurs when a program allocates memory from the operating system but fails to release the memory after it is finished working with the memory. This problem is compounded when the program is intended to run for a long time, such as a service that runs in the background. To combat this problem, the .NET Framework uses nondeterministic finalization. Instead of relying on the applications to deallocate the unused memory, the framework uses a garbage collection object. The garbage collector periodically scans for unused memory blocks and returns them to the operating system.

Improved Security Model

Implementing security in today's highly distributed, Internet-based applications is an extremely important issue. In the past, security has focused on the user of the application. Security identities were checked when users logged in to an application, and their identities were passed along as the application made calls to remote servers and databases. This type of security model has proven to be inefficient and complicated to implement for today's enterprise-level, loosely coupled systems. In an effort to make security easier to implement and more robust, the .NET Framework uses the concept of code identity and code access.

When an assembly is created, it is given a unique identity. When a server assembly is created, you can grant access permissions and rights. When a client assembly calls a server assembly, the runtime will check the permissions and rights of the client and grant or deny access to the server code accordingly. Because each assembly has an identity, you can also restrict access to the assembly through the operating system. If a user downloads a component from the Web, for example, you can restrict the component's ability to read and write files on the user's system.

Components of the .NET Framework

Now that you have seen some of the major goals of the .NET Framework, let's take a look at the components it comprises.

Common Language Runtime

The fundamental component of the .NET Framework is the CLR. The CLR manages the code being executed and provides for a layer of extraction between the code and the operating system. Built into the CLR are mechanisms for the following:

- Loading code into memory and preparing it for execution

- Converting the code from the intermediate language to native code

- Managing code execution

- Managing code and user-level security

- Automating deallocation and release of memory

- Debugging and tracing code execution

- Providing structured exception handling

Framework Base Class Library

Built on top of the CLR is the .NET Framework base class library. Included in this class library are reference types and value types that encapsulate access to the system functionality. *Types* are data structures. A reference type is a complex type—for example, classes and interfaces. A value type is simple type—for example, integer or Boolean. Programmers use these base classes and interfaces as the foundation on which they build applications, components, and controls. The base class library includes types that encapsulate data structures, perform basic input/output operations, invoke security management, manage network communication, and perform many other functions.

Data and XML Classes

Built on top of the base classes are classes that support data management. This set of classes is commonly referred to as ADO.NET. Using the ADO.NET object model, programmers can access and manage data stored in a variety of data storage structures through managed providers. Microsoft has written and tuned the ADO.NET classes and object model to work efficiently in a loosely coupled, disconnected, multitiered environment. Under the hood, ADO.NET works with data in an XML-structured format. Using this type of structure instead of a binary format makes it much easier to pass data using the Hypertext Transfer Protocol (HTTP) and to share data between disparate systems. Another advantage of ADO.NET is that it not only exposes the data from the database, but also exposes the metadata associated with the data. Data is exposed as a sort of mini-relational database. This means that you can get the data and work with it while disconnected from the data source and later synchronize the data with the data source.

Microsoft has provided support for several data providers. Data stored in Microsoft SQL Server 7.0 and later can be accessed through the native SQL data provider. OLEDB and Open Database Connectivity (ODBC) managed providers are two generic providers for systems currently exposed through the OLEDB or ODBC standard APIs. Because these managed data providers do not interface directly with the database engine but rather talk to the unmanaged provider, which then talks to the database engine, using non-native data providers is less efficient and robust than using a native provider. Because of the extensibility of the .NET Framework and Microsoft's commitment to open-based standards, many data storage vendors now supply native data providers for their systems.

ADO.NET is heavily dependent on XML to store, manipulate, and pass data and metadata. Rich support is provided by ADO.NET to manipulate, search, and transform XML data. In fact, programmers using ADO.NET can work with any data storage device on any platform that can expose its data in a standard XML format. You can also read in an XML data structure, expose it as a relational data structure for clients to work with and manipulate, and then convert it back to an XML format for data storage or transport.

Web Forms and Services

The .NET Framework exposes a base set of classes that can be used on a web server to create user interfaces and services exposed to web-enabled clients. These classes are collectively referred to as ASP.NET. Using ASP.NET, you can develop one user interface that can dynamically respond to the type of client device making the request. At runtime, the .NET Framework takes care of discovering the type of client making the request (browser type and version) and exposing an appropriate interface. The GUIs for web applications running on a Windows client have become more robust because the .NET Framework exposes much of the API functionality that previously had been exposed only to traditional Windows Forms-based C++ and VB applications. Another improvement in web application development using the .NET Framework is that server-side code can be written in any .NET-compliant language. Prior to .NET, server-side code had to be written in a scripting language such as VBScript or JScript.

Incorporated into ASP.NET are base class and interface support for creating web-based services. Microsoft's vision is that web services will provide functionality similar to the components developed using previous versions of Visual C++ (VC++) and VB. Because these components were based on binary standards, it was not easy to communicate with the components through firewalls and across the Internet. The proprietary nature of the components also limited the types of clients that could effectively use and interact with the components. Microsoft has addressed these limitations by exposing web services through Internet standards such as XML and SOAP. The current version of web services components can easily interact and expose their services to any client that is XML-enabled and can communicate via HTTP.

Windows Forms

Understanding that not all applications built with the .NET Framework will be web applications, Microsoft has exposed a rich set of classes for building Windows GUI applications. Microsoft has wrapped functionality previously exposed through cryptic API calls into the object-oriented class structure of the .NET Framework. In the past, developing Windows GUIs in VC++ was dramatically different than developing them in VB. Although developing GUIs in VB was easy and could be accomplished very quickly, VB developers were isolated and not fully exposed to the underlying features of the Windows API. Because Windows GUI development has been incorporated into the .NET Framework set of base classes, such development has become consistent across the various .NET-enabled programming languages. Microsoft has also exposed advanced Windows GUI functionality equally among the .NET-compliant languages.

Windows Services

Microsoft has supplied .NET developers with a set of classes and interfaces that greatly eases the ability to interact with Windows services. For example, creating applications that interact with the Windows event logging system or system performance monitors has become a much improved, consistent programming experience. You can also easily create and deploy your own services that plug into the Windows service manager and automatically run in the background while the computer runs.

Working with the .NET Framework

To work with the .NET Framework, you should understand how it is structured and how managed code is compiled and executed. .NET applications are organized and packaged into *assemblies*. All code executed by the .NET runtime must be contained in an assembly.

Understanding Assemblies and Manifests

The assembly contains the code, resources, and a manifest (metadata about the assembly) needed to run the application. Assemblies can be organized into a single file, where all this information is incorporated into a single dynamic link library (DLL) file or executable (EXE) file, or multiple files where the information is incorporated into separate DLL files, graphics files, and a manifest file. One of the main functions of an assembly is to form a boundary for types, references, and security. Another important function of the assembly is to form a unit for deployment.

One of the most crucial portions of an assembly is the manifest; in fact, every assembly must contain a manifest. The purpose of the manifest is to describe the assembly. It contains such things as the identity of the assembly, a description of the classes and other data types the assembly exposes to clients, any other assemblies this assembly needs to reference, and security details needed to run the assembly.

By default, when an assembly is created, it is marked as private. A copy of the assembly must be placed in the same directory or a `bin` subdirectory of any client assembly that uses it. If the assembly must be shared among multiple client assemblies, it is placed in the GAC, a special Windows folder. To convert a private assembly into a shared assembly, you must run a utility program to create encryption keys, and you must sign the assembly with the keys. After signing the assembly, you must use another utility to add the shared assembly into the GAC. By mandating such stringent requirements for creating and exposing shared assemblies, Microsoft is trying to ensure that naming collisions and malicious tampering of shared assemblies will not occur.

Referencing Assemblies and Namespaces

To make the .NET Framework more manageable, Microsoft has given it a hierarchical structure. This hierarchical structure is organized into what are referred to as *namespaces*. By organizing the framework into namespaces, the chances of naming collisions are greatly reduced. Organizing related functionality of the framework into namespaces also greatly enhances its usability for developers. For example, if you want to build a window's GUI, it is a pretty good bet the functionality you need exists in the `System.Windows.Forms` namespace.

All of the .NET Framework classes reside in the System namespace. The System namespace is further subdivided by functionality. The functionality required to work with a database is contained in the System.Data namespace. Some namespaces run several levels deep; for example, the functionality used to connect to a SQL Server database is contained in the System.Data.SqlClient namespace.

An assembly may be organized into a single namespace or multiple namespaces. Several assemblies may also be organized into the same namespace.

To gain access to the classes in the .NET Framework, you need to reference the assembly that contains the namespace in your code. Then you can access classes in the assembly by providing their fully qualified names. For example, if you want to add a text box to a form, you create an instance of the System.Windows.Forms.TextBox class, like so:

```
Private WithEvents textBox1 as System.Windows.Forms.TextBox
```

Fortunately, in VB, you can use the imports statement so that you do not need to continually reference the fully qualified name in the code:

```
Imports System.Windows.Forms
Private WithEvents textBox1 as TextBox
```

Compiling and Executing Managed Code

When .NET code is compiled, it is converted into a .NET portable executable (PE) file. The compiler translates the source code into Microsoft intermediate language (MSIL) format. MSIL is CPU-independent code, which means it needs to be further converted into native code before executing.

Along with the MSIL code, the PE file includes the metadata information contained within the manifest. The incorporation of the metadata in the PE file makes the code *self-describing*. There is no need for additional type library or Interface Definition Language (IDL) files.

Because the source code for the various .NET-compliant languages is compiled into the same MSIL and metadata format based on a common type system, the .NET platform supports language integration. This is a step beyond Microsoft's COM components, where, for example, client code written in VB could instantiate and use the methods of a component written in C++. With .NET language integration, you could write a .NET class in VB that inherits from a class written in C# and then overrides some of its methods.

Before the MSIL code in the PE file is executed, a .NET Framework just-in-time (JIT) compiler converts it into CPU-specific native code. To improve efficiency, the JIT compiler does not convert all the MSIL code into native code at the same time. MSIL code is converted on an as-needed basis. When a method is executed, the compiler checks to see if the code has already been converted and placed in cache. If it has, the compiled version is used; otherwise, the MSIL code is converted and stored in the cache for future calls.

Because JIT compilers are written to target different central processing units (CPUs) and operating systems, developers are freed from needing to rewrite their applications to target various platforms. It is conceivable that the programs you write for a Windows server platform will also run on a Unix server. All that is needed is a JIT compiler for the Unix architecture.

Using the Visual Studio Integrated Development Environment

You can write VB code using a simple text editor and compile it with a command-line compiler. You will find, however, that programming enterprise-level applications using a text editor can be frustrating and inefficient. Most programmers who code for a living find an integrated development environment (IDE) invaluable in terms of ease of use and increased productivity. Microsoft has developed an exceptional IDE in Visual Studio (VS). Integrated into VS are many features that make programming for the .NET Framework more intuitive, easier, and more productive. VS includes the following:

- Editor features such as automatic syntax checking, autocompletion, and color highlighting

- One IDE for all .NET languages

- Extensive debugging support, including the ability to set breakpoints, step through code, and view and modify variables

- Integrated help documentation

- Drag-and-drop GUI development

- XML and HTML editing

- Automated deployment tools that integrate with Windows Installer

- The ability to view and manage servers from within the IDE

- A fully customizable and extensible interface

The following activities will introduce you to some of the many features available in the VS IDE. As you work through these steps, don't worry about the coding details. Just concentrate on getting used to working within the VS IDE. You'll learn more about the code in upcoming chapters.

Activity 5-1. Touring VS

In this activity, you will become familiar with the following:

- Customizing the IDE

- Creating a .NET project and setting project properties

- Using the various editor windows in the VS IDE

- Using the auto syntax check and autocompletion features of the VS IDE

- Compiling assemblies with the VS IDE

Customizing the IDE

To customize the IDE, follow these steps:

1. Launch VS by selecting Start ➤ Programs ➤ Microsoft Visual Studio 2005.

Note If this is the first time you have launched VS, you will be asked to choose a default development setting. Choose the visual development settings.

2. You will be presented with the Start Page. The Start Page contains several panes, including one titled MSDN: Visual Basic, which has links to recent VB articles posted on the MSDN (Microsoft Developer Network) web site. Clicking one of these links will launch a browser window hosted inside VS, which will open the article on the MSDN site. The Getting Started pane includes links to the VS documentation. Clicking a documentation link launches the Microsoft Document Explorer. Take some time to investigate the information and the various links exposed to you on the Start Page.

3. Microsoft has taken considerable effort to make VS a customizable design environment. You can customize just about every aspect of the layout, from the various windows and menus down to the color coding used in the code editor. Select Tools ➤ Options to open the Options dialog box, shown in Figure 5-1, which allows you to customize many aspects of the IDE.

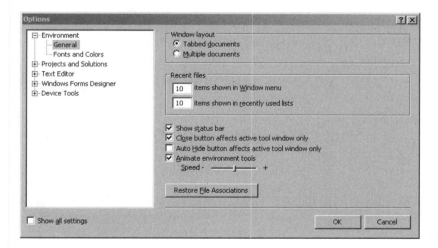

Figure 5-1. *VS Options dialog box*

4. Click Projects and Solutions in the category list on the left side of the dialog box. You are presented with options to change the default location of projects and what happens when you build and run a project. Select the Always Show Solution option and the Show Output Window When Build Starts option.

5. Investigate some of the other customizable options available. Close the Options dialog box when you are finished by clicking the OK button.

Creating a New Project

To create a new project, follow these steps:

1. On the Start Page, in the Recent Projects pane, click the Create Project link, which launches the New Project dialog box. (You can also choose File ➤ New ➤ Project to open this dialog box.)

2. The New Project dialog box allows you to create various projects using built-in templates. There are templates for creating VB projects, VC# projects, deployment projects, as well as many others, depending on what options you chose when installing VS.

3. In the Project Types pane, expand the Visual Basic node and select the Windows node, as shown in Figure 5-2. Observe the various VB project templates. There are templates for creating various types of Windows applications, including Windows Forms-based applications, class libraries, and console applications.

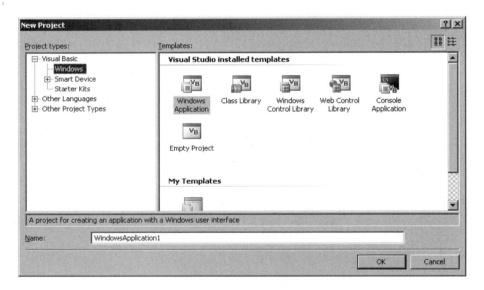

Figure 5-2. *VS New Project dialog box*

4. Click the Windows Application template. Change the name of the application to DemoChapter5 and click the OK button.

When the project opens, you will be presented with a form designer for a default form (named Form1) that has been added to the project. To the right of this window, you should see the Solution Explorer.

Investigating the Solution Explorer and Class View

The Solution Explorer displays the projects and files that are part of the current solution, as shown in Figure 5-3. By default, when you create a project, a solution is created with the same name as the project. The solution contains some global information, project-linking information, and customization settings, such as a task list and debugging information. A solution may contain more than one related project.

Figure 5-3. *Solution Explorer*

■**Note** If you do not see the solution node, select Tools ➤ Options and click Projects and Solutions. Select the Always Show Solution option.

Under the solution node is the project node. The project node organizes the various files and settings related to a project. The project file organizes this information in an XML document, which contains references to the class files that are part of the project, any external references needed by the project, and compilation options that have been set. Under the project node is a My Project node and the class file for the Form1 class.

To practice using the Solution Explorer and some VS features and views, follow these steps:

1. Right-click the My Project node and select Open. This launches the Project Properties window. Along the left side of the window are several tabs you can use to explore and set various application settings.

2. Select the Application tab, as shown in Figure 5-4. Notice that, by default, the assembly name and root namespace are set to the name of the project. Form1 has also been designated as the startup object.

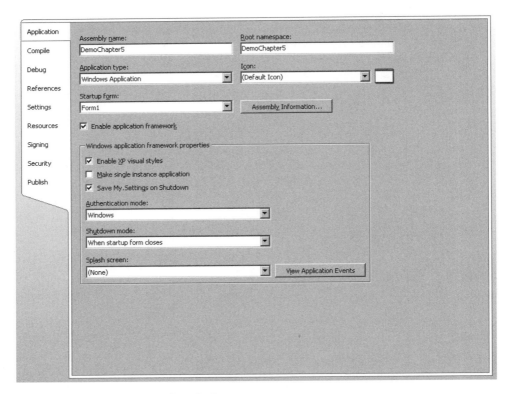

Figure 5-4. *VS Project Properties window*

3. Select the References tab. This tab shows the external assemblies referenced by the application. Notice that several references have been included by default. The default references depend on the type of project. For example, since this is a Windows Application project, a reference to the System.Windows.Forms namespace is included by default.

4. Explore some of the other tabs in the Project Properties window. Close the window when you are finished by clicking on the x in the upper-right corner of the window.

5. The Form1 class file under the Solution Explorer's project node has a .vb extension to indicate it is written in VB code. By default, the name of the file has been set to the same name as the form. Double-click the file in the Solution Explorer, and the form is shown in Design View. Click the View Code button in the toolbar at the top of the Solution Explorer, and the code editor for the Form1 class will open.

6. Select View ➤ Other Windows ➤ Class View to launch the Class View window. The top part of the Class View window organizes the project files in terms of the namespace hierarchy. Expanding the DemoChap5 root node reveals two subnodes: a References node and the DemoChap5 namespace node. A namespace node is designated by the {} symbol to the left of the node name.

Tip You can show or hide the various types of nodes shown in the Class View window by altering the settings in the Class View Settings drop-down list at the top of the Class View window. For this exercise, choose all the options except the Show Hidden Types and Members option.

7. Listed under the namespace node are the classes that belong to the namespace. Currently, there is one class, Form1. Expanding the Form1 node reveals a Base Types folder. Expanding Base Types shows the classes and interfaces inherited and implemented by the Form1 class, as shown in Figure 5-5. You can further expand the nodes to show the classes and interfaces inherited and implemented by the Form base class.

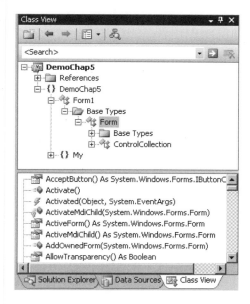

Figure 5-5. *Expanded nodes in the Class View*

8. The bottom section of the Class View window is a listing of the class's methods, properties, and events. Select the Form node in the top section of the Class View window. Notice the considerable number of methods, properties, and events listed in the bottom section of the window.

9. Right-click the DemoChap5 project node and select Add ➤ Class. Name the class DemoClass1 and click the Add button. If the class code is not visible in the code editor, double-click the DemoClass1 node in the Class View window to display it. Wrap the class definition code in a namespace declaration as follows:

```
Namespace MyDemoNamespace
    Public Class DemoClass1
    End Class
End Namespace
```

10. Notice the updated hierarchy in the Class View. DemoClass1 now belongs to the MyDemoNamespace, which belongs to the DemoChapter5 namespace. The fully qualified name of DemoClass1 is now DemoChapter5.MyDemoNamespace.DemoClass1.

11. Add the following code to the DemoClass1 definition:

```
Namespace MyDemoNamespace
    Public Class DemoClass1
        Inherits System.Collections.CaseInsensitiveComparer
    End Class
End Namespace
```

As you add the code, notice the auto selection drop-down list provided (see Figure 5-6). Pressing the Tab key will select the current item on the list.

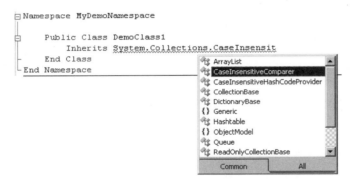

Figure 5-6. *Code selection drop-down list*

12. A Bases Types node has been added beneath the DemoClass1 node in the Class View. Expand this node, and you will see the base CaseInsensitiveComparer class node. Select this node, and you will see the methods and properties of the CaseInsensitiveComparer class in the lower section of the Class View window.

13. Right-click the Compare method of the CaseInsensitiveComparer class node and choose Browse Definition. (You can also initiate this step by double-clicking the Compare method node in the Class View.) The Object Browser window is opened as a tab in the main window, and information about the Compare method is displayed. Notice it takes two object arguments, compares them, and returns an integer value based on the result (see Figure 5-7).

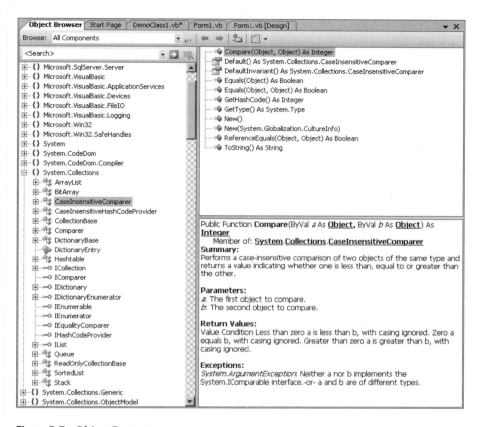

Figure 5-7. *Object Browser*

14. The Object Browser enables you to explore the object hierarchies and to view information about items and methods within the hierarchy. Take some time to explore the Object Browser. When you are finished, close the Object Browser and close the Class View window.

Exploring the Toolbox and Properties Window

To explore the VS Toolbox and Properties window, follow these steps:

1. In the Solution Explorer window, double-click the `Form1.vb` node. This brings up the `Form1` design tab in the main editing window. Locate the Toolbox tab to the left of the main editing window. Hover the cursor over the tab, and the Toolbox window should expand, as shown in Figure 5-8. In the upper-right corner of the Toolbox, you should see the Auto Hide icon, which looks like a thumbtack. Click the icon to turn off the auto hide feature.

Figure 5-8. *VS Toolbox*

2. Under the All Windows Forms node of the Toolbox are controls that you can drag-and-drop onto your form to build the GUI. There are also other nodes that contain nongraphical components that help make some common programming tasks easier to create and manage. For example, the Data node contains controls for accessing and managing data stores. Scroll down the Toolbox window and observe the various controls exposed by the designer.

3. Under the All Windows Forms node, select the Label control. Move the cursor over the form; it should change to a crosshairs pointer. Draw a label on the form by clicking, dragging, and then releasing the mouse. In a similar fashion, draw a TextBox control and a Button control on the form. Figure 5-9 shows how the form should look.

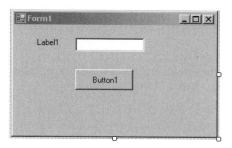

Figure 5-9. *Sample form layout*

4. Turn the auto hide feature of the Toolbox back on by clicking the Auto Hide (thumbtack) icon in the upper-right corner of the Toolbox window.

5. Locate the Properties tab to the right of the main editing window, or select View ➤ Properties Window to open the Properties window. The Properties window displays the properties of the currently selected object in the Design View. You can also edit many of the object's properties through this window.

6. In the Form1 design window, click Label1. The Label1 control should be selected in the drop-down list at the top of the Properties window (see Figure 5-10). Locate the Text property, and change it to **Enter your password:**.

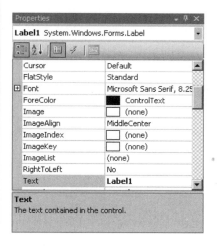

Figure 5-10. *VS Properties window*

■ **Note** You may need to resize the label on the form to see all the text.

---

7. Set the PasswordChar property of TextBox1 to *. Change the Text property of Button1 to **OK**. (Click the control on the form or use the drop-down list at the top of the Properties window to see the control's properties.)

8. Save the project by choosing File ➤ Save All.

Building and Executing the Assembly

To build and execute the assembly, follow these steps:

1. In the Solution Explorer, click `Form1`. At the top of the Solution Explorer, click the View Code toolbar button. The code editor for `Form1` will be displayed in the main editing window.

2. In the left drop-down list at the top of the code editor, select the Button1 control. In the right drop-down list, select the click event. A method that handles the button click event is added to the code editor.

3. Add the following code to the method. This code will display the password entered in TextBox1 on the title bar of the form:

```
Me.Text = "Your password is " & txtBox
```

4. Press Enter to move the cursor to the next line of code. You should see a blue squiggly line appear under the word `txtBox`. The auto syntax check feature indicates that `txtBox` is not a recognized word. Change `txtBox` to `TextBox1.Text`:

```
Me.Text = "Your password is " & TextBox1.Text
```

5. Move the cursor to the next line of code. The blue squiggly line should disappear.

6. Select Build ➤ Build Solution. The Output window shows the progress of compiling the assembly (see Figure 5-11). Once the assembly has been compiled, it is ready for execution. (If you cannot locate the Output window, select View menu ➤ Other Windows ➤ Output.)

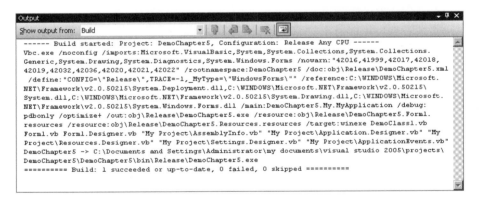

Figure 5-11. *Progress of build displayed in the Output window*

7. Select Debug ➤ Start Debugging. This runs the assembly in debug mode. Once the form loads, enter a password and click the OK button. You should see a message box containing the password. Close the message box, and then close the form.

8. Select File ➤ Save All, and then exit VS by selecting File ➤ Exit.

Activity 5-2. Using the Debugging Features of VS

In this activity, you will become familiar with the following:

- Setting breakpoints and stepping through the code

- Using the various debugging windows in the VS IDE

- Locating and fixing build errors using the Error List window

■**Note** If you have not already done so, download the starter files from the Source Code area of the Apress web site (www.apress.com).

Stepping Through Code

To step through your code, follow these steps:

1. Start VS. Select File ➤ Open ➤ Project.

2. Navigate to the `Activity5_2Starter` folder, click the `Act5_2.sln` file, and then click Open.

3. When the project opens, it will contain a form and a class file. You will use these files to test some of the debugging features available in VS.

4. In the Solution Explorer, right-click `Form1` and select View Code. Locate the `btnLoadList_Click` method. This code instantiates an instance of the `List` class, calls the `ListNumbers` method, and then fills the ListBox control with a list of numbers returned from the method.

5. To set a breakpoint, place the cursor on the declaration line of the `btnLoadList_Click` method, right-click, and choose Breakpoint ➤ Insert Breakpoint. A red dot will appear in the left margin to indicate that a breakpoint has been set (see Figure 5-12).

```
Form1.vb   Form1.vb [Design]                                                        ▾ ✕
btnLoadList                              ▾    Click                                    ▾
blic Class Form1
    Private Sub btnLoadList_Click(ByVal sender As System.Object, ByVal e As System.Event
        Dim objList As List = New List()
        Dim NumberList As System.Collections.ArrayList = New System.Collections.ArrayLis
        Dim Item As Integer
        lstNumbers.Items.Clear()
        NumberList = objList.ListNumbers
        For Each Item In NumberList
            Debug.WriteLine(lstNumbers.Items.Count)
            lstNumbers.Items.Add(Item)
        Next
    End Sub
d Class
```

Figure 5-12. *Setting a breakpoint in the code editor*

6. Select Debug ➤ Start Debugging. When the form appears, click the Load List button. Program execution will pause at the breakpoint. A yellow arrow indicates the next line of code that will be executed.

7. Select View ➤ Toolbars and click the Debug toolbar. (A check next to the toolbar name indicates it is visible.) To step through the code one line at a time, select the Step Into button on the Debug toolbar (see Figure 5-13). (You can also choose Debug ➤ Step Into.) Continue stepping through the code until you get to the ListNumbers function in the List class.

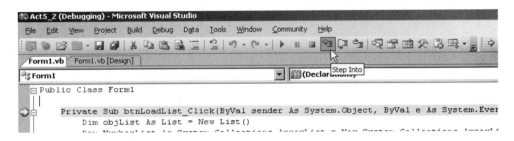

Figure 5-13. *Using the Debug toolbar*

8. Step through the code until the for-next loop has looped a couple of times. At this point, you are probably satisfied this code is working and want to step out of this method. On the Debug toolbar, click the Step Out button. You should return to the btnLoadList_Click method of Form1.

9. Continue stepping through the code until the for-next loop has looped a couple of times. At this point, you may want to return to runtime mode. To do this, click the Continue button on the Debug toolbar.

10. When the form appears, click the Load List button to enter break mode again. Step through the code until you get to the line that calls the ListNumbers method of the objList object:: NumberList = objList.ListNumbers.

11. On the Debug toolbar, choose the Step Over button. This will execute the method and reenter break mode after execution returns to the calling code. After stepping over the method, continue stepping through the code for several lines, and then choose the Stop button on the Debug toolbar. Click the red dot in the left margin to remove the breakpoint.

Setting Conditional Breakpoints

To set conditional breakpoints, follow these steps:

1. In the Solution Explorer, right-click List and select View Code. Locate the ListNumbers method. Set a breakpoint on the following line of code:

```
NumberList.Add(i)
```

2. Open the Breakpoints window by selecting Debug ➤ Windows ➤ Breakpoints. (You can also press Ctrl+Alt+B to open the Breakpoints window.) You should see the breakpoint you just set listed in the Breakpoints window (see Figure 5-14).

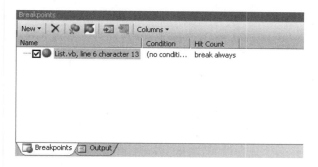

Figure 5-14. *Breakpoints window*

3. Right-click the breakpoint in the Breakpoints window and select Condition. You will see the Breakpoint Condition dialog box. Enter i = 3 as the condition expression and click the OK button (see Figure 5-15).

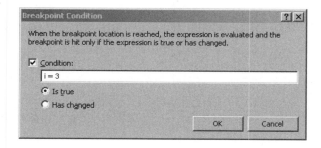

Figure 5-15. *Breakpoint Condition dialog box*

4. Select Debug ➤ Start. When the form appears, click the Load List button. Program execution will pause, and you will see a yellow arrow indicating the next line that will be executed.

5. Select Debug ➤ Windows➤ Locals. The Locals window is displayed at the bottom of the screen (see Figure 5-16). The value of i is displayed in the Locals window. Verify that it is 3. Step through the code using the Debug toolbar, and watch the value of i change in the Locals window. Click the Stop Debugging button in the Debug toolbar.

Locals			▾ 및 ✕
Name	Value	Type	
⊞ ◆◈ Me	{Act5_2.List}	Act5_2.List	
◆ i	3	Integer	
◈ ListNumbers	Nothing	System.Collections.ArrayList	
⊞ ◈ NumberList	Count = 2	System.Collections.ArrayList	

Locals | Immediate Window

Figure 5-16. *Locals window*

6. Locate the Output window at the bottom of your screen and click the Breakpoints tab. Right-click the breakpoint in the Breakpoints window and select Condition. Clear the current condition by clearing the Condition check box, and then click the OK button.

7. Right-click the breakpoint in the Breakpoints window and select Hit Count. Set the breakpoint to break when the hit count equals 4, and then click OK.

8. Select Debug ➤ Start. When the form appears, click the Load List button. Program execution will pause. A yellow arrow indicates the next line of code that will execute.

9. Right-click the NumberList statement and select Add Watch. A Watch window will be displayed with NumberList in it. Notice that NumberList is a System.Collections.ArrayList type. Click the plus sign next to NumberList. Click the plus sign next to the Items entry. Verify that the array contains three items (see Figure 5-17). Step through the code, and watch the array fill with items. Click the Stop button in the Debug toolbar.

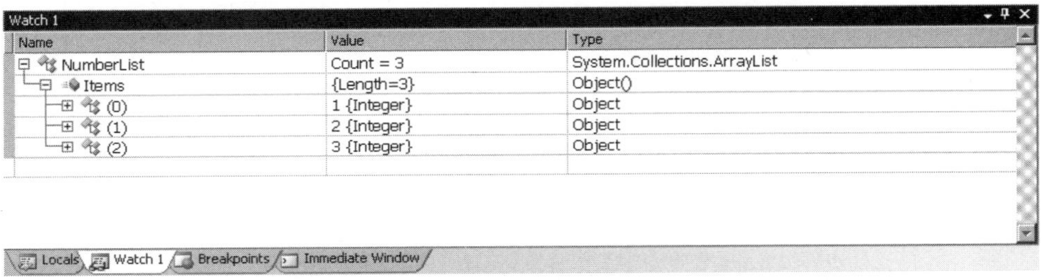

Name	Value	Type
NumberList	Count = 3	System.Collections.ArrayList
Items	{Length=3}	Object()
(0)	1 {Integer}	Object
(1)	2 {Integer}	Object
(2)	3 {Integer}	Object

Locals / Watch 1 / Breakpoints / Immediate Window

Figure 5-17. *The Watch window*

10. To find out more about the System.Collections.ArrayList type, highlight the code statement in the code editor and press the F1 key. A Help window is displayed with information about the type.

Locating and Fixing Build Errors

To locate and fix build errors, follow these steps:

1. In the Solution Explorer, right-click Form1 and select View Code. Locate the btnLoadList_Click method. Locate the following line of code and comment it out by placing a single quote in front of it, as shown here:

```
'Dim Item As Integer
```

2. Select Build ➤ Build Solution. A message box indicates that there were build errors and asks if you want to continue. Select no. The Error List window will appear at the bottom of the screen, indicating a build error (see Figure 5-18).

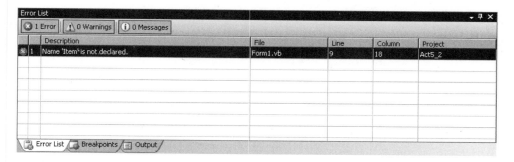

Figure 5-18. *Locating build errors with the Error List window*

3. Double-click the line containing the build error in the Error List window. The corresponding code will become visible in the code editor.

4. Uncomment the line you commented in step 1 by deleting the single quote. Select Build ➤ Build Solution. This time, the Output window is displayed at the bottom of the screen, indicating that there were no build errors.

5. Save the project and exit VS.

Summary

This chapter introduced you to the fundamentals of the .NET Framework. You reviewed some of the underlying goals of the .NET Framework. You also looked at how the .NET Framework is structured and how code is compiled and executed by the CLR. These concepts are relevant and consistent across all .NET-compliant programming languages. In addition, you explored some of the features of the Visual Studio integrated development environment.

The next chapter is the first in a series that looks at how the OOP concepts—such as class structure, inheritance, and polymorphism—are implemented in VB code.

CHAPTER 6

■ ■ ■

Creating Classes

In the previous chapter, you looked at how the .NET Framework was developed and how programs execute under the framework. That chapter introduced you to the VS IDE, and you gained some familiarity with working in it. You are now ready to start coding! This chapter is the first of a series that will introduce you to how classes are created and used in VB. It covers the basics of creating and using classes. You will create classes, add attributes and methods, and instantiate object instances of the classes in client code.

After reading this chapter, you should be familiar with the following:

- How objects used in OOP depend on class definition files

- The important role encapsulation plays in OOP

- How to define the properties and methods of a class

- The purpose of class constructors

- How to use instances of classes in client code

- The process of overloading class constructors and methods

- How to create and test class definition files with VS

Introducing Objects and Classes

In OOP, you use objects in your programs to encapsulate the data associated with the entities with which the program is working. For example, a human resources application needs to work with employees. Employees have attributes associated with them that need to be tracked. You may be interested in such things as the employee names, addresses, departments, and so on. Although you track the same attributes for all employees, each employee has unique values for these attributes. In the human resources application, an Employee object obtains and modifies the attributes associated with an employee. In OOP, the attributes of an object are referred to as *properties*.

Along with the properties of the employees, the human resource application also needs an established set of *behaviors* exposed by the Employee object. For example, one behavior of an employee of interest to the human resources department is the ability to request time off. In OOP, objects expose behaviors through *methods*. The Employee object contains a RequestTimeOff method that encapsulates the implementation code.

The properties and methods of the objects used in OOP are defined through *classes*. A class is a blueprint that defines the attributes and behaviors of the objects that are created as instances of the class. If you have completed the proper analysis and design of the application, you should be able to refer to the UML design documentation to determine which classes need to be constructed and the properties and methods these classes will contain. The UML class diagram contains the initial information you need to construct the classes of the system.

To demonstrate the construction of a class using VB, you will look at the code for a simple Employee class. The Employee class will have properties and methods that encapsulate and work with employee data as part of a fictitious human resources application.

Defining Classes

Let's walk through the source code needed to create a class definition. The first line of code defines the code block as a class definition using the keyword Class followed by the name of the class. The keyword Public is an access modifier that makes this class available to all client code. The class definition block ends with the End Class statement. The code block is structured like this:

```
Public Class Employee
......
End Class
```

Creating Class Properties

After defining the starting and ending point of the class code block, the next step is to define the instance variables contained in the class. These variables hold the data that an instance of your class will manipulate. The Private keyword ensures that these instance variables can be manipulated only by the code inside the class. Here are the instance variable definitions:

```
Private _empID As Integer
Private _loginName As String
Private _password As String
Private _department As String
Private _fullName As String
```

When a user of the class (*client code*) needs to query or set the value of these instance variables, public properties are exposed to them. Inside the property block of code are a Set block and a Get block. The Get block returns the value of the private instance variable to the user of the class. This code provides a readable property. The Set block provides a write-enabled property; it passes a value sent in by the client code to the corresponding private instance variable. Here is an example of a property block:

```
Public Property FullName()
      Get
           Return _fullName
      End Get
      Set(ByVal Value)
          _fullName = Value
      End Set
End Property
```

Newcomers to OOP often ask why you need to go through so much work to get and set properties. Couldn't you just create public instance variables that the user could read and write to directly? The answer lies in one of the fundamental tenets of OOP: *data encapsulation*. Data encapsulation means that the client code does not have direct access to the data. When working with the data, the client code must use clearly defined properties and methods accessed through an instance of the class. The following are some of the benefits of encapsulating the data in this way:

- Preventing unauthorized access to the data

- Ensuring data integrity through error checking

- Creating read-only or write-only properties

- Isolating users of the class from changes in the implementation code

For example, you could check to make sure the password is at least six characters long:

```
Public Property Password() As String
      Get
            Return _password
      End Get
      Set(ByVal Value As String)
          If Len(Value) >= 6 then
              _password = Value
          Else
              Throw New Exception _
           ("Password must be at least 6 characters.")
          End If
      End Set
End Property
```

Restricting Property Access

By using the `ReadOnly` keyword and eliminating the `Set` block inside the `Property` block, you create a read-only property. The following code shows how to make the `EmployeeID` property read-only:

```
Public ReadOnly Property EmployeeID() As Integer
      Get
            Return _empID
      End Get
End Property
```

Conversely, if you use the `WriteOnly` keyword and eliminate the `Get` block, you create a write-only property. The following code shows a `password` property that is defined as write-only:

```
Public WriteOnly Property Password() As String
        Set(ByVal Value As String)
            _password = Value
        End Set
End Property
```

Creating Class Methods

Class methods define the behaviors of the class. Class methods take the form of either a function or a subprocedure. A function returns a value back to the calling code. A subprocedure does not return a value. For example, the following defines a subprocedure for the Employee class that verifies employee logins:

```
Public Sub Login(ByVal loginName As String, ByVal password As String)
        'Data normally retrieved from database.
        'Hardcoded for demo only.
        If loginName = "Smith" And password = "js" Then
            _empID = 1
            Department = "IS"
            FullName = "Jerry Smith"
        ElseIf loginName = "Jones" And password = "mj" Then
            _empID = 2
            Department = "HR"
            FullName = "Mary Jones"
        Else
            Throw New Exception("Login incorrect.")
        End If
End Sub
```

When client code calls the Login method of the class, the login name and password are checked. If they match a current employee, the instance of the class is populated with attributes of the employee. If the login name and password do not match a current employee, an exception is passed back to the client code.

Note Exception handling is an important part of application processing. For more information about exceptions, see Appendix B.

The following AddEmployee function is another method of the Employee class. It's called when an employee needs to be added to the database, and it returns the newly assigned employee ID to the client. The method also populates the object instance of the Employee class with the attributes of the newly added employee.

```
Public Function AddEmployee(ByVal loginName As String, _
    ByVal password As String, ByVal department As String, _
    ByVal fullName As String) As Integer
        'Data normally saved to database.
```

```
      _empID = 3
      LoginName = loginName
      Password = password
      Department = department
      FullName = fullName
      Return EmployeeID
End Function
```

Activity 6-1. Creating the Employee Class

In this activity, you will become familiar with the following:

- Creating a VB class definition file using VS

- Creating and using an instance of the class from VB client code

Note If you have not already done so, download the starter files from the Source Code area of the Apress web site (www.apress.com).

Defining the Employee Class

To create the Employee class, follow these steps:

1. Start VS. Select File ➤ Open ➤ Project.

2. Navigate to the Activity6_1Starter folder, click the Act6_1.sln file, and click Open. When the project opens, it will contain a login form. You will use this form later to test the Employee class you create.

3. Select Project ➤ Add Class. In the Add New Item dialog box, rename the class file to Employee.vb, and then click Open. VS adds the Employee.vb file to the project and adds the following class definition code to the file:

```
Public Class Employee
End Class
```

4. Enter the following code to add the private instance variables to the class definition file:

```
Private _empID As Integer
Private _loginName As String
Private _password As String
Private _securityLevel As Integer
```

5. Add the following public properties to access the private instance variables defined in step 4:

```
Public ReadOnly Property EmployeeID() As Integer
    Get
        Return _empID
    End Get
End Property
```

```vb
Public Property LoginName() As String
    Get
        Return _loginName
    End Get
    Set(ByVal Value As String)
        _loginName = Value
    End Set
End Property
Public Property Password() As String
    Get
        Return _password
    End Get
    Set(ByVal Value As String)
        _password = Value
    End Set
End Property
Public ReadOnly Property SecurityLevel() As Integer
    Get
        Return _securityLevel
    End Get
End Property
```

6. Add the following Login method to the class definition:

```vb
Public Sub Login(ByVal loginName As String, ByVal password As String)
            LoginName = loginName
            Password = password
        'Data normally retrieved from database.
        'Hardcoded for demo only
        If loginName = "Smith" And password = "js" Then
            _empID = 1
            _securityLevel = 2
        ElseIf loginName = "Jones" And password = "mj" Then
            _empID = 2
            _securityLevel = 4
        Else
            Throw New Exception("Login incorrect.")
        End If
    End Sub
```

7. Select Build ➤ Build Solution. Make sure there are no build errors in the Error List window. If there are, fix them, and then rebuild.

Testing the Employee Class

To test the Employee class, follow these steps:

1. Open frmLogin in the code editor and locate the btnLogin click event code.

■Tip Double-clicking the Login button in the form designer will also bring up the event code in the code editor.

---

2. Declare and instantiate a variable of type Employee called oEmployee:

    ```
    Dim oEmployee As Employee = New Employee()
    ```

3. Call the Login method of the oEmployee object, passing in the values of the login name and the password from the text boxes on the form:

    ```
    oEmployee.Login(txtName.Text, txtPassword.Text)
    ```

4. Show a message box stating the user's security level retrieved by reading the SecurityLevel property of the oEmployee object:

    ```
    MessageBox.Show ("You have security clearence level " & _

    oEmployee.SecurityLevel.ToString)
    ```

5. Select File ➤ Save All.

6. Select Build ➤ Build Solution. Make sure there are no build errors in the Error List window. If there are, fix them, and then rebuild.

7. Select Debug ➤ Start to run the project. Test the login form by entering a login name of **Smith** and a password of **js**. You should get a message indicating a security level of 2. Try entering your name and a password of **pass**. You should get a message indicating the login failed.

8. After testing the login procedure, close the form, which, in turn, will stop the debugger.

Using Constructors

In OOP, you use *constructors* to perform any processing that needs to occur when an object instance of the class becomes instantiated. For example, you could initialize properties of the object instance or establish a database connection. When an object instance of a class is instantiated by client code, a constructor method called New is executed. The following constructor is used in the Employee class to initialize the properties of an object instance of the Employee class. An employee ID is passed in to the constructor to retrieve the values from data storage.

```
Public Sub New(ByVal empID As Integer)
    _empID = empID

        'retrieval of data is hardcoded for testing purposes only
```

```
        If _empID = 1 Then
            LoginName = "Smith"
            Password = "js"
            Department = "IS"
            FullName = "Jerry Smith"
        ElseIf _empID = 2 Then
            LoginName = "Jones"
            Password = "mj"
            Department = "HR"
            FullName = "Mary Jones"
        Else
            Throw New Exception("Invalid EmployeeID")
        End If
End Sub
```

Using Destructors

Microsoft has incorporated automatic memory management into the CLR in the form of a system garbage collector (GC) class. When an object is created in code, the CLR allocates the memory from the *managed heap*. The managed heap is a portion of the system's memory reserved for the CLR. Periodically, the GC checks the managed heap for objects that are no longer referenced, and it releases the memory. Although using an automated GC process has many advantages for .NET developers, it has a downside: programmers do not know when an object will be garbage collected.

When the GC cleans up an object, it executes a destructor method (in .NET languages, this is the Finalize method) for the object. This is referred to as *nondeterministic finalization*. Because of the time delay between when an object is no longer referenced and when it gets garbage collected, relying on a destructor to clean up system resources such as database connections may, in some instances, cause performance problems. You could force the collection of an object, thereby forcing the execution of the Finalize method, by calling the Collect method of the GC system class. However, this in itself causes significant processing overhead and a degradation of system performance.

To get around these problems, if you need to run cleanup code, Microsoft recommends that you create a custom method that the client code will call when it no longer needs the object reference. The following code implements a custom Dispose method that cleans up resources. A call to the Dispose method is also added to the Finalize method of the class, so that if the client forgets to call the Dispose method, it will be called when an object instance is garbage collected:

```
Public Sub Dispose()
    'Clean up code goes here.
End Sub
Protected Overrides Sub Finalize()
    Dispose()
End Sub
```

Note Implementing a custom `Dispose` method is not trivial. For example, error checking should be included so that an error is not triggered when the `Dispose` method is called a second time. I suggest you thoroughly review the .NET Framework documentation before attempting to create a `Dispose` method.

Overloading Methods

The ability to *overload* methods is a useful feature of OOP languages. You overload methods in a class by defining multiple methods that have the same name but contain different signatures. A *method signature* is a combination of the name of the method and its parameter type list. If you change the parameter type list, you create a different method signature. For example, the parameter type lists can contain a different number of parameters or different parameter types. The compiler will determine which method to execute by examining the parameter type list passed in by the client.

Note Changing how a parameter is passed (in other words, from `byVal` to `byRef`) does not change the method signature. Altering the return type of the method also does not create a unique method signature. For a more detailed discussion of method signatures and passing arguments, refer to Appendix A.

Suppose you want to provide two methods of the `Employee` class that will allow you to add an employee to the database. The first method assigns a username and password to the employee when the employee is added. The second method adds the employee information but defers the assignment of username and password until later. You can easily accomplish this by overloading the `AddEmployee` method of the `Employee` class, as the following code demonstrates.

```
Public Function AddEmployee(ByVal loginName As String, _ _
    ByVal password As String, ByVal department As String, _
    ByVal fullName As String) As Integer
    'Data normally saved to database.
    _empID = 3
    LoginName = loginName
    Password = password
    Department = department
    FullName = fullName
    Return EmployeeID
End Function
Public Function AddEmployee(ByVal department As String,  _
    ByVal fullName As String) As Integer
    'Data normally saved to database.
    _empID = 3
    LoginName = ""
    Password = ""
```

```
        Department = department
        FullName = fullName
        Return EmployeeID
End Function
```

Because the parameter type list of the first method (string, string) differs from the parameter type list of the second method (string, string, string, string), the compiler can determine which method to invoke.

A common technique in OOP is to overload the constructor of the class. For example, when an instance of the Employee class is created, one constructor could be used for new employees and another could be used for current employees, by passing in the employee ID when the class instance is instantiated by the client. The following code shows the overloading of a class constructor.

```
Public Sub New()
        _empID = -1
 End Sub
 Public Sub New(ByVal empID As Integer)
    _empID = empID
        'retrieval of data is hardcoded for testing purposes only.
        If empID = 1 Then
            LoginName = "Smith"
            Password = "js"
            Department = "IS"
            FullName = "Jerry Smith"
        ElseIf empID = 2 Then
            LoginName = "Jones"
            Password = "mj"
            Department = "HR"
            FullName = "Mary Jones"
        Else
            Throw New Exception("Invalid EmployeeID")
        End If
 End Sub
```

When client code instantiates an instance of the class, the compiler will examine the arguments passed and determine which constructor to use.

Activity 6-2. Overloading Methods and Constructors

In this activity, you will become familiar with the following:

- Creating and overloading the class constructor method

- Using overloaded constructors of a class from client code

- Overloading a method of a class

- Using overloaded methods of a class from client code

Creating and Overloading Class Constructors

To create and overload class constructors, follow these steps:

1. Start VS. Select File ➤ Open ➤ Project.

2. Navigate to the `Activity6_2Starter` folder, click the `Act6_2.sln` file, and then click Open. When the project opens, it will contain a `frmEmployeeInfo` form that you will use to test the `Employee` class. The project also includes the `Employee.vb` file, which contains the `Employee` class definition code.

3. Open `Employee.vb` in the code editor and examine the code. The class contains several properties pertaining to employees that need to be maintained.

4. After the property declaration code, add the following private method to the class. This method simulates the generation of a new employee ID.

```
Private Function GetNextID() As Integer
     'simulates the retrieval of next
     'available id from database.
     Return 100
End Function
```

5. Locate the default class constructor `Sub New()`, and add code that calls the `GetNextID` method and assigns the return value to the private instance variable `_empID`:

```
Public Sub New()
    _empID = GetNextID()
End Sub
```

6. Overload the default constructor method by adding a second `Sub New` method with an integer parameter of `empID`:

```
Public Sub New(ByVal empID As Integer)
     'Constructor for existing employee
End Sub
```

7. Add the following code, which simulates extracting the employee data from a database and assigns the data to the instance properties of the class:

```
'Simulates retrieval from database
If empID = 1 Then
    _empID = empID
    LoginName = "smith"
    Password = "js"
    SSN = 123456789
    Department = "IS"
ElseIf empID = 2 Then
    _empID = empID
    LoginName = "jones"
    Password = "mj"
    SSN = 987654321
    Department = "HR"
```

```
Else
    Throw New Exception("Invalid Employee ID")
End If
```

8. Select Build ➤ Build Solution. Make sure there are no build errors in the Error List window. If there are, fix them, and then rebuild.

Testing the Employee Class Constructors

To test the Employee class constructors, follow these steps:

1. Open the frmEmployeeInfo code in the code editor and locate the btnNewEmp click event code.

2. Declare and instantiate a variable of type Employee called oEmployee:

```
Dim oEmployee As Employee = New Employee()
```

3. Show a message informing the user that a new employee ID has been generated and employee information can be updated to the database:

```
MessageBox.Show("A new employee id has been generated of " & _
        oEmployee.EmployeeID & "." & vbCrLf & _
        "Fill in the values for the " & _
        "new employee and press update.")
```

4. Update the EmployeeID text box with the employee ID and disable the EmployeeID text box:

```
txtEmpID.Text = oEmployee.EmployeeID.ToString
txtEmpID.Enabled = False
'clear the remaining text boxes.
txtLoginName.Text = ""
txtPassword.Text = ""
txtSSN.Text = ""
txtDepartment.Text = ""
```

5. Select Build ➤ Build Solution. Make sure there are no build errors in the Error List window. If there are, fix them, and then rebuild.

6. Locate the btnExistingEmp click event code.

7. Declare and instantiate a variable of type Employee called oEmployee. Retrieve the employee ID from the txtEmpID text box and pass it as an argument in the constructor:

```
Dim oEmployee As Employee = New Employee(CInt(txtEmpID.Text))
```

8. Show a message informing the user that information for the employee has been retrieved, and employee information can be changed and updated to the database:

```
MessageBox.Show ("Information for Employee ID " & _
oEmployee.EmployeeID & "." & vbCrLf & _
"Make any necessary changes for the " & _
"employee and press update.")
```

9. Update the EmployeeID text box with the employee ID and disable the EmployeeID text box:

```
txtEmpID.Text = oEmployee.EmployeeID.ToString
txtEmpID.Enabled = False
```

10. Fill in the remaining text boxes with the values of the Employee object's properties:

```
txtLoginName.Text = oEmployee.LoginName
txtPassword.Text = oEmployee.Password
txtSSN.Text = oEmployee.SSN.ToString
txtDepartment.Text = oEmployee.Department
```

11. Select Build ➤ Build Solution. Make sure there are no build errors in the Error List window. If there are, fix them, and then rebuild.

12. Select Debug ➤ Start to run the project and test the code.

13. When the EmployeeInfo form is displayed, click the New Employee button. You should get a message box stating a new employee ID has been generated.

14. Click the Reset button to clear and enable the txtEmpID text box.

15. Enter a value of **1** for the employee ID and click the Get Existing Employee button. The information for the employee is displayed on the form.

16. After testing the constructors, close the form, which will stop the debugger.

Overloading a Class Method

To overload a class method, follow these steps:

1. Open the Employee.vb code in the code editor.

2. Add the following Update method to the class definition file. This method simulates the updating of the employee security information to a database.

```
Public Function Update(ByVal lgName As String, _
    ByVal pWord As String) As String
    LoginName = lgName
    Password = pWord
    Return "Security Info Updated."
End Function
```

3. Add a second Update method to simulate the updating of the employee human resources data to a database:

```
Public Function Update(ByVal  SSNumber As Integer, _
    ByVal dpt As String) As String
    SSN = SSNumber
    Department = dpt
    Return "HR Info Updated."
End Function
```

4. Select Build ➤ Build Solution. Make sure there are no build errors in the Error List window. If there are, fix them, and then rebuild.

Testing the Overloaded Update Method

To test the overloaded Update method, follow these steps:

1. Open the frmEmployeeInfo code in the code editor and locate the btnUpdateSI click event code.

2. Declare and instantiate a variable of type Employee called oEmployee. Retrieve the employee ID from the txtEmpID text box and pass it as an argument in the constructor:

   ```
   Dim oEmployee As Employee = New Employee(CInt(txtEmpID.Text))
   ```

3. Call the Update method, passing the values of the login name and password from the text boxes. Show the method return message to the user in a message box:

   ```
   MessageBox.Show (oEmployee.Update(txtLoginName.Text, txtPassword.Text))
   ```

4. Update the login name and password text boxes with the property values of the Employee object:

   ```
   txtLoginName.Text = oEmployee.LoginName
   txtPassword.Text = oEmployee.Password
   ```

5. Add similar code to the btnUpdateHR click event procedure to simulate updating the human resources information:

   ```
   Dim oEmployee As Employee = New Employee(CInt(txtEmpID.Text))
   MessageBox.Show (oEmployee.Update(CInt(txtSSN.Text), txtDepartment.Text))
   txtSSN.Text = oEmployee.SSN.ToString
   txtDepartment.Text = oEmployee.Department
   ```

6. Select Build ➤ Build Solution. Make sure there are no build errors in the Error List window. If there are, fix them, and then rebuild.

7. Select Debug ➤ Start to run the project and test the code.

8. Enter a value of **1** for the employee ID and click the Get Existing Employee button.

9. Change the values for the security information and click the Update button.

10. Change the values for the human resources information and click the Update button.

11. You should see that the correct Update method is called, in accordance with the parameters passed to it. After testing the Update method, close the form.

Summary

This chapter gave you a firm foundation in creating and using classes in VB code. Now that you are comfortable constructing and using classes, you are ready to look at implementing some of the more advanced features of OOP. In the next chapter, you will concentrate on how inheritance and polymorphism are implemented in VB code. As an object-oriented programmer, it is important for you to become familiar with these concepts and learn how to implement them in your programs.

CHAPTER 7

Creating Class Hierarchies

In the previous chapter, you looked at how to create classes, add attributes and methods, and instantiate object instances of the classes in client code. This chapter introduces you to *inheritance*. Inheritance is one of the most powerful and fundamental features of any OOP language. Using inheritance, you create base classes that encapsulate common functionality. Other classes can be derived from these base classes. The derived classes inherit the properties and methods of the base classes, and extend the functionality as needed.

Another fundamental OOP feature introduced in this chapter is *polymorphism*. Polymorphism allows a base class to define methods that will be implemented by any derived classes. The base class defines the message signature that derived classes must adhere to, but the implementation code of the method is left up to the derived class. The power of polymorphism lies in the fact that clients know they can implement methods of classes of the base type in the same fashion. Even though the internal processing of the method may be different, the client knows the inputs and outputs of the methods will be the same.

After reading this chapter, you should be familiar with the following:

- How to create and use base classes

- How to create and use derived classes

- How access modifiers control inheritance

- How to override base class methods

- How to implement interfaces

- How to implement polymorphism through inheritance and through interfaces

Understanding Inheritance

One of the most powerful features of any OOP language is inheritance. Inheritance is the ability to create a base class with properties and methods that can be used in classes derived from the base class.

Creating Base and Derived Classes

The purpose of inheritance is to create a base class that encapsulates properties and methods needed in multiple derived classes of the same type. For example, you could create a base class Account. A GetBalance method is defined in the Account class. You can then create two separate classes: a SavingsAccount and a CheckingAccount class. Because the SavingsAccount and the CheckingAccount class use the same logic to retrieve balance information, they inherit the GetBalance method from the base class Account. This enables you to create one common code base that is easier to maintain and manage.

Derived classes are not limited to the properties and methods of the base class, however. The derived classes define methods and properties that must be made unique to them. For example, when withdrawing money from a checking account, the business rules require that a minimum balance be maintained. A minimum balance is not required when withdrawing money from a savings account. In this case, each of the derived classes contains its own unique definition of a Withdraw method.

To create a derived class in VB code, you use the Inherits keyword along with the name of the base class when defining the derived class. The following code demonstrates the creation of a CheckingAccount class derived from an Account base class.

```
Public Class Account
    Private _lngAccountNumber As Long
    Public Property AccountNumber() As Long
        Get
            Return _lngAccountNumber
        End Get
        Set(ByVal Value As Long)
            _lngAccountNumber = Value
        End Set
    End Property
    Public Function GetBalance() As Double
        'Code to retrieve account balance from database
    End Function
End Class

Public Class CheckingAccount
    Inherits Account
    Private _dblMinBalance As Double
    Public Sub Withdraw(ByVal Amount As Double)
        'Code to withdraw from account
    End Sub
End Class
```

The following code could be implemented by a client creating an object instance of CheckingAccount. Notice that to the client, there is no distinction made between the call to the GetBalance method and the call to the Withdraw method. In this case, the client has no knowledge of the Account class; instead, both methods appear to have been defined by CheckingAccount.

```
Dim oCheckAccount As CheckingAccount = New CheckingAccount()
Dim dblBalance as Double
```

```
oCheckAccount.AccountNumber = 1000
dblBalance = oCheckAccount.GetBalance()
oCheckAccount.Withdraw(500)
```

Creating an Abstract Class

At this point in the example, a client can access the GetBalance method through an instance of the derived CheckingAccount class or directly through an instance of the base Account class. Sometimes, you may want to have a base class that cannot be instantiated by client code. Access to the methods and properties of the class must be through a derived class. In this case, you construct the base class using the MustInherit modifier. The following code shows the Account class definition with the MustInherit keyword added:

```
Public MustInherit Class Account
```

This makes the Account class an *abstract* class. An abstract class is a class that defines the interfaces of the methods and properties that will be inherited by the derived classes. Because an abstract class does not contain any implementation code, only the interface definitions, it cannot be instantiated directly. For clients to gain access to the GetBalance method, they must instantiate an instance of the derived CheckingAccount class.

Creating a Sealed Class

By default, all classes can be inherited. When creating classes that can be inherited, you must take care that they are not modified in such a way that derived classes no longer function as intended. If you are not careful, you can create complex inheritance chains that are hard to manage and debug. For example, suppose you create a derived CheckingAccount class based on the Account class. Another programmer can come along and create a derived class based on the CheckingAccount and use it in ways you never intended. (This could easily occur in large programming teams with poor communication and design.)

By using the NotInheritable modifier, you can create classes that you know will not be derived from. This type of class is often referred to as a *sealed* or *final* class. By making a class not inheritable, you avoid the complexity and overhead associated with altering the code of base classes. The following code demonstrates the use of the NotInheritable modifier when constructing a class definition:

```
Public NotInheritable Class CheckingAccount
```

Using Access Modifiers in Base Classes

When setting up class hierarchies using inheritance, you must manage how the properties and methods of your classes are accessed. Two access modifiers you have looked at so far are Public and Private. If a method or property of the base class is exposed as Public, it is accessible by both the derived class and any client of the derived class. If you expose the property or method of the base class as Private, it is not accessible directly by the derived class or the client.

You may want to expose a property or method of the base class to a derived class, but not to a client of the derived class. In this case, you use the Protected access modifier. The following code demonstrates the use of the Protected access modifier:

```
Protected Function GetBalance() As Double
          'Code to retrieve account balance from database
End Function
```

By defining the GetBalance method as Protected, it becomes accessible to the derived class CheckingAccount but not to the client code accessing an instance of the CheckingAccount class.

Activity 7-1. Creating and Using Base and Derived Classes with VS

In this activity, you will become familiar with the following:

- Creating a base class and derived classes

- Using access modifiers in the base class

- Creating an abstract base class

Creating the Account Class

To create the Account class, follow these steps:

1. Start VS. Select File ➤ Open ➤ Project.

2. Navigate to the Activity7_1Starter folder, click the Act7_1.sln file, and then click Open. When the project opens, it will contain a teller form. You will use this form later to test the classes you will create.

3. Select Project ➤ Add Class.

4. In the Add New Item dialog box, rename the class file to Account.vb, and click Open. The Account.vb file is added to the project, and the Account class definition code is added to the file.

5. Add the following code to the class definition file to create the private instance variable:

```
Private _intAccountNumber As Integer
```

6. Add the following GetBalance method to the class definition:

```
Public Function GetBalance(ByVal AccountNumber As Integer) As Double
    _ intAccountNumber = AccountNumber
    'Data normally retrieved from database. Hardcoded for demo only
    If _intAccountNumber = 1 Then
        Return 1000
    ElseIf _intAccountNumber = 2 Then
        Return 2000
    Else
        Throw New Exception("Account number incorrect.")
    End If
End Function
```

7. After the Account class, add the following code to create the CheckingAccount and SavingsAccount derived classes:

```
Public Class CheckingAccount
     Inherits Account
End Class
Public Class SavingsAccount
     Inherits Account
End Class
```

8. Select Build ➤ Build Solution. Make sure there are no build errors in the Error List window. If there are, fix them, and then rebuild.

Testing the Classes

To test the classes, follow these steps:

1. Open the frmTeller form in the code editor and locate the btnGetBalance click event code.

2. Inside the event procedure, prior to the Try block, declare and instantiate a variable of type CheckingAccount called oCheckingAccount, a variable of type SavingsAccount called oSavingsAccount, and a variable of type Account called oAccount:

```
Dim oCheckingAccount As CheckingAccount = New CheckingAccount()
Dim oSavingsAccount As SavingsAccount = New SavingsAccount()
Dim oAccount As Account = New Account()
```

3. Depending on which radio button is selected, call the GetBalance method of the appropriate object and pass the account number value from the Account Number text box. Show the return value in the Balance text box. Place the following code in the Try block prior to the Catch statement:

```
If rdbChecking.Checked Then
    txtBalance.Text = oCheckingAccount.GetBalance _
        (CInt(txtAccountNumber.Text)).ToString
ElseIf rdbSavings.Checked Then
    txtBalance.Text = oSavingsAccount.GetBalance _
        (CInt(txtAccountNumber.Text)).ToString
ElseIf rdbGeneral.Checked Then
    txtBalance.Text = oAccount.GetBalance _
        (CInt(txtAccountNumber.Text)).ToString
End If
```

4. Select Build ➤ Build Solution. Make sure there are no build errors in the Error List window. If there are, fix them, and then rebuild.

5. Select Debug ➤ Start to run the project. Enter an account number of **1** and click the Get Balance button for the Checking Account type. You should get a balance of 1,000. Test the other account types. You should get the same result, since all classes are using the same GetBalance function defined in the base class.

6. After testing, close the form, which will stop the debugger.

Creating a Protected Method

At this point, the GetBalance method of the base class is public, which means that it can be accessed by client code of the derived classes. You will alter this so that the GetBalance method can be accessed only by the code of the derived classes and not by clients of the derived classes. To alter the GetBalance method, follow these steps:

1. Locate the GetBalance method of the Account class.

2. Change the access modifier of the GetBalance method from Public to Protected.

3. Switch to the frmTeller code editor and locate the btnGetBalance click event code.

4. Hover the cursor over the call to the GetBalance method of the oCheckingAccount object. You will see a warning stating that it is a protected function and not accessible in this context.

5. Comment out the code between the Try and the Catch statements.

6. Switch to the Account.vb code editor.

7. Add code to create the following private instance variable to the SavingsAccount class definition file:

```
Private _dblBalance As Double
```

8. Add the following Withdraw method to the SavingsAccount class. This function calls the protected method of the Account base class:

```
Public Function Withdraw(ByVal AccountNumber As Integer, _
    ByVal Amount As Double) As Double
    _dblBalance = GetBalance(AccountNumber)
    If _dblBalance >= Amount Then
        _dblBalance -= Amount
        Return _dblBalance
    Else
        Throw New Exception("Not enough funds.")
    End If
End Function
```

9. Select Build ➤ Build Solution. Make sure there are no build errors in the Error List window. If there are, fix them, and then rebuild.

Testing the Withdraw Method

To test the Withdraw method, follow these steps:

1. Open the frmTeller form in the code editor and locate the btnWithdraw click event code.

2. Inside the event procedure, prior to the Try block, declare and instantiate a variable of type SavingsAccount called oSavingsAccount:

```
Dim oSavingsAccount As SavingsAccount = New SavingsAccount()
```

3. Call the Withdraw method of the oSavingsAccount. Pass the account number value from the Account Number text box and the withdrawal amount from the Amount text box. Show the return value in the Balance text box. Place the following code in the Try block prior to the Catch statement:

```
txtBalance.Text = oSavingsAccount.withdraw _
(CInt(txtAccountNumber.Text), CDbl(txtAmount.Text)).ToString
```

4. Select Build ➤ Build Solution. Make sure there are no build errors in the Error List window. If there are, fix them, and then rebuild.

5. Select Debug ➤ Start to run the project.

6. Test the `Withdraw` method of the `SavingsAccount` class. Enter an account number of **1** and a withdrawal amount of **200**. Click the Withdraw button. You should get a resulting balance of 800.

7. Enter an account number of **1** and a withdrawal amount of **2000**. Click the Withdraw button. You should get an insufficient funds message.

8. After testing the `Withdraw` method, close the form, which will stop the debugger.

Creating an Abstract Class

At this point, the `Account` base class is public, which means that it can be instantiated by client code of the derived classes. You will alter this so that the `Account` base class can be accessed only by the code of the derived classes and cannot be instantiated and accessed by clients of the derived classes. To create the abstract class, follow these steps:

1. Locate the `Account` class definition in the `Account.vb` code.

2. Add the `MustInherit` keyword to the class definition code.

   ```
   Public MustInherit Class Account
   ```

3. Select Build ➤ Build Solution. You should receive a build error in the Error List window. Find the line of code causing the error:

   ```
   Dim oAccount As Account = New Account()
   ```

4. Comment out the line of code, and select Build ➤ Build Solution again. It should now build without any errors.

5. Save and close the project.

Overriding Methods of the Base Class

When a derived class inherits a method from the base class, it inherits the implementation of the method defined in the base class. As the designer of the base class, you may want to allow a derived class its own unique implementation of the method. This is known as *overriding* the base class method.

By default, the derived class cannot override the implementation code of the base class. To allow overriding of a method of the base class, you include the keyword `Overridable` in the method definition. In the derived class, you define a method with the same method signature and indicate it is overriding a base class method with the `Overrides` keyword. The following code demonstrates the creation of an overridable `Deposit` method in the `Account` base class:

```
Public Overridable Sub Deposit(ByVal Amount As Double)
    'Base class implementation code
End Sub
```

To override the Deposit method in the derived CheckingAccount class, use the following code:

```
Public Overrides Sub Deposit(ByVal dblAmount As Double)
    'Derived class implementation code
End Sub
```

One caveat is to watch for when a derived class inherits from the base class and a second derived class inherits from the first derived class. When a method overrides a method in the base class, it becomes overridable by default. To limit an overriding method from being overridden farther up the inheritance chain, you must include the NotOverridable keyword in front of the Overrides keyword in the method definition of the derived class. The following code in the CheckingAccount class prevents the overriding of the Deposit method if the CheckingAccount class is derived from:

```
Public NotOverridable Overrides Sub Deposit(ByVal Amount As Double)
    'Derived class implementation code
End Sub
```

When you indicate that a base class method is overridable, derived classes have the option of overriding the method or using the implementation provided by the base class. In some cases, you may want to use a base class method as a template for the derived classes. The base class has no implementation code but is used to define the method signatures used in the derived classes. Remember that this type of class is referred to as an *abstract* base class. You define the class with the MustInherit keyword, and then define the method with the MustOverride keyword. The following code is used to create an abstract Account base class:

```
Public MustInherit Class Account
    'Other code here . . .
    Public MustOverride Sub Deposit(ByVal Amount As Double)
End Class
```

Notice that because there is no implementation code defined in the base class for the Deposit method, the End Sub statement is omitted.

Calling the Derived Class Method

A situation may arise in which you are calling an overridable method in the base class from another method of the base class, and the derived class overrides the method of the base class. When a call is made to the base class method from an instance of the derived class, the base class will call the overridden method of the derived class. The following code shows an example of this situation. A CheckingAccount base class contains an overridable GetMinBalance method. The InterestBearingCheckingAccount class, inheriting from the CheckingAccount class, overrides the GetMinBalance method.

```
Public Class CheckingAccount
    Private _dblBalance As Double = 2000
```

```
    Public ReadOnly Property Balance()
        Get
            Return _dblBalance
        End Get
    End Property
    Public Overridable Function GetMinBalance() As Double
        'This function is overidden in a derived class
        'Base class functionality implemented here
        Return 200
    End Function
    Public Overridable Sub Withdraw(ByVal Amount As Double)
        Dim dblMinBalance As Double = GetMinBalance()
        If dblMinBalance < (Balance - Amount) Then
            _dblBalance -= Amount
        Else
            Throw New Exception("Minimum balance error.")
        End If
    End Sub
End Class
Public Class InterestBearingCheckingAccount
    Inherits CheckingAccount
    Public Overrides Function GetMinBalance() As Double
        'This function is overidden
        'Derived class functionality implemented here
        Return 1000
    End Function
End Class
```

A client instantiates an object instance of the InterestBearingCheckingAccount class and calls the Withdraw method. In this case, the overridden GetMinimumBalance method of the InterestBearingCheckingAccount class is executed, and a minimum balance of 1,000 is used:

```
Private oInterestBearingChecking As InterestBearingCheckingAccount = _
    New InterestBearingCheckingAccount()
oInterestBearingChecking.Withdraw(500)
```

When the call was made to the Withdraw method, you could have prefaced it with the Me qualifier:

```
Dim dblMinBalance As Double = Me.GetMinBalance()
```

Because the Me qualifier is the default qualifier if none is used, the code would execute the same way as previously demonstrated. The most derived class implementation (that has been instantiated) of the method is executed. In other words, if a client instantiates an instance of the InterestBearingCheckingAccount class, as was demonstrated previously, the base class's call to GetMinimumBalance is made to the derived class's implementation. On the other hand, if a client instantiates an instance of the CheckingAccount class, the base class's call to GetMinimumBalance is made to its own implementation.

Calling the Current Class Method

There may be times when you want to make sure the base class will call its own method implementation, even though the client is using an object instance of the derived class. In this situation, the MyClass qualifier prefaces the call to the overridden base class method. In the following code, a call is made to a method that determines the account's average balance for the month. Depending on the result, the CalculateInterest method of the class will either call its own implementation of the GetInterestRate method or the derived class's implementation.

```
Public Class CheckingAccount
    Public Function GetAverageBalance() As Double
        Dim dblAverageBalance as Double
        'Determine average monthly balance
        Return dblAverageBalance
    End Function
    Public Overridable Function GetInterestRate() As Single
        Dim sngInterestRate as Single
        'Retrieve current rate
        Return sngInterestRate
    End Function
    Public Sub CalculateInterest(ByVal Amount As Double)
        Dim sngInterestRate as Single
          If GetAverageBalance() < 1000 then
                'Call the current class method
                sngInterestRate = MyClass.GetInterestRate()
          Else
                'Call the derived class method
                sngInterestRate = Me.GetInterestRate()
        End If
            'Code continues. . .
    End Sub
End Class
```

Be careful not to confuse the MyClass qualifier with the Me qualifier. The Me qualifier is the default qualifier if none is used. When the Me qualifier is used, the most derived class implementation of the method is executed. This is different from the MyClass qualifier, which will use the current class's implementation.

Calling the Base Class Implementation

In some cases, you may want to develop a derived class method that still uses the implementation code in the base class but also augments it with its own implementation code. In this case, you create an overriding method in the derived class and call the code in the base class using the MyBase qualifier. The following code demonstrates the use of the MyBase qualifier:

```
Public Overrides Sub Deposit(ByVal Amount As Double)
    'Derived class implementation code
    'Call to base class implementation
    MyBase.Deposit(Amount)
End Sub
```

This technique is particularly useful if the base class has overloaded constructors that you need to call. In this case, you call the overloaded constructor from the derived class's constructor using the MyBase qualifier.

One important point to remember is that a call to the base class constructor must be the first executable code statement in the derived class's constructor. The following code shows the process of calling the base class's constructor from a derived class's constructor:

```
Public Sub New()
    'Call to base constructor
    MyBase.new()
    'Derived class constructor code
    _minBalance = 100
End Sub
```

Activity 7-2. Overriding Base Classes

In this activity, you will become familiar with the following:

- Overriding methods of a base class

- Using the MyBase and MyClass qualifiers in base and derived classes

Overriding the Account Class

To override the Account class, follow these steps:

1. Start VS. Select File ➤ Open ➤ Project.

2. Navigate to the Activity7_2Starter folder, click the Act7_2.sln file, and then click Open. When the project opens, it will contain a teller form. You will use this form later to test the classes you will create. The project also contains a BankClasses.vb file. This file contains code for the Account base class and the derived classes SavingsAccount and CheckingAccount.

3. Examine the Withdraw method defined in the base class Account. This function checks to see whether there are sufficient funds in the account and, if there are, updates the balance. You will override this function in the CheckingAccount class to ensure that a minimum balance is maintained.

4. Change the Withdraw method definition in the Account class to indicate it is overridable:

    ```
    Public Overridable Function Withdraw(ByVal Amount As Double) As Double
    ```

5. Add the following GetMinimumBalance method to the CheckingAccount class definition:

    ```
    Public Function GetMinimumBalance() As Double
        Return 200
    End Function
    ```

6. Add the following overriding Withdraw method to the CheckingAccount class definition. This method adds a check to see that the minimum balance is maintained after a withdrawal.

    ```
    Public Overrides Function Withdraw(ByVal Amount As Double) As Double
        If dblBalance >= Amount + GetMinimumBalance() Then
    ```

```
                dblBalance -= Amount
                Return dblBalance
        Else
                Throw New Exception("Not enough funds.")
        End If
End Function
```

7. Select Build ➤ Build Solution. Make sure there are no build errors in the Error List window. If there are, fix them, and then rebuild.

Testing the Withdraw Methods

To test the `Withdraw` methods, follow these steps:

1. Open the `frmTeller` form in the code editor and locate the `btnWithdraw` click event code.

2. Depending on which radio button is selected, call the `Withdraw` method of the appropriate object and pass the value of the `txtAmount` text box. Show the return value in the `txtBalance` text box:

```
If rdbChecking.Checked Then
    txtBalance.Text = __
        oCheckingAccount.Withdraw(CDbl(txtAmount.Text)).ToString
ElseIf rdbSavings.Checked Then
    txtBalance.Text = __
        oSavingsAccount.Withdraw(CDbl(txtAmount.Text)).ToString
End If
```

3. Select Build ➤ Build Solution. Make sure there are no build errors in the Error List window. If there are, fix them, and then rebuild.

4. Select Debug ➤ Start to run the project.

5. Enter an account number of **1**, choose the Checking option button, and click the Get Balance button. You should get a balance of 1000.

6. Enter a withdrawal amount of **200** and click the Withdraw button. You should get a resulting balance of 800.

7. Enter a withdrawal amount of **700** and click the Withdraw button. You should get an insufficient funds message, because the resulting balance would be less than the 200 minimum balance.

8. Enter an account number of **1**, choose the Savings option button, and click the Get Balance button. You should get a balance of 1000.

9. Enter a withdrawal amount of **600** and click the Withdraw button. You should get a resulting balance of 400.

10. Enter a withdrawal amount of **400** and click the Withdraw button. You should get a resulting balance of 0, because there is no minimum balance for the savings account that uses the `Account` base class's `Withdraw` method.

11. After testing, close the form, which will stop the debugger.

Using the MyBase Qualifier

At this point, the `Withdraw` method of the `CheckingAccount` class overrides the `Account` class's `Withdraw` method. None of the code in the base class's method is executed. You will now alter the code so that when the `CheckingAccount` class's code is executed, it also executes the base class's `Withdraw` method. Follow these steps:

1. Locate the `Withdraw` method of the `Account` class.

2. Change the implementation code so that it decrements the balance by the amount passed to it:

```
Public Overridable Function Withdraw _
    (ByVal Amount As Double) As Double
    dblBalance -= Amount
    Return dblBalance
End Function
```

3. Change the `Withdraw` method of the `CheckingAccount` class so that after it checks for sufficient funds, it calls the `Withdraw` method of the `Account` base class:

```
Public Overrides Function Withdraw(ByVal Amount As Double) As Double
    If dblBalance >= Amount + GetMinimumBalance() Then
        Return MyBase.Withdraw(Amount)
    Else
        Throw New Exception("Not enough funds.")
    End If
End Function
```

4. Add a `Withdraw` method to the `SavingsAccount` class that is similar to the `Withdraw` method of the `CheckingAccount` class but does not check for a minimum balance:

```
Public Overrides Function Withdraw(ByVal Amount As Double) As Double
    If dblBalance >= Amount Then
        Return MyBase.Withdraw(Amount)
    Else
        Throw New Exception("Not enough funds.")
    End If
End Function
```

5. Select Build ➤ Build Solution. Make sure there are no build errors in the Error List window. If there are, fix them, and then rebuild.

Testing the Withdraw Method

To test the `Withdraw` method, follow these steps:

1. Select Debug ➤ Start.

2. Enter an account number of **1**, choose the Checking option button, and click the Get Balance button. You should get a balance of 1000.

3. Enter a withdrawal amount of **600** and click the Withdraw button. You should get a resulting balance of 400.

4. Enter a withdrawal amount of **300** and click the Withdraw button. You should get an insufficient funds message, because the resulting balance would be less than the 200 minimum.

5. Enter an account number of **1**, choose the Savings option button, and click the Get Balance button. You should get a balance of 1000.

6. Enter a withdrawal amount of **600** and click the Withdraw button. You should get a resulting balance of 400.

7. Enter a withdrawal amount of **300** and click the Withdraw button. You should get a resulting balance of 100, because there is no minimum balance for the savings account that uses the Account base class's Withdraw method.

8. After testing, close the form, which will stop the debugger.

Using the MyClass Qualifier

To demonstrate the use of the MyClass qualifier, you will create an InterestCheckingAccount class to represent an interest-earning checking account. It will derive from the CheckingAccount class. To create InterestCheckingAccount, follow these steps:

1. Alter the GetMinimumBalance method of the CheckingAccount class so that it is overridable.

2. Add the following code to create the InterestCheckingAccount class.

```
Public Class InterestCheckingAccount
    Inherits CheckingAccount
    Public Overrides Function GetMinimumBalance() As Double
        Return 400
    End Function
End Class
```

3. Replace the existing code in the Withdraw method of the CheckingAccount class with following code. This code makes a call to the GetMinimumBalance method of the derived InterestCheckingAccount class and the GetMinimumBalance method of the base CheckingAccount class, and uses the larger return in the calculation.

```
Dim dblMinBalance As Double
If GetMinimumBalance() >= MyClass.GetMinimumBalance Then
    dblMinBalance = GetMinimumBalance ()
Else
    dblMinBalance = MyClass.GetMinimumBalance
End If

If dblBalance >= Amount + dblMinBalance Then
    Return MyBase.Withdraw(Amount)
Else
    Throw New Exception("Not enough funds.")
End If
```

4. Select Build ➤ Build Solution. Make sure there are no build errors in the Error List window. If there are, fix them, and then rebuild.

Testing the GetMinimumBalance Methods

To test the `GetMinimumBalance` methods, follow these steps:

1. Open the `frmTeller` form in the code editor. Locate and uncomment the following line of code located near the top of the file:

```
Private oInterestCheckingAccount As _
InterestCheckingAccount = New InterestCheckingAccount()
```

2. Locate the `btnBalance` click event and uncomment the following `ElseIf` block of code. This will call the `GetBalance` method for the `oInterestCheckingAccount` object:

```
ElseIf rdbInterestChecking.Checked Then
    oInterestCheckingAccount.AccountNumber = _
    CInt(txtAccountNumber.Text)
    txtBalance.Text = _
    oInterestCheckingAccount.GetBalance().ToString
```

3. Change the `If` block in the `btnWithdraw` event to call the `Withdraw` method of the `oInterestCheckingAccount` object if the `InterestChecking` radio button is selected:

```
If rdbChecking.Checked Then
    txtBalance.Text = _
    oInterestCheckingAccount.Withdraw(CDbl(txtAmount.Text)).ToString
ElseIf rdbInterestChecking.Checked Then
    txtBalance.Text = _
    oInterestCheckingAccount.Withdraw(CDbl(txtAmount.Text)).ToString
ElseIf rdbSavings.Checked Then
    txtBalance.Text = _
    oSavingsAccount.Withdraw(CDbl(txtAmount.Text)).ToString
End If
```

4. Select Build ➤ Build Solution. Make sure there are no build errors in the Error List window. If there are, fix them, and then rebuild.

5. Select Debug ➤ Start to run the application.

6. Enter an account number of **1**, choose the Interest Checking option button, and click the Get Balance button. You should get a balance of 1000.

7. Enter a withdrawal amount of **400** and click the Withdraw button. You should get a resulting balance of 600.

8. Enter a withdrawal amount of **300** and click the Withdraw button. You should get an insufficient funds message, because the resulting balance would be less than the 400 minimum set in the `InterestCheckingAccount` class.

9. Close the form, which will stop the debugger.

10. Change the return value of the `InterestCheckingAccount` class's `getMinimumBalance` method to 100.

11. Select Build ➤ Build Solution. Make sure there are no build errors in the Error List window. If there are, fix them, and then rebuild.

12. Select Debug ➤ Start to run the application.

13. Enter an account number of **1**, choose the Interest Checking option button, and click the Get Balance button. You should get a balance of 1000.

14. Enter a withdrawal amount of **500** and click the Withdraw button. You should get a resulting balance of 500.

15. Enter a withdrawal amount of **200** and click the Withdraw button. You should get a balance of 300, which is more than the minimum of 200 set by the CheckingAccount class's GetMinimumBalance method.

16. Enter a withdrawal amount of **150** and click the Withdraw button. You should get an insufficient funds message, because the resulting balance would be less than the 200 minimum set in the CheckingAccount class. Remember that the code you added to the CheckingAccount class's Withdraw method calls both the CheckingAccount class's GetMinimumBalance method and the InterestCheckingAccount class's GetMininmumBalance method, and uses the greater value.

17. Close the form, which will stop the debugger. Exit VS.

Overloading Methods of the Base Class

Methods inherited by the derived class can be *overloaded*. You overload a method by using the keyword Overloads when defining the method. The method signature of the overloaded class must use the same name as the overloaded method, but the parameter lists must differ. This is the same as when you overload methods of the same class, except that the Overloads keyword is optional and usually omitted. The following code demonstrates the overloading of a derived method:

```
Public Class Account
    Public Sub Withdraw(ByVal Amount As Double)
        'Implementation code
    End Sub
End Class
Public Class CheckingAccount
    Inherits Account
    Public Overloads Sub Withdraw(ByVal Amount As Double, _
        ByVal MinimumBalance As Double)
        'Implementation code
    End Sub
End Class
```

Using Shadowing

When a derived class inherits a method from the base class, it may *shadow* the method instead of overriding the method. If a method is defined in the derived class with the same method signature as the method of the base class, it effectively hides the method of the base class. In this situation, not only is the method of the base class hidden, but so are any overloaded methods in the base class. The following code shows how shadowing can occur when the Overrides keyword is left out of the overriding method:

```
Public Class Account
    Public Overridable Sub Withdraw(ByVal Amount As Double)
        'Implementation code
    End Sub
    Public Overridable Sub Withdraw(ByVal Amount As Double, _
        ByVal MinimumBalance As Double)
        'Implementation code
    End Sub
End Class
Public Class CheckingAccount
    Inherits Account
    Public Sub Withdraw(ByVal Amount As Double, _
        ByVal MinimumBalance As Double)
        'Implementation code
    End Sub
End Class
```

Although the IDE will issue a warning, the code will still compile. If you intend to shadow a base class method, you should explicitly use the Shadows keyword in the definition of the shadowing method of the derived class:

```
Public Shadows Sub Withdraw(ByVal Amount As Double, _
    ByVal MinimumBalance As Double)
    'Implementation code
End Sub
```

Implementing Interfaces

As you saw earlier, you can create an abstract base class that does not contain any implementation code but defines the method signatures that must be used by any class that inherits from the base class. When using an abstract class, the derived classes must provide the implementation code for the inherited methods. You could use another technique to accomplish a similar result. In this case, instead of defining an abstract class, you define an interface that defines the method signatures.

■Note Interfaces can also define properties and events.

Classes that implement the interface are contractually required to implement the interface signature definition and cannot alter it. This technique is useful to ensure that client code using the classes know which methods are available, how they should be called, and the return values to expect. The following code shows how you declare an interface definition:

```
Public Interface IAccount
    Function GetAccountInfo() As String
End Interface
```

A class implements the interface by using the Implements keyword. When a class implements an interface, it must provide implementation code for all methods defined by the interface. The following code demonstrates how a CheckingAccount class and a SavingsAccount class implement the IAccount interface. Notice that the keyword Implements indicates the class implements the interface, and it is also used to indicate when a method of the class is implementing a method of the interface:

```
Public Class CheckingAccount
    Implements IAccount
    Public Function GetAccountInfo() As String _
        Implements IAccount.getAccountInfo
        Return "Printing Checking Account Info"
    End Function
End Class
Public Class SavingsAccount
    Implements IAccount
    Public Function GetAccountInfo() As String _
        Implements IAccount.getAccountInfo
        Return "Printing Savings Account Info"
    End Function
End Class
```

Because implementing an interface and inheriting from an abstract base class are similar, you might ask why you should bother using an interface. The main advantage of using interfaces is that a class can implement multiple interfaces. The .NET Framework does not support inheritance from more than one class. As a workaround to multiple inheritance, the ability to implement multiple interfaces was introduced. Another advantage to implementing interfaces is that at compile-time, clients can instantiate an object instance based on an interface. During runtime, any object of a class type that implements the interface can be used. This is the basis for a type of polymorphism, which is discussed in the next section.

Understanding Polymorphism

Polymorphism is the ability of objects based on different classes to respond to the same method call using their own unique method implementation. This simplifies client code because the client code does not need to worry about which class type it is referencing, as long as the class types implement the same method interfaces.

For example, suppose you want all account classes to contain a GetAccountInfo method with the same interface definition but different implementations based on account type. Client code could loop through a collection of account-type classes, and the compiler would determine at runtime which specific account-type implementation needs to be executed. If you later added a new account type that implements the GetAccountInfo method, you would not need to alter the existing client code.

You can achieve polymorphism either by using inheritance or by implementing interfaces. The following code demonstrates the use of inheritance. First, you define the base and derived classes:

```
Public MustInherit Class Account
    Public MustOverride Function GetAccountInfo() As String
End Class

Public Class CheckingAccount
    Inherits Account
    Public Overrides Function GetAccountInfo() As String
        Return "Printing Checking Account Info"
    End Function
End Class

Public Class SavingsAccount
    Inherits Account
    Public Overrides Function GetAccountInfo() As String
        Return "Printing Savings Account Info"
    End Function
End Class
```

You can then create a collection class to hold a collection of classes of type Account:

```
Imports System.Collections.CollectionBase
Public Class AccountCollection
    Inherits CollectionBase
    Public Sub add(ByVal value As Object)
        list.Add(value)
    End Sub
    Public Sub remove(ByVal value As Object)
        list.Remove(value)
    End Sub
End Class
```

You can then loop through the collection class and call the GetAccountInfo method:

```
Dim oAccountCollection As AccountCollection = New AccountCollection()
Dim oCheckAccount As Account = New CheckingAccount()
Dim oSavingsAccount As Account = New SavingsAccount()
oAccountCollection.add(oCheckAccount)
oAccountCollection.add(oSavingsAccount)

Dim oItem as Account
For Each oItem In oAccountCollection
    MessageBox.Show(oItem.GetAccountInfo)
Next
```

You can also achieve a similar result by using interfaces. Instead of inheriting from the base class Account, you define and implement an IAccount interface:

```
Public Interface IAccount
    Function GetAccountInfo() As String
End Interface

Public Class CheckingAccount
    Implements IAccount
    Public Function GetAccountInfo() As String _
        Implements IAccount.GetAccountInfo
        Return "Printing Checking Account Info"
    End Function
End Class

Public Class SavingsAccount
    Implements IAccount
    Public Function GetAccountInfo() As String _
        Implements IAccount.GetAccountInfo
        Return "Printing Savings Account Info"
    End Function
End Class
```

You can then use the collection class to hold a collection of interfaces of type IAccount:

```
Dim oAccountCollection As AccountCollection = New AccountCollection()
Dim oCheckAccount As IAccount = New CheckingAccount()
Dim oSavingsAccount As IAccount = New SavingsAccount()
oAccountCollection.add(oCheckAccount)
oAccountCollection.add(oSavingsAccount)
```

You can then loop through the collection class and call the GetAccountInfo method:

```
For Each oItem as IAccount In oAccountCollection
    MessageBox.Show(oItem.GetAccountInfo)
Next
```

Activity 7-3. Investigating Polymorphism

In this activity, you will become familiar with the following:

- Creating polymorphism through inheritance

- Creating polymorphism through interfaces

Implementing Polymorphism Using Inheritance

To implement polymorphism using inheritance, follow these steps:

1. Start VS. Select File ➤ Open ➤ Project.

2. Navigate to the `Activity7_3Starter` folder, click the `Act7_3.sln` file, and then click Open. When the project opens, it will contain a teller form. You will use this form later to test the classes you will create. The project also includes a `BankClass.vb` file. This file contains code for an `AccountCollection` class, which you will use to hold a collection of objects declared as type `Account`.

3. Examine the code for the `AccountCollection` class. Notice that it inherits from a base class `CollectionBase` from the `System.Collections` namespace. This base class included in the CLR provides functionality for working with strongly typed collections.

4. After the code for the `AccountCollection` class, add the code to create an abstract base class with a `MustOverride` method `GetAccountInfo` that takes no parameters and returns a string:

```
Public MustInherit Class Account
    Public MustOverride Function GetAccountInfo() As String
End Class
```

5. Add the following code to create two derived classes: `CheckingAccount` and `SavingsAccount`. These classes will override the `GetAccountInfo` method of the base class.

```
Public Class CheckingAccount
    Inherits Account
    Public Overrides Function GetAccountInfo() As String
        Return "Printing Checking Account Info"
    End Function
End Class

Public Class SavingsAccount
    Inherits Account
    Public Overrides Function GetAccountInfo() As String
        Return "Printing Savings Account Info"
    End Function
End Class
```

6. Select Build ➤ Build Solution. Make sure there are no build errors in the Error List window. If there are, fix them, and then rebuild.

Testing the Polymorphic Method

To test the polymorphic method, follow these steps:

1. Open the `frmTeller` form in the code editor and locate the `btnAccountInfo` click event code.

2. Instantiate an instance of the `AccountCollection` as type `AccountCollection`:

```
Dim oAccountCollection As AccountCollection = _
    New AccountCollection()
```

3. Instantiate an instance of the `CheckingAccount` and `SavingsAccount` as type `Account`. By instantiating these as the base type class, you are exposing only the common functionality inherited from the base class. You can now work with these objects generically in your client code:

```
Dim oCheckAccount As Account = _
    New CheckingAccount()
Dim oSavingsAccount As Account = _
    New SavingsAccount()
```

4. Add the oCheckingAccount and oSavingsAccount to the collection using the Add method of the oAccountCollection:

```
oAccountCollection.add(oCheckAccount)
oAccountCollection.add(oSavingsAccount)
```

5. Loop through the collection and call the GetAccountInfo method of each object in the collection:

```
For Each oItem as Account In oAccountCollection
    MessageBox.Show(oItem.GetAccountInfo)
Next
```

6. Select Build ➤ Build Solution. Make sure there are no build errors in the Error List window. If there are, fix them, and then rebuild.

7. Select Debug ➤ Start to run the project.

8. Click the Account Info button. You should see a message box for each object in the collection implementing its own version of the GetAccountInfo method.

9. After testing the polymorphism, close the form, which will stop the debugger.

Implementing Polymorphism Using an Interface

To implement polymorphism using an interface, follow these steps:

1. View the code for the BankClass.vb file in the code editor.

2. Comment out the code for the Account, CheckingAccount, and SavingsAccount classes.

3. Define an interface IAccount that contains the GetAccountInfo method:

```
Public Interface IAccount
    Function GetAccountInfo() As String
End Interface
```

4. Change the Add method of the AccountCollection class so that it accepts items of type IAccount:

```
Public Sub Add(ByVal Item as IAccount)
    List.Add(Item)
End Sub
```

5. Add the following code to create two classes: CheckingAccount and SavingsAccount. These classes will implement the IAccount interface.

```
Public Class CheckingAccount
    Implements IAccount
    Public Function GetAccountInfo() As String _
```

```
        Implements IAccount.GetAccountInfo
            Return "Printing Checking Account Info"
        End Function
    End Class
    Public Class SavingsAccount
        Implements IAccount
        Public Function GetAccountInfo() As String _
            Implements IAccount.GetAccountInfo
                Return "Printing Savings Account Info"
        End Function
    End Class
```

6. Select File ➤ Save All.

Testing the Polymorphic Method

To test the polymorphic method, follow these steps:

1. Open the `frmTeller` form in the code editor and locate the `btnAccountInfo` click event code.

2. Change the code so that `oCheckingAccount`, `oSavingsAccount`, and `oItem` are instantiated as type `IAccount`:

```
Dim oAccountCollection As AccountCollection = _
    New AccountCollection()
Dim oCheckAccount As IAccount = _
    New CheckingAccount()
Dim oSavingsAccount As IAccount = _
    New SavingsAccount()
oAccountCollection.Add(oCheckAccount)
oAccountCollection.Add(oSavingsAccount)

For Each oItem As IAccount In oAccountCollection
    MessageBox.Show(oItem.GetAccountInfo)
Next
```

3. Select Build ➤ Build Solution. Make sure there are no build errors in the Error List window. If there are, fix them, and then rebuild.

4. Select Debug ➤ Start to run the project.

5. Click the Account Info button. You should see a message box for each object in the collection implementing its own version of the `GetAccountInfo` method.

6. After testing the polymorphism, close the form, which will stop the debugger. Exit VS.

Summary

This chapter gave you a firm foundation in OOP's most powerful features: inheritance and polymorphism. Being able to implement these features is fundamental to becoming a successful object-oriented programmer, regardless of the language you use.

In the next chapter, you will take a closer look at how the objects in your applications collaborate. The topics covered include how objects pass messages to one another, how events drive your programs, how data is shared among instances of a class, and how exceptions are handled.

CHAPTER 8

■ ■ ■

Implementing Object Collaboration

In the previous chapter, you looked at how class hierarchies are created in VB. That chapter also introduced the concepts of inheritance, polymorphism, and interfaces. In this chapter, you will look at how the objects of the application work together to perform the tasks required. You will see how objects communicate through messaging and how application processing initiates through events. Another important concept reviewed in this chapter is how the objects respond and communicate exceptions that may occur as they carry out their assigned tasks.

After reading this chapter, you should be familiar with the following:

- The process of object communication through messaging

- The different types of messaging that can occur

- How objects can respond to events and publish their own events

- How to use delegation in VB applications

- The process of issuing and responding to exceptions

- How to create shared data and procedures among several instances of the same class

- How to issue message calls asynchronously

Communicating Through Messaging

One of the advantages of OOP is that the applications you create function in much the same way people function in the real world. You can think of your application as an organization similar to a company. In large organizations, the employees have specialized functions they perform. For example, one person is in charge of accounts payable processing, and another is responsible for the accounts receivable operations. When an employee needs to request a service—paid time off (PTO), for example—the employee (the client) sends a message to her manager (the server). This client/server request can involve just two objects, or it can be a complex chain of client/server requests. For example, the employee requests the PTO from her manager, who, in turn, checks with the human resources (HR) department to see if the employee has enough accumulated time. In this case, the manager is both a server to the employee and a client to the HR department.

Defining Method Signatures

When a message passes between a client and server, the client may or may not expect a response back. For example, when an employee requests PTO, she expects a response indicating approval or denial. However, when the accounting department issues paychecks, the staff members do not expect everyone in the company to issue a response e-mail thanking them!

A common requirement when a message is issued is to include information needed to carry out the request. When an employee requests PTO, her manager expects her to provide him with the dates she is requesting off. In OOP terminology, you refer to the name of the method (requested service) and the input parameters (client-supplied information) as the *method signature.*

The following code demonstrates how methods are defined in VB. A method that returns a value is defined as a function procedure. If the method does not return a value, it is defined as a subprocedure.

```
Public Function AddEmployee(ByVal empName As String, . . .) _
    As Integer
        'Code to save data to database
    . . .
End Function
Public Sub Login(ByVal loginName As String, . . .)
        'Code to retrieve data from database
            . . .
End Sub
```

Passing Parameters

When a method is defined in the class, you also must indicate how the parameters are passed. Parameters may be passed *by value* or *by reference.*

If you choose to pass the parameters by value, a copy of the parameter data is passed from the client to the server. The server works with the copy and, if changes are made to the data, the server must pass the copy back to the client so that the client can choose to discard the changes or replicate the changes. Returning to the company analogy, think about the process of updating your employee file. The HR department does not give you direct access to the file. It sends you a copy of the values in the file, you make changes to the copy, and then you send it back to the HR department. The HR department then decides whether to replicate these changes to the actual employee file.

Another way you can pass parameters is by reference. In this case, the client does not pass in a copy of the data, but instead passes a reference to where the data is located. Using the previous example, instead of sending you a copy of the data in your employee file when you want to make updates, the HR department informs you where the file is located and tells you to go get it and make the changes. In this case, clearly it would be better to pass the parameters by value. The following code shows how you define the method to pass values by reference:

```
Public Function AddEmployee(ByRef empName As String, . . .) _
    As Integer
        'Code to save data to database
. . .
End Function
```

> **■Note** Because the default method of passing parameters is by value, if you omit the byVal keyword, VS inserts it automatically.

In highly distributed applications, it is advantageous to pass parameters by value instead of by reference. Passing parameters by reference can cause increased overhead, because when the server object must work with parameter information, it needs to make calls across processing boundaries and the network. Passing values by reference is also less secure when maintaining data integrity. The client is opening a channel for the data to be manipulated without the client's knowledge or control.

On the other hand, passing values by reference may be the better choice when the client and server are in the same process space (they occupy the same cubicle, so to speak) and have a clearly established trust relationship. In this situation, allowing direct access to the memory storage location and passing the parameters by reference may offer a performance advantage over passing the parameters by value. The other situation where passing parameters by reference may be advantageous is if the object is a complex data type, such as another object. In this case, the overhead of copying the data structure and passing it across process and network boundaries outweighs the overhead of making repeated calls across the network.

> **■Note** The .NET Framework addresses the problem of complex data types by allowing you to efficiently copy and pass those types by serializing and deserializing them in an XML structure.

Understanding Event-Driven Programming

So far, you have been looking at messaging between the objects in which the client initiates the message interaction. If you think about how you interact with objects in real life, you often receive messages in response to an event that has occurred. For example, when the sandwich vendor comes into the building, a message is issued over the intercom informing employees that the event has occurred. This type of messaging is referred to as *broadcast messaging*. The server issues the message, and the clients decide to ignore or respond to the message.

Another way this event message could be issued is by the receptionist issuing an e-mail to interested employees when the sandwich vendor shows up. In this case, the interested employees would subscribe to receive the event message with the receptionist. This type of messaging is often referred to as *subscription-based messaging*.

Applications built with the .NET Framework are object-oriented, event-driven programs. If you trace the client/server processing chains that occur in your applications, you can identify the event that kicked off the processing. In the case of Windows applications, the user interacting with a GUI usually initiates the event. For example, a user might initiate the process of saving data to a database by clicking a button. Classes in applications can also initiate events. A security class could broadcast an event message when an invalid login is detected. You can also subscribe to external events. You could create a web service that would issue an event notification when a change occurs in the stock market. You could write an application that subscribes to the service and responds to the event notification.

In VB, if you want to issue event messages, you add an event definition to the class definition file. The interface associated with an event procedure is similar to a subprocedure. You can pass parameters with the message notification, but you do not expect a response back. When you want to raise the event, you execute the RaiseEvent statement. The following code shows how you define and raise an event in a server class:

```
Public Class Data
    Public Event DataUpdate(ByVal Msg As String)
    Public Sub SaveInfo()
        Try
            RaiseEvent DataUpdate("Data has been updated")
        Catch
            RaiseEvent DataUpdate("Data could not be updated")
        End Try
    End Sub
End Class
```

If a client wants to subscribe to the events of the server, it must use the WithEvents keyword when declaring an instance of the server class. The object instance of the server class must also be declared with class-level scope. Once the object instance of the server has been declared, any of the methods of the client class can be used to handle the event, as long as the argument list matches the list passed by the event message. The following code shows a form class handling an event message issued by the server class:

```
Public Class Form2
    Inherits System.Windows.Forms.Form
    Dim WithEvents oData As Data

    Private Sub oData_DataSaved(ByVal Msg As String) _
        Handles oData.DataUpdate
            MessageBox.Show(Msg)
    End Sub

    Private Sub btnSave_Click(ByVal sender As System.Object, _
        ByVal e As System.EventArgs) Handles btnSave.Click
            oData = New Data()
            oData.SaveInfo()
    End Sub
End Class
```

■**Note** The VS form designer uses the WithEvents keyword when declaring object instances of Windows controls placed on a form.

Activity 8-1. Issuing and Responding to Event Messages

In this activity, you will become familiar with the following:

- Creating and raising events from a server class

- Handling events from client classes

- Handling GUI events

Adding and Raising Event Messaging in the Class Definition

To add and raise event messaging in the class definition file, follow these steps:

1. Start VS. Select File ➤ New ➤ Project.

2. Choose a Windows Application project. Name the project Act8_1.

3. A default form is included in the project. Add controls to the form and change the property values, as listed in Table 8-1. Your completed form should look similar to Figure 8-1.

Figure 8-1. *The completed login form*

Table 8-1. *Login Form and Control Properties*

Object	Property	Value
Form1	Name	frmLogin
	Text	Login
Label1	Name	lblName
	Text	Name:
Label2	Name	lblPassword
	Text	Password:
Textbox1	Name	txtName
	Text	(empty)
Textbox2	Name	txtPassword
	Text	(empty)
	PasswordChar	*
Button1	Name	btnLogin
	Text	Login
Button2	Name	btnClose
	Text	Close

4. Select Project ➤ Add Class. Name the class Employee. Open the Employee class code in the code editor.

5. Inside the class declaration, add the following line of code to define the LogLogin event procedure. You will use this event to track employee logins to your application.

```
Public Event LogLogin(ByVal LoginName As String, _
    ByVal Status As Boolean)
```

6. Add the following Login method to the class, which will raise the LogLogin event:

```
Public Sub Login(ByVal strLoginName As String, _
    ByVal strPassword As String)
    'Data normally retrieved from database
    'Hardcoded for demo only
    If strLoginName = "Smith" And strPassword = "js" Then
        RaiseEvent LogLogin(strLoginName, True)
    Else
        RaiseEvent logLogin(strLoginName, False)
    End If
End Sub
```

Receiving Events in the Client Class Using the WithEvents Declaration

To receive events in the client class using the WithEvents declaration, follow these steps:

1. Open the frmLogin class code in the code editor.

2. At the top of the form class code, declare an object instance of the Employee class, including the WithEvents keyword:

```
Private WithEvents oEmployee As Employee
```

3. At the top of the code editor, choose the oEmployee object in the left drop-down list. In the right drop-down list, choose the LogLogin event.

4. Notice the handles keyword at the end of the oEmployee_LogLogin method. This assigns the method as a handler for the LogLogin event message. In this event handler method, add the following code:

```
MessageBox.Show(" Login status: " & Status)
```

5. At the top of the code editor, choose the btnLogin object in the left drop-down list. In the right drop-down list, choose the click event.

6. In the event handler method btnLogin_Click, add the following code to call the Login method of the Employee object:

```
oEmployee = New Employee()
oEmployee.Login(txtName.Text, txtPassword.Text)
```

7. In the Solution Explorer, select the project node. Right-click the project node and select Properties. In the Property Pages dialog box, change the startup object to `frmLogin`.

8. Select Build ➤ Build Solution. Make sure there are no build errors in the Error List window. If there are, fix them, and then rebuild.

9. Select Debug ➤ Start to run the project.

10. To test to make sure the `LogLogin` event message is raised, enter a login name of **Smith** and a password of **js**. This should trigger a login status of true.

11. After testing the `LogLogin` event, close the form, which will stop the debugger.

Receiving Events in the Client Class Using the AddHandler Method

To receive events in the client class using the `AddHandler` method, follow these steps:

1. Open the `frmLogin` class code in the code editor.

2. Comment out the `oEmployee` declaration added previously.

```
'Private WithEvents oEmployee As Employee
```

3. Delete the following code from the `oEmployee_LogLogin` method declaration:

```
Handles oEmployee.LogLogin
```

4. Comment out the following line of code in the `btnLogin_Click` method:

```
'oEmployee = New Employee()
```

5. Add the following code after the line of code commented out in step 4:

```
Dim oEmployee As Employee = New Employee()
AddHandler oEmployee.LogLogin, AddressOf oEmployee_LogLogin
```

6. Select Build ➤ Build Solution. Make sure there are no build errors in the Error List window. If there are, fix them, and then rebuild.

7. Select Debug ➤ Start to run the project. Test to make sure the `LogLogin` event message is raised when you log in.

8. After testing the `LogLogin` event, close the form.

9. Select File ➤ Save All.

Handling Multiple Events with One Method

To handle multiple events with one method, follow these steps:

1. Open `frmLogin` in the form designer by right-clicking the `frmLogin` node in the Solution Explorer and choosing View Designer.

2. From the Toolbox, add a MenuStrip control to the form. Click where it says "Type Here" and enter **&File** for the top-level menu and **E&xit** for its submenu. (See Figure 8-2.)

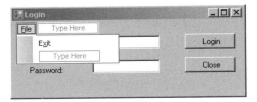

Figure 8-2. *Adding the MenuStrip control*

3. Open the `frmLogin` class code in the code editor and locate the `btnClose_Click` method.

4. Change the name of the method to `FormClose` and add a handler for the `ExitToolStripMenuItem` click event:

```
Private Sub FormClose(ByVal sender As Object, _
ByVal e As System.EventArgs) _
Handles btnClose.Click, ExitToolStripMenuItem.Click
    Me.Close()
End Sub
```

5. Select Build ➤ Build Solution. Make sure there are no build errors in the Error List window. If there are, fix them, and then rebuild.

6. Select Debug ➤ Start to run the project. Test `mnuExit` and `btnClose`.

7. After testing, close the form.

8. Save the project, and then exit VS.

Understanding Delegation

Delegation is when you request a service from a server by making a method call. The server then reroutes this service request to another method, which services the request. The delegate class can examine the service request and dynamically determine at runtime where to route the request. Returning to the company analogy, when a manager receives a service request, she often delegates it to a member of her department. (In fact, many would argue that a common trait among successful managers is the ability to know when and how to delegate responsibilities.)

Using Delegation

When creating a delegated method, you define the delegated method's signature. Because the delegate function does not actually service the request, it does not contain any implementation code. The following code shows a delegated method used to compare integer values:

```
Delegate Function CompareInt(ByVal I1 As Integer, _
    ByVal I2 As Integer) As Boolean
```

Once the delegated method's signature is defined, you can then create the methods that will be delegated to. These methods must have the same parameters and return types as the delegated method. The following code shows two methods, which the delegated method will delegate to:

```
Private Function AscendOrder(ByVal I1 As Integer, _
    ByVal I2 As Integer) As Boolean
    If I1 < I2 Then
        Return True
    End If
End Function
Private Function DescendOrder(ByVal I1 As Integer, _
    ByVal I2 As Integer) As Boolean
    If I1 > I2 Then
        Return True
    End If
End Function
```

Once the delegate and its delegating methods have been defined, you are ready to use the delegate. The following code shows a portion of a sorting routine that determines which delegated method to call depending on a SortType passed in as a parameter:

```
Public Sub SortIntegers(ByVal SortDirection As SortType, _
    ByVal intArray() As Integer)
    Dim CheckOrder As CompareInt
    If SortDirection = SortType.Ascending Then
        CheckOrder = New CompareInt(AddressOf AscendOrder)
    Else
        CheckOrder = New CompareInt(AddressOf DescendOrder)
    End If
        'Code contines . . .
End Sub
```

Using delegating techniques, the same sorting routine can be called by clients to implement descending and ascending sorting of integers.

Using Delegation to Implement Event Handlers

As you saw in Activity 8-1, another way of implementing event handlers is by using the AddHandler statement. AddHandler takes two parameters: the name of the event being handled and the name of the delegating method that will handle the event. The following code shows how to use the AddHandler statement to handle the DataUpdate event message defined in the Data class:

```
Public Class Form1
    Inherits System.Windows.Forms.Form

    Private Sub Save_click(ByVal sender As System.Object, _
        ByVal e As System.EventArgs) Handles btnSave.Click
```

```
        Dim oData As Data = New Data()
        AddHandler oData.DataUpdate, AddressOf oData_DataUpdate
        oData.SaveInfo()
    End Sub

    Private Sub oData_DataUpdate(ByVal Msg As String)
        MessageBox.Show(Msg)
    End Sub
End Class
```

The advantage of implementing event handlers using this method is that you do not need to declare the class instance variable with class-level scope, and you can dynamically add and remove event handlers at runtime.

Activity 8-2. Implementing Delegation in VB

In this activity, you will become familiar with the following:

- Creating and implementing a delegated method

- Filtering event messages in an event handler

Creating Delegated Methods

To create delegated methods, follow these steps:

1. Start VS. Select File ➤ New ➤ Project.

2. Choose a Windows Application project. Name the project Act8_2.

3. A default form is included in the project. Add controls to the form and change the property values, as listed in Table 8-2. Your completed form should look similar to Figure 8-3.

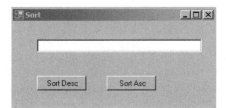

Figure 8-3. *The completed sort form*

Table 8-2. *Sort Form and Control Properties*

Object	Property	Value
Form1	Name	frmSort
	Text	Sort
Textbox1	Name	txtList
	Text	(empty)
Button1	Name	btnSortDesc
	Text	Sort Desc
Button2	Name	btnSortAsc
	Text	Sort Asc

4. Select Project ➤ Add Class. Name the class Sort and open the Sort class code in the code editor. You will investigate delegation by creating a method that will sort a list of comma-delimited words in ascending or descending order.

5. Add the following code to create a public enumeration SortType that will be used in the Sort method:

```
Public Enum SortType
    Ascending = 1
    Descending = 2
End Enum
```

6. Create the delegated method signature using the following code. You will delegate to one of two methods depending on the sort direction chosen.

```
Delegate Function CompareStrings(ByVal String1 As String, _
    ByVal String2 As String) As Boolean
```

7. Add CompareAscending and CompareDescending methods, which will be delegated to in your main Sort method:

```
Private Function CompareAscending(ByVal String1 As String, _
    ByVal String2 As String) As Boolean
    If String.Compare(String1, String2, True) < 1 Then
        Return True
    End If
End Function
Private Function CompareDescending(ByVal String1 As String, _
    ByVal String2 As String) As Boolean
    If String.Compare(String1, String2, True) > 0 Then
        Return True
    End If
End Function
```

8. Create a `SortString` method that will delegate to the correct compare function depending on the sort type requested. This function takes an array of strings, sorts the strings, and returns the sorted array to the client:

```
Public Function SortStrings(ByVal SortDirection As SortType, _
    ByVal SortArray() As String) As String()
...
End Function
```

9. The first thing you need to do in the Sort function is to determine which direction to implement the sort and point to the appropriate function that must be delegated to:

```
Dim CheckOrder As CompareStrings
If SortDirection = SortType.Ascending Then
    CheckOrder = New CompareStrings(AddressOf CompareAscending)
Else
    CheckOrder = New CompareStrings(AddressOf CompareDescending)
End If
```

10. The next part of the Sort function implements a sort on the string array by comparing adjacent values and switching the order if needed:

```
Dim OuterCount, InnerCount As Integer
Dim TempValue As String
For OuterCount = 0 To UBound(SortArray)
    For InnerCount = OuterCount + 1 To UBound(SortArray)
        If Not CheckOrder(SortArray(OuterCount), _
            SortArray(InnerCount)) Then
                TempValue = SortArray(OuterCount)
                SortArray(OuterCount) = SortArray(InnerCount)
                SortArray(InnerCount) = TempValue
        End If
    Next
Next
Return SortArray
```

11. In the Solution Explorer, select the project node. Right-click the project node and select Properties. In the Property Pages dialog box, change the startup object to `frmSort`.

12. Select Build ➤ Build Solution. Make sure there are no build errors in the Error List window. If there are, fix them, and then rebuild.

Testing the Sort Routine and Filtering Events in the Client Class

To test the sort routine and filter events in the client class, follow these steps:

1. Open the `frmSort` class code in the code editor.

2. Add the following Sort method to the form class code. This method handles clicking either the `btnSortAsc` button or the `btnSortDes` button. You can determine which button has been clicked by examining the `sender` parameter, which is passed in with the event message:

```
Private Sub Sort(ByVal sender As System.Object, _
    ByVal e As System.EventArgs) Handles btnSortDesc.Click, _
        btnSortAsc.Click
. . .
End Sub
```

3. Declare and instantiate an object instance of the Sort class. Declare a string array and populate it by using the Split function to separate a list of strings entered in the text box.

```
Dim oSort As Sort = New Sort()
Dim _Array() As String = Split(TxtList.Text, ",")
```

4. Check the event message sender object, call the SortStrings method of the oSort object, and pass the appropriate SortType:

```
If sender Is btnSortAsc Then
    Array = oSort.SortStrings _
        (Act8_2.Sort.SortType.Ascending, _Array)
ElseIf sender Is btnSortDesc Then
    Array = oSort.SortStrings _
        (Act8_2.Sort.SortType.Descending, _Array)
End If
```

5. Using the Join method, populate the txtList with a comma-delineated list of the sorted array:

```
txtList.Text = Join(_Array, ",")
```

6. Select Build ➤ Build Solution. Make sure there are no build errors in the Error List window. If there are, fix them, and then rebuild.

7. Select Debug ➤ Start to run the project. Test the sorting by entering a comma-delimited list of strings in the text box and clicking the sort ascending button. Then click the sort descending button.

8. After testing, close the form.

9. Save the project, and then exit VS.

Handling Exceptions in the .NET Framework

Your applications should be able to gracefully handle exceptions that may occur during application processing. *Exceptions* are things that you do not expect to occur during normal processing. For example, you may be trying to save data to a database over the network when the connection fails, or a user may be trying to save to the floppy drive without a disk in the drive.

The .NET Framework uses a structured exception handling mechanism. The following are some of the benefits of this structured exception handling:

- Common support and structure across all .NET languages

- Support for the creation of protected blocks of code

- The ability to filter exceptions to create efficient robust error handling

- Support of termination handlers to guarantee that cleanup tasks are completed, regardless of any exceptions that may be encountered

The .NET Framework also provides an extensive number of exception classes used to handle common exceptions that might occur. For example, the FileNotFoundException class encapsulates information such as the file name, error message, and the source for an exception that is thrown when there is an attempt to access a file that does not exist. In addition, the .NET Framework allows the creation of application-specific exception classes used to handle common exceptions that may be unique to your application.

Using the Try-Catch Block

When creating code that could end up causing an exception, you should place it in a Try block. Code placed inside the Try block is considered protected. If an exception occurs while the protected code is executing, code processing is transferred to the Catch block, where it is handled. The following code shows a method of a class that tries to read from a file that does not exist. When the exception is thrown, it is caught in the Catch block.

```
Imports System.IO
Public Class Reader
    Private strFilePath As String
    Property FilePath() As String
        Get
            Return strFilePath
        End Get
        Set(ByVal Value As String)
            strFilePath = Value
        End Set
    End Property
    Public Function ReadText() As String
        Dim sr As StreamReader
        Dim strFileText As String
        Try
            sr = File.OpenText(strFilePath)
            strFileText = sr.ReadToEnd()
            sr.Close()
            Return strFileText
        Catch
            Return "Error! File not found."
        End Try
    End Function
End Class
```

All Try blocks require at least one nested Catch block. You can use the Catch block to catch all exceptions that may occur in the Try block, or you can use it to filter exceptions based on the type of exception. This enables you to dynamically respond to different exceptions based on the exception type. The following code demonstrates filtering exceptions based on the different exceptions that could occur when trying to read a text file from disk:

```
. . .
Try
    sr = File.OpenText(strFilePath)
    strFileText = sr.ReadToEnd()
    sr.Close()
    Return strFileText
Catch e As DirectoryNotFoundException
    Return e.Message
Catch e As FileNotFoundException
    Return e.Message
Catch
    Return "An unhandled error has occurred!"
End Try
. . .
```

Adding a Finally Block

Additionally, you can nest a `Finally` block at the end of the `Try` block. Unlike the `Catch` block, the use of the `Finally` block is optional. The `Finally` block is for any cleanup code that needs to occur, even if an exception is encountered. For example, you may need to close a database connection or release a file. When the code of the `Try` block is executed and an exception occurs, processing will jump to the appropriate `Catch` block. After the `Catch` block executes, the `Finally` block will execute. If the `Try` block executes and no exception is encountered, the `Catch` blocks do not execute, but the `Finally` block will still get processed. The following code shows a `Finally` block being used to close a connection to a SQL Server database:

```
Public Sub MakeConnection()
    Dim myConnString As String
  Dim myConnection As SqlConnection = Nothing
    Try
        myConnString = "user id=sa;" & _
            "password=;database=northwind;server=myserver"
        myConnection = New SqlConnection(myConnString)
        myConnection.Open()
        'Code to interact with database . . .
    Catch myException As SqlException
        Dim myErrors As SqlErrorCollection = myException.Errors
        Dim i As Integer
        For i = 0 To myErrors.Count - 1
            MessageBox.Show("Index #" & i & ControlChars.Cr & _
                "Error: " & myErrors(i).ToString() & ControlChars.Cr)
        Next i
    Finally
        If myConnection IsNot Nothing Then
            myConnection.Close()
        End If
    End Try
End Sub
```

Throwing Exceptions

During code execution, when an exception occurs that does not fit into one of the predefined system exception classes, you can throw your own exception. You normally throw your own exception when the error will not cause problems with execution, but rather with the processing of your business rules. For example, you could look for an order date that is in the future and throw an invalid date range exception. When you throw an exception, you are creating an instance of the System.Exception class. The following code shows an example of throwing a custom exception:

```
Public Sub LogOrder(ByVal OrderNumber As Long, _
    ByVal OrderDate As Date)
    Try
        If OrderDate > Now() Then
            Throw New Exception _
                ("Order date cannot be in the future.")
        End If
        'Processing code. . .
    Catch
        'Exception handler code . . .
    End Try
End Sub
```

Nesting Exception Handling

In some cases, you may be able to correct an exception that occurred and continue processing the rest of the code in the Try block. For example, a division by zero error may occur, and it would be acceptable to assign the result a value of zero and continue processing. In this case, a Try-Catch block could be nested around the line of code that would cause the exception. After the exception is handled, processing would return to the line of code in the outer Try-Catch immediately after the nested Try block. The following code demonstrates nesting one Try block within another:

```
Try
    Try
        Y1 = X1 / X2
    Catch e As DivideByZeroException
        Y1 = 0
    End Try
    'Rest of processing code . . .
Catch
    'Outer exception processing . . .
End Try
```

■**Note** For more information about handling exceptions and the .NET Framework exception classes, refer to Appendix B.

Accessing Shared Properties and Methods

When you declare an object instance of a class, it instantiates its own instances of the properties and methods defined by the class. For example, if you had a counting routine that incremented a counter and you instantiated two object instances of the class, the counters of each object would be independent of each other. If you increment one counter, it would have no effect on the other counter. Normally, this object independence is the behavior you want. However, sometimes you may want different object instances of a class accessing shared variables. For example, you may want to build in a counter that logs how many of the object instances have been instantiated. In this case, you would create a shared property value in the class definition. The following code demonstrates how you create a shared TaxRate property in a class definition:

```
Public Class AccountingUtilities
    Private Shared _TaxRate As Single = 0.06
    Public Shared ReadOnly Property TaxRate() As Single
        Get
            Return _TaxRate
        End Get
    End Property
End Class
```

To access the shared property, you do not create an object instance of the class, but refer to the class directly. The following code shows a client accessing the shared TaxRate property defined previously:

```
Public Class Purchase
    Public Function CalculateTax(ByVal PurchasePrice As Double) _
        As Double
        Return PurchasePrice * AccountingUtilities.TaxRate
    End Function
End Class
```

Shared methods are useful if you have utility functions that clients need to access but do not want the overhead of creating an object instance of a class to gain access to the method. Note that shared methods can access only shared properties. The following code shows a shared method used to count the number of users currently logged in to an application:

```
Public Class UserLog
    Private Shared _UserCount As Integer
    Public Shared Sub IncrementUserCount()
        _UserCount += 1
    End Sub
    Public Shared Sub DecrementUserCount()
        _UserCount -= 1
    End Sub
End Class
```

When client code accesses a shared method, it does so by referencing the class directly and does not need to create an object instance of the class. The following code demonstrates accessing the shared method defined previously:

```
Public Class User
...
    Public Sub Logon(ByVal UserName As String, _
        ByVal UserPassword As String)
        'Code to check logon credentials
        'if successful . . .
        UserLog.IncrementUserCount()
    End Sub
. . .
End Class
```

Although you may not use shared properties and methods often when creating the classes in your applications, they are useful when creating base class libraries and are used throughout the .NET Framework system classes. The following code demonstrates the use of the Compare method of the System.String class. This is a shared method that compares two strings alphabetically. It returns a positive value if the first string is greater, a negative value if the second string is greater, or zero if the strings are equal:

```
Public Function CheckStringOrderAscending(ByVal String1 As String, _
ByVal String2 As String) As Boolean
    If String.Compare(String1, String2, True) >= 0 Then
        Return True
    End If
End Function
```

Activity 8-3. Implementing Exception Handling and Shared Methods in VB

In this activity, you will become familiar with the following:

- Creating and calling shared methods of a class

- Using structured exception handling in VB

Creating Shared Methods

To create the shared methods, follow these steps:

1. Start VS. Select File ➤ New ➤ Project.

2. Choose a Windows Application project. Name the project Act8_3.

3. A default form is included in the project. Add controls to the form and change the property values, as listed in Table 8-3. Your completed form should look similar to Figure 8-4.

Figure 8-4. *The completed logger form*

Table 8-3. *Logger Form and Control Properties*

Object	Property	Value
Form1	Name	frmLogger
	Text	Logger
Textbox1	Name	txtLogPath
	Text	c:\LogTest.txt
Textbox2	Name	txtLogInfo
	Text	Test Message
Button1	Name	btnLogInfo
	Text	Log Info

4. Select Project ➤ Add Class. Name the class Logger.

5. Because you will be using the System.IO class within the Logger class, add an Imports statement to the file:

```
Imports System.IO
Public Class Logger
. . .
End Class
```

6. Add a shared LogWrite function to the class. This function will write information to a log file. To open the file, you will create a FileStream object. You will create a StreamWriter object to write the information to the file.

```
Public Shared Function LogWrite(ByVal LogFilePath As String, _
    ByVal LogInfo As String) As String
    Dim oFileStream As FileStream = _
        New FileStream(LogFilePath, FileMode.Open, FileAccess.Write)
    Dim oStreamWriter As StreamWriter = _
        New StreamWriter(oFileStream)
    oFileStream.Seek(0, SeekOrigin.End)
    oStreamWriter.WriteLine(Now)
    oStreamWriter.WriteLine(LogInfo)
    oStreamWriter.WriteLine()
```

```
        oStreamWriter.Close()
        Return "Info logged"
    End Function
```

7. Open `frmLogger` in the code editor. In the right object drop-down list, choose `btnLogInfo`. In the left drop-down list, choose the click event. Add the following code, which runs the `LogWrite` method of the `Logger` class and displays the results in the form's text property. Note that because you designated the `LogWrite` method as shared (in step 6), the client does not need to create an object instance of the `Logger` class. Shared methods are accessed directly through a class reference.

```
Private Sub btnLogInfo_Click(ByVal sender As System.Object, _
    ByVal e As System.EventArgs) Handles btnLogInfo.Click
        Me.Text = Logger.LogWrite(txtLogPath.Text, txtLogInfo.Text)
End Sub
```

8. In the Solution Explorer, select the project node. Right-click the project node and select Properties. In the Property Pages dialog box, change the startup object to `frmLogger`.

9. Select Build ➤ Build Solution. Make sure there are no build errors in the Error List window. If there are, fix them, and then rebuild.

10. Select Debug ➤ Run. When the form launches, click the Log Info button. You should get an unhandled exception message of type `System.IO.FileNotFoundException`. Stop the debugger.

Creating the Structured Exception Handler

To create the structured exception handler, follow these steps:

1. Open the `Logger` class code in the code editor.

2. Locate the `LogWrite` method and add a `Try-Catch` block around the current code. In the `Catch` block, return a string stating the logging failed:

```
Try
    Dim oFileStream As FileStream = New FileStream _
        (strLogFilePath, FileMode.Open, FileAccess.Write)
    . . . rest of code
Catch
    Return "Logging failed!"
End Try
```

3. Select Build ➤ Build Solution. Make sure there are no build errors in the Error List window. If there are, fix them, and then rebuild.

4. Select Debug ➤ Run. When the form launches, click the Log Info button. This time, you should not get the exception message because it was handled by the `LogWrite` method. You should see the message *Login Failed!* in the form's caption. Close the form.

Filtering Exceptions

To filter exceptions, follow these steps:

1. Alter the Catch block to return different messages depending on which exception is thrown:

```
Catch e As FileNotFoundException
    Return "Logging failed! Could not find the file."
Catch e As IOException
    Return "Logging failed! No disk in drive."
Catch
    Return "Logging failed!"
End Try
```

2. Select Build ➤ Build Solution. Make sure there are no build errors in the Error List window. If there are, fix them, and then rebuild.

3. Select Debug ➤ Start to run the project. Test the FileNotFoundException catch by clicking the Log Info button. Test the IOException by changing the file path to the A drive and clicking the Log Info button. These errors should be caught and the appropriate message presented in the form's caption.

4. After testing, close the form.

5. Using Notepad, create the LogTest.txt file on the C drive and close the file.

6. Select Debug ➤ Start to run the project. Test the WriteLog method by clicking the Log Info button. This time, the form's caption should indicate the log write was successful.

7. Stop the debugger.

8. Open the LogTest.txt file using Notepad and verify that the information was logged.

9. Save the project, and then exit VS.

Using Asynchronous Messaging

When objects interact by passing messages back and forth, they can pass the message *synchronously* or *asynchronously*.

When a client object makes a synchronous message call to a server object, the client suspends processing and waits for a response back from the server before continuing. Synchronous messaging is the easiest to implement and is the default type of messaging implemented in the .NET Framework. However, sometimes this is an inefficient way of passing messages. For example, the synchronous messaging model is not well suited for long-running file reading and writing, making service calls across slow networks, and message queuing in disconnected client scenarios. To more effectively handle these types of situations, the .NET Framework provides the plumbing needed to pass messages between objects asynchronously.

When a client object passes a message asynchronously, the client can continue processing. After the server completes the message request, the response information will be sent back to the client.

If you think about it, you interact with objects in the real world both synchronously and asynchronously. A good example of synchronous messaging is when you are in the checkout line at the grocery store. When the clerk cannot determine the price of one of the items, he calls the manager for a price check and suspends the checkout process until a result is returned. An example of an asynchronous message call is when the clerk notices that he is running low on change. He alerts the manager that he will need change soon, but he can continue to process his customer's items until the change arrives.

In the .NET Framework, when you want to call a method of the server object asynchronously, you first need to create a delegate. Instead of making the call directly to the server, the call is passed to the delegate. When a delegate is created, the compiler also creates two methods you can use to interact with a server class asynchronously. These methods are called BeginInvoke and EndInvoke. The BeginInvoke method takes the parameters defined by the delegate plus an AsyncCallback delegate. The delegate is used to pass a callback method that the server will call and to return information to the client when the asynchronous method completes. Another parameter that can be sent in the BeginInvoke method is a context object that the client can use to keep track of the context of the asynchronous call. When the client calls the BeginInvoke method, it returns a reference to an object that implements the IAsynchResult interface. The BeginInvoke method also starts the execution of the asynchronous method call on a different thread from the main thread used by the client when initiating the call. The EndInvoke method takes the parameters and the IAsyncResult object returned by the BeginInvoke method and blocks the thread used by the BeginInvoke method until a result is returned. When the results are returned by the asynchronous method, the EndInvoke method intercepts the results and passes them back to the client thread that initiated the call.

■**Note** The method of the server class is not altered to enable a client to call its methods asynchronously. It is up to the client to decide whether to call the server asynchronously and implement the functionality required to make the call.

The following code demonstrates the process needed to make a call to a server method asynchronously. In this example, the client code is making a call to a server method over a slow connection to read log information. The first step is to define a delegate type that will be used to make the call:

```
Private Delegate Function AsyncReadLog(ByVal FilePath As String) As String
```

The next step is to declare a variable of the delegate type and instantiate it, passing in the address of the method you are calling asynchronously:

```
Private LogReader As AsyncReadLog = _
    New AsyncReadLog(AddressOf Logger.LogRead)
```

■**Note** Because the LogRead method of the Logger class is a shared method, you can call it directly.

You then declare a variable of type AsyncCallback and instantiate it, passing in the address of the method that you have set up to process the results of the asynchronous call. The AsyncCallback class is a member of the System.Runtime.Remoting.Messaging namespace:

```
Dim aCallBack As AsyncCallback = _
    New AsyncCallback(AddressOf Me.LogReadCallBack)
```

You are now ready to call the server method asynchronously by implementing the `BeginInvoke` method of the delegate type. You need to declare a variable of type `IAsyncResult` to capture the return value and pass the parameters required by the server method and a reference to the `AsyncCallback` object declared previously:

```
Dim ar As IAsyncResult = _
LogReader.BeginInvoke(txtLogPath.Text, aCallBack, Nothing)
```

You can now implement the callback method in the client, which needs to accept an input parameter of type `IAsyncCallback` that will be passed to it. Inside this method, you will make a call to the delegate's `EndInvoke` method. This method takes the same parameters passed into the `BeginInvoke` method, as well as the `IAsyncCallback` object type returned by the `BeginInvoke` method. In this case, you are displaying the results of the call in a message box:

```
Public Sub LogReadCallBack(ByVal ar As IAsyncResult)
    MessageBox.Show(LogReader.EndInvoke(txtLogPath.Text, ar))
End Sub
```

■Note You can also use the BackgroundWorker component to call methods using a thread separate from the UI thread. For more information about using the BackgroundWorker thread, consult the VS help files.

Activity 8-4. Calling Methods Asynchronously

In this activity, you will become familiar with the following:

- Creating shared methods

- Calling methods synchronously

- Calling methods asynchronously

Creating the Shared Method and Calling It Synchronously

To create the shared method and call it synchronously, follow these steps:

1. Start VS. Select File ➤ Open ➤ Project.

2. Open the solution file you completed in Act8_3.

3. Add the buttons shown in Table 8-4 to the `frmLogger` form. Figure 8-5 shows the completed form.

Figure 8-5. *The completed logger form for synchronous and asynchronous reading*

Table 8-4. *Additional Buttons for the Logger Form*

Object	Property	Value
Button1	Name	btnSyncRead
	Text	Sync Read
Button2	Name	btnAsyncRead
	Text	Async Read
Button3	Name	btnMessage
	Text	Message

4. Open the Logger class in the code editor.

5. Recall that because you are using the System.IO namespace within the Logger class, you added an Imports statement to the file. You are also going to use System.Threading namespace, so add an Imports statement to include this namespace:

```
Imports System.IO
Imports System.Threading
Public Class Logger
. . .
End Class
```

6. Add a shared LogRead function to the class. This function will read information from a log file. To open the file, you will create a FileStream object. You will use a StreamReader object to read the information from the file. You are also using the Thread class to suspend processing for three seconds to simulate a long call across a slow network.

```
Public Shared Function LogRead(ByVal FilePath As String) As String
    Dim sr As StreamReader
    Dim strFileText As String
    Try
        sr = File.OpenText(FilePath)
        strFileText = sr.ReadToEnd()
        sr.Close()
        Thread.Sleep(3000)
        Return strFileText
    Catch e As DirectoryNotFoundException
```

```
            Return e.Message
        Catch e As FileNotFoundException
            Return e.Message
        Catch
            Return "Error! Could not load file."
        End Try
    End Function
```

7. Open `frmLogger` in the code editor. In the right object drop-down list, choose `btnSyncRead`. In the left drop-down list, choose the click event. Add code that calls the `LogRead` method of the `Logger` class and displays the results in a message box. Note that because you designated the `LogRead` method as shared, the client does not need to create an object instance of the `Logger` class. Shared methods are accessed directly through a class reference.

```
Private Sub btnSyncRead_Click(ByVal sender As System.Object, _
    ByVal e As System.EventArgs) Handles btnSyncRead.Click
        MessageBox.Show(Logger.LogRead(txtLogPath.Text))
End Sub
```

8. Open `frmLogger` in the code editor. In the right object drop-down list, choose `btnMessage`. In the left drop-down list, choose the click event. Add code that displays a message box:

```
Private Sub btnMessage_Click(ByVal sender As System.Object, _
    ByVal e As System.EventArgs) Handles btnMessage.Click
        MessageBox.Show("Hello, Asynchronous World!")
End Sub
```

9. Select Build ➤ Build Solution. Make sure there are no build errors in the Error List window. If there are, fix them, and then rebuild.

10. Select Debug ➤ Run. When the form launches, click the Sync Read button. After clicking the Sync Read button, try clicking the Message button. You should not get a response when clicking the Message button because you called the `ReadLog` method synchronously. After the `ReadLog` method returns a result, the Message button will respond when clicked.

11. When you have finished testing, close the form.

Calling a Method Asynchronously

To call a method asynchronously, follow these steps:

1. Open the `frmLogger` class code in the code editor.

2. After the class definition statement at the beginning of the class file, add code to create a delegate function definition that will be used to make the asynchronous call:

```
Private Delegate Function AsyncReadLog _
    (ByVal FilePath As String) As String
```

3. On the next line, declare a `LogReader` variable of the delegate type and instantiate it, passing the address of the `LogRead` method of the `Logger` class:

```
Private LogReader As AsyncReadLog = _
    New AsyncReadLog(AddressOf Logger.LogRead)
```

4. Create a callback method that will be used to retrieve the results of the asynchronous message call. This method needs to accept a parameter of type `IAsyncResult`:

```
Public Sub LogReadCallBack(ByVal ar As IAsyncResult)
    . . .
End Sub
```

5. At the top of the code editor, in the right object drop-down list, choose `btnAsyncRead`. In the left drop-down list, choose the click event. Add code that declares a variable of type `AsyncCallback` and instantiate it, passing in the address of the `LogReadCallBack` method you created. On the next line of code, call the `BeginInvoke` method of the `LogReader` delegate, passing in the file path and the `AsyncCallback` variable. Capture the return value in a variable of type `IAsyncResult`.

```
Private Sub btnAsyncRead_Click(ByVal sender As System.Object, _
    ByVal e As System.EventArgs) Handles btnAsyncRead.Click
    Dim aCallBack As AsyncCallback = New AsyncCallback _
        (AddressOf Me.LogReadCallBack)
    Dim ar As IAsyncResult = LogReader.BeginInvoke _
        (txtLogPath.Text, aCallBack, Nothing)
End Sub
```

6. Add code to the `LogReadCallBack` method that calls the `EndInvoke` method of the `LogReader` delegate, passing in the file path and the `IAsyncResult` parameter. Display the results in a message box.

```
Public Sub LogReadCallBack(ByVal ar As IAsyncResult)
    MessageBox.Show(LogReader.EndInvoke(ar))
End Sub
```

7. Select Build ➤ Build Solution. Make sure there are no build errors in the Error List window. If there are, fix them, and then rebuild.

8. Select Debug ➤ Run. When the form launches, click the Async Read button. After clicking the Async Read button, click the Message button. This time, you should get a response, because you called the `ReadLog` method asynchronously.

9. When you have finished testing, close the form.

10. Save the project, and then exit VS.

Summary

This chapter described how the objects in your applications collaborate. You saw how objects pass messages to one another, how events drive your programs, how instances of a class share data, and how to handle exceptions.

In the next chapter, you will look at collections and arrays. Collections and arrays organize similar objects into a group. Working with collections is one of the most common programming constructs you will need to apply in your applications. You will examine some of the basic types of collections available in the NET Framework and become familiar with how to employ collections in your code.

■■■

CHAPTER 9

Working with Collections

In the previous chapter, you looked at how objects collaborate and communicate in object-oriented programs. That chapter introduced the concepts of messaging, events, delegation, exception handling, and asynchronous programming. In this chapter, you will look at how collections of objects are organized and processed. The .NET Framework contains an extensive set of classes and interfaces for creating and managing collections of objects. You will look at the various types of collection structures, what they are designed for, and when to use which. You will also look at how to use generics to create highly reusable, efficient collections.

After reading this chapter, you should be familiar with the following:

- The various types of collections exposed by the .NET Framework

- How to work with arrays and array lists

- How to use hash tables and dictionaries

- How to implement queues and stacks

- How to create strongly typed and generic-based collections

Introducing the .NET Framework Collection Types

Programmers frequently need to work with collections. For example, if you are working with employee time records in a payroll system, you need to group the records by employee, loop through the records, and add up the hours for each. In fact, you used a collection in the previous chapter (Activity 8-2) when you parsed a comma-delimited string into an array of strings in order to sort it alphabetically.

All collections need a basic set of functionality, such as adding objects, removing objects, and iterating through their objects. In addition to the basic set, some collections need additional specialized functionality. For example, a collection of help desk e-mail requests needs to implement a first-in, first-out functionality when adding and removing items from the collection.

The .NET Framework provides a variety of basic and specialized collection classes for you to use. The System.Collections namespace contains interfaces and classes that define various collections of objects, such as lists, queues, hash tables, and dictionaries. Table 9-1 describes some of the commonly used collection classes. If you do not find a collection class with the functionality you need, you can extend a .NET Framework class to create your own specialized collection.

Table 9-1. *Commonly Used Collection Classes*

Class	Description
Array	Provides the base class for language implementations that support strongly typed arrays
ArrayList	Represents a weakly typed list of objects using an array whose size is dynamically increased as required
SortedList	Represents a collection of key/value pairs that are sorted by the keys and are accessible by key and by index
Queue	Represents a first-in, first-out (FIFO) collection of objects
Stack	Represents a simple last-in, first-out (LIFO), nongeneric collection of objects
Hashtable	Represents a collection of key/value pairs that are organized based on the hash code of the key
CollectionBase	Provides the abstract base class for a strongly typed collection
DictionaryBase	Provides the abstract base class for a strongly typed collection of key/value pairs

Table 9-2 describes some of the interfaces implemented by these collection classes.

Table 9-2. *Collection Class Interfaces*

Interface	Description
ICollection	Defines size, enumerators, and synchronization methods for all nongeneric collections
IComparer	Exposes a method that compares two objects
IDictionary	Represents a nongeneric collection of key/value pairs
IDictionaryEnumerator	Enumerates the elements of a nongeneric dictionary
IEnumerable	Exposes the enumerator, which supports a simple iteration over a nongeneric collection
IEnumerator	Supports a simple iteration over a nongeneric collection
IList	Represents a nongeneric collection of objects that can be individually accessed by index

In this chapter, you will work with each of the commonly used collection classes, beginning with the Array and ArrayList classes.

Working with Arrays and Array Lists

An *array* is one of the simplest data structures in computer programming. An array holds data elements of the same data type. For example, you can create an array of integers, strings, or dates.

You access the elements of an array through its *index*. The index is an integer representing the position of the element in the index. For example, an array of strings representing the days of the week has the following index values:

Index	Value
0	Sunday
1	Monday
2	Tuesday
3	Wednesday
4	Thursday
5	Friday
6	Saturday

This days of the week example is a *one-dimensional array*, which means the index is represented by a single integer. Arrays can also be multidimensional. The index of an element of a *multidimensional array* is a set of integers equal to the number of dimensions. For example, Figure 9-1 shows a seating chart, which represents a two-dimensional array, where the student's name (value) is referenced by the ordered pair of row number, seat number (index).

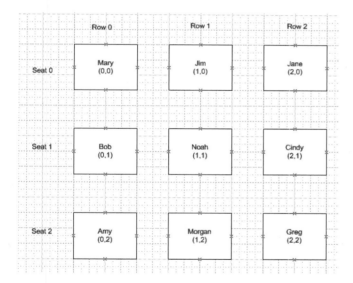

Figure 9-1. *A two-dimensional array*

Although you cannot explicitly derive from the Array class, you implement array functionality when declaring an explicit type. For example, the following code declares an array of type Integer:

```
Dim intArray() As Integer = {1, 2, 3, 4, 5}
```

Once the type is declared as an array, the properties and methods of the Array class are exposed. Some of the functionality includes querying for the upper and lower bounds of the array, updating the elements of the array, and copying the elements of the array. The Array class contains many shared methods used to work with arrays, such as methods for clearing, reversing, and sorting the elements of an array.

The following code demonstrates declaring and working with an array of integers. It also uses several shared methods exposed by the Array class.

```
Dim intArray() As Integer = {1, 2, 3, 4, 5}
Console.WriteLine("********* Upper Bound ")
Console.WriteLine(intArray.GetUpperBound(0))
Console.WriteLine("********* Array elements ")
For Each i As Integer In intArray
    Console.WriteLine(i)
Next
Array.Reverse(intArray)
Console.WriteLine("********* Array reversed ")
For Each i As Integer In intArray
    Console.WriteLine(i)
Next
Array.Clear(intArray, 2, 2)
Console.WriteLine("********* Elements 2 and 3 cleared ")
For Each i As Integer In intArray
    Console.WriteLine(i)
Next
intArray(4) = 9
Console.WriteLine("********* Elements 4 reset ")
For Each i As Integer In intArray
    Console.WriteLine(i)
Next
Console.ReadLine()
```

Figure 9-2 shows the output of this code in the Quick Console window.

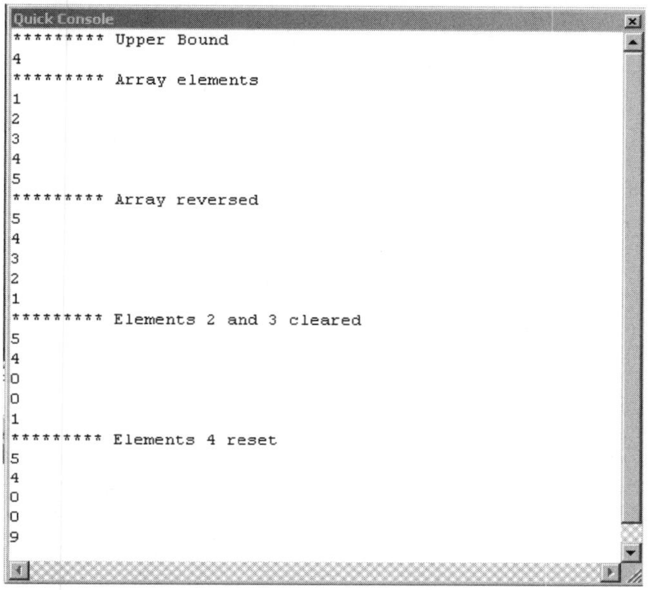

Figure 9-2. *One-dimensional array output*

You can also create multidimensional arrays, as the following code demonstrates. It declares and fills a two-dimensional array.

```
Dim int2DArray(2, 2) As Integer
For i As Integer = 0 To int2DArray.GetUpperBound(0)
    For x As Integer = 0 To int2DArray.GetUpperBound(1)
        int2DArray(i, x) = i + x
    Next
Next
'Print the index and value of the elements
For i As Integer = 0 To int2DArray.GetUpperBound(0)
    For x As Integer = 0 To int2DArray.GetUpperBound(1)
        Console.WriteLine("index(" & i & "," & x & ")" & _
            ControlChars.Tab & "Value " & int2DArray(i, x))
    Next
Next
```

Figure 9-3 shows the output of this code in the Quick Console window.

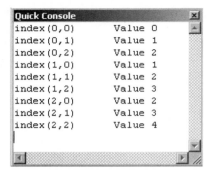

Figure 9-3. *Two-dimensional array output*

When working with collections, you often do not know the number of items contained in the collection until runtime. While an array can be resized using the Redim statement, that is not an efficient or convenient way of working with dynamic arrays. This is where the ArrayList class fits in. The capacity of an *array list* automatically expands as required, with the memory reallocation and copying of elements performed automatically. The ArrayList class also provides methods for adding, inserting, or removing a range of elements, which Array does not provide. The following code demonstrates storing a list of names in an array list. Notice that the capacity of the list expands dynamically as more names are added.

```
Dim nameList As New ArrayList
nameList.Add("Bob")
nameList.Add("Dan")
nameList.Add("Wendy")
Console.WriteLine("***** Original Capacity ")
Console.WriteLine(nameList.Capacity)
Console.WriteLine("***** Original Values ")
For Each item As Object In nameList
        Console.WriteLine(item)
Next
Console.WriteLine("***** Insert two names ")
nameList.Insert(nameList.IndexOf("Dan"), "Cindy")
nameList.Insert(nameList.IndexOf("Wendy"), "Jim")
Console.WriteLine("***** New Capacity ")
Console.WriteLine(nameList.Capacity)
Console.WriteLine("***** New Values ")
For Each item As Object In nameList
        Console.WriteLine(item)
Next
```

Figure 9-4 shows the output in the Quick Console window.

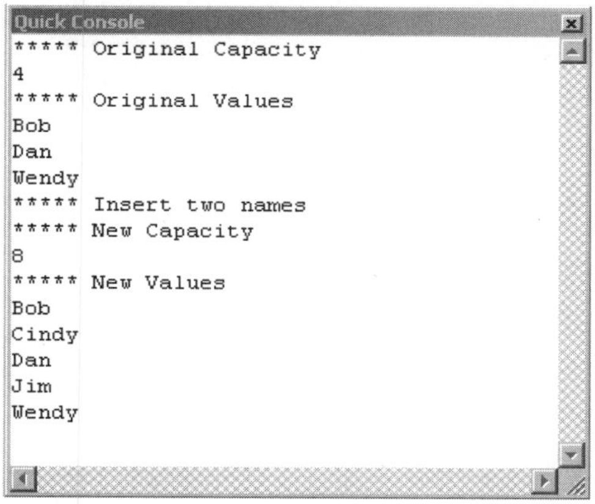

```
Quick Console                                    ×
***** Original Capacity
4
***** Original Values
Bob
Dan
Wendy
***** Insert two names
***** New Capacity
8
***** New Values
Bob
Cindy
Dan
Jim
Wendy
```

Figure 9-4. *The ArrayList output*

Although, in many cases, working with an ArrayList is easier than working with an Array, the ArrayList can have only one dimension. Also, an Array of a specific type has better performance than an ArrayList, because the elements of ArrayList are of type Object.

Activity 9-1. Working with Arrays and ArrayLists

In this activity, you will become familiar with the following:

- Creating and using arrays

- Working with multidimensional arrays

- Working with array lists

Creating and Using Arrays

To create and populate an array, follow these steps:

1. Start VS. Select File ➤ New ➤ Project.

2. Choose a Console Application project. Name the project Act9_1. The console application contains a module called Module1 with a Main procedure. The Main procedure is the first procedure that is accessed when the application is launched.

3. Create the following subprocedure in Module1. This procedure prints the values of the array passed to it to the console window.

```
Sub PrintArray(ByVal intArray() As Integer, ByVal msg As String)
    Console.Write(msg & New String(" "c, 20 - msg.Length))
    For Each i As Integer In intArray
        Console.Write(i & ",")
    Next
    Console.WriteLine()
End Sub
```

4. Add the following code to the Sub Main procedure. This code creates and populates an array of integers. It then reads the upper bound of the array, writes out the values to the console, reverses the array, and writes out the values again.

```
Sub Main()
    Dim intArray() As Integer = {1, 2, 3, 4, 5}
    PrintArray(intArray, "Initial Array")
    Console.WriteLine("UpperBound=" & intArray.GetUpperBound(0))
    Array.Reverse(intArray)
    PrintArray(intArray, "Reversed")
    Console.ReadLine()
End Sub
```

5. Select Debug ➤ Start to run the project. You should see a Quick Console window launched with the output shown in Figure 9-5. If you don't see a Quick Console window, select Tools ➤ Options and make sure the option to redirect all console output to the Quick Console window is selected, as shown in Figure 9-6. After viewing the output, stop the debugger.

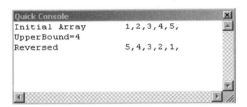

Figure 9-5. *The Quick Console output for the array of integers*

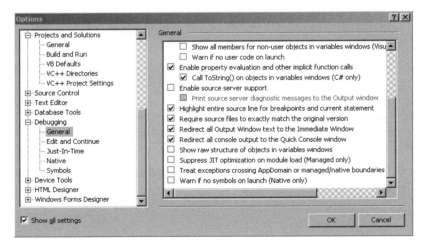

Figure 9-6. *Select the option to redirect all console output to the Quick Console window in the Options dialog box*

■**Note** The Quick Console window may be hiding behind the regular console window.

---

6. Add the following code above the `Console.ReadLine` code in the `Sub Main` procedure. This code clears the values of the array, starting at index 2 and stopping at index 4. It then sets the value of the fourth item in the array to 9.

```
Array.Clear(intArray, 2, 2)
PrintArray(intArray, "Array.Clear(a,2,2)")
intArray(3) = 9
PrintArray(intArray, "a(3)=9")
```

7. Select Debug ➤ Start to run the project. You should see the Quick Console window launched with the additional output shown, as in Figure 9-7. After viewing the output, stop the debugger.

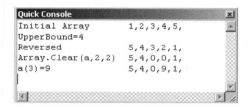

Figure 9-7. *Output after clearing and resetting the array*

Working with Multidimensional Arrays

To create and populate a multidimensional array, follow these steps:

1. In the Solution Explorer, right-click the solution node and select Add ➤ New Project. Add a new Windows Application and name it `DrawTest`.

2. Right-click the `Form1` node in the Solution Explorer and choose View Code.

3. At the top of the code editor, choose the `(Form1 Events)` in the left drop-down list. In the right drop-down list, choose the `Paint` event.

4. In the event handler method `Form1_Paint`, add the following code to populate an array of x-y coordinates.

```
Dim pointArray(4, 1) As Integer
For i As Integer = 0 To pointArray.GetUpperBound(0)
    pointArray(i, 0) = 100
    pointArray(i, 1) = 50 * i
Next
```

5. After the array is populated, add the following code to draw lines on the form from the top-left corner of the form to each point.

```
Dim bit As Bitmap = New Bitmap(Me.Width, Me.Height)
Dim g As Graphics = Graphics.FromImage(bit)
Dim myPen As Pen = New Pen(Color.Blue, 3)
For i As Integer = 0 To pointArray.GetUpperBound(0)
    Me.CreateGraphics.DrawLine(myPen, 0, 0, _
        pointArray(i, 0), pointArray(i, 1))
    Me.CreateGraphics.DrawString("P" & i & "(" & _
        pointArray(i, 0) & "," & pointArray(i, 1) & ")", _
        New Font(FontFamily.GenericSansSerif, 12), Brushes.DarkGreen, _
        pointArray(i, 0), pointArray(i, 1))
Next
```

6. In the Solution Explorer, select the DrawTest project node. Right-click the project node and select Set as StartUp Project.

7. Select Debug ➤ Start to run the project. You should see the Form1 window launched with the output, as shown in Figure 9-8. After viewing the output, stop the debugger.

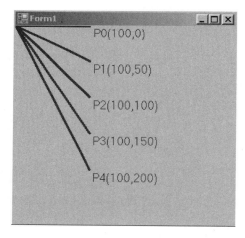

Figure 9-8. *Form1 output with a multidimensional array*

■Note For more information about graphics and drawing, refer to the System.Drawing namespace topic in the VS help files.

Working with Array Lists

Although the multidimensional array you just created works, it is probably more intuitive to store the points in a point structure and organize them into an ArrayList structure. To create and populate an array list, follow these steps:

1. In the event handler method Form1_Paint, add the following code to the end of the procedure. This code populates an array list of points.

```
Dim pointList As New ArrayList
For i As Integer = 0 To 4
    Dim pt As New Point(200, 35 * i)
    pointList.Add(pt)
Next
```

2. After the array list is populated, add the following code to draw lines on the form from the top-left corner of the form to each point.

```
myPen.Color = Color.Cyan
For Each item As Point In pointList
    Me.CreateGraphics.DrawLine(myPen, 0, 0, _
        item.X, item.Y)
    Me.CreateGraphics.DrawString("P" & pointList.IndexOf(item) & "(" & _
        item.X & "," & item.Y & ")", _
        New Font(FontFamily.GenericSansSerif, 12), Brushes.DarkRed, _
        item.X, item.Y)
Next
```

3. Select Debug ➤ Start to run the project. You should see the Form1 window launched with the output, as shown in Figure 9-9. After viewing the output, stop the debugger.

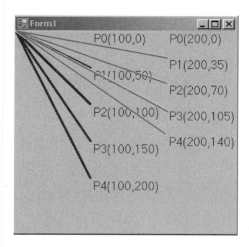

Figure 9-9. *Form1 output with an array list*

4. One advantage of the ArrayList class is that you can add and remove items from it dynamically. To see this in action, comment out the current code and add the following code to the Form1_Paint event.

```
Dim pointList As New ArrayList
For i As Integer = 0 To 4
    Dim pt As New Point(200, 35 * i)
    pointList.Add(pt)
Next
For Each item As Point In pointList
    Me.CreateGraphics.DrawString("P" & pointList.IndexOf(item) & "(" & _
        item.X & "," & item.Y & ")", _
        New Font(FontFamily.GenericSansSerif, 12), Brushes.DarkRed, _
        50, item.Y)
Next
pointList.RemoveAt(1)
pointList.Insert(2, New Point(150, 250))
For Each item As Point In pointList
    Me.CreateGraphics.DrawString("P" & pointList.IndexOf(item) & "(" & _
        item.X & "," & item.Y & ")", _
        New Font(FontFamily.GenericSansSerif, 12), Brushes.MediumBlue, _
        150, item.Y)
Next
```

5. Select Debug ➤ Start to run the project. You should see the Form1 window launched with the output shown in Figure 9-10. After viewing the output, stop the debugger.

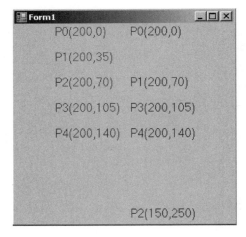

Figure 9-10. *Form1 output after adding and removing array list items*

Programming with Stacks and Queues

Two special types of collections often used in programming are the stack and the queue. A *stack* represents a last-in, first-out (LIFO) collection of objects. A *queue* represents a first-in, first-out (FIFO) collection of objects.

A good example of a stack is maintaining an approval list for an expense. When the expense is submitted up through a chain of managers, a stack maintains the list. Upon approval from the top-level manager, the next manager is retrieved from the list and sent a notification. The items on the list are retrieved in the reverse order of how they were added. Another example of using a stack occurs when a program executes a series of function calls. A stack maintains the addresses of the functions, and execution returns to the functions in the reverse order in which they were called. When placing items in a stack, you use the push method. The pop method removes items from the stack. The peek method returns the object at the top of the stack without removing it.

An application servicing help desk requests is a good example of when to use a queue. A collection maintains a list of help desk requests sent to the application. When requests are retrieved from the collection for processing, the first ones in should be the first ones retrieved. The Queue class uses the enqueue and dequeue methods to add and remove items. It also implements the peek method to return the item at the beginning of the queue without removing the item.

The following code demonstrates adding and removing items from a stack and a queue.

```
Dim approvalStack As New Stack()
For i As Integer = 0 To 5
    approvalStack.Push("mgr" + i.ToString)
Next
Console.WriteLine("items in the stack ...")
For Each item As Object In approvalStack
    Console.WriteLine(item)
Next
Console.WriteLine(approvalStack.Pop + _
        " has been removed from the stack.")
Console.WriteLine("items left in the stack ...")
For Each item As Object In approvalStack
    Console.WriteLine(item)
Next
Console.ReadLine()
Dim requestQueue As New Queue()
For i As Integer = 0 To 5
    requestQueue.Enqueue("req" + i.ToString)
Next
Console.WriteLine("items in the queue ...")
For Each item As Object In requestQueue
    Console.WriteLine(item)
Next
Console.WriteLine(requestQueue.Dequeue + _
    " has been removed from the queue.")
Console.WriteLine("items left in the queue ...")
For Each item As Object In requestQueue
    Console.WriteLine(item)
Next
Console.ReadLine ()
```

Figure 9-11 shows the output in the Quick Console window.

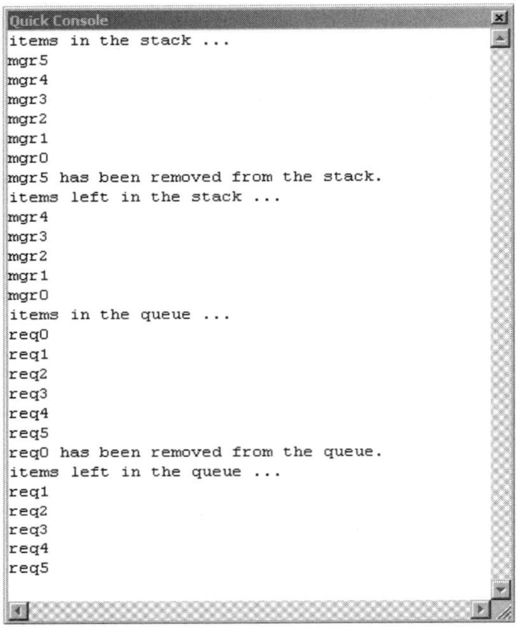

Figure 9-11. *Stack and queue output*

Using Hash Tables and Dictionary Entries

You often need to search through a collection for a particular item. If the items are stored in an Array or ArrayList structure, you need to loop through the entire collection until you find what you're looking for. As the collection grows, this becomes very inefficient. A better way to organize large collections is to group the items into subgroups based on an attribute of the item. For example, you can organize a baseball card collection into subgroups based on teams or positions played. You represent this type of collection in the .NET Framework by using a Hashtable collection.

Each element in the hash table is a DictionaryEntry structure, which consists of a key/value pair. The hash table organizes the elements of the collection into buckets. A *bucket* is a virtual subgroup of elements associated with a hash code, generated using a hash function and based on the key of the element. Organizing the items into the buckets makes searching and retrieving easier and faster.

The following code demonstrates creating and loading a hash table with customer information. The customer ID is used as the key, and the company name is used as the value. After loading the hash table, the key is used to search for a customer. The value is used to find all customers whose names start with the letter *C*.

> **■Note** The customer information for the example is retrieved from a SQL database using ADO.NET. Chapter 10 covers data access using ADO.NET.

```vb
Dim customerTable As New Hashtable
'get data from database
Dim queryString As String = _
    "SELECT CustomerID, CompanyName FROM dbo.Customers;"
Dim connectionString As String = _
    "Data Source=DRCSRVO1;" & _
    "Initial Catalog=Northwind;Integrated Security=True"
Using connection As New _
    Data.SqlClient.SqlConnection(connectionString)
    Dim command As New Data.SqlClient.SqlCommand _
        (queryString, connection)
    connection.Open()
    Dim reader As Data.SqlClient.SqlDataReader
    reader = command.ExecuteReader()

    While reader.Read()
        'add names to arraylist
        customerTable.Add(reader("CustomerID"), reader("CompanyName"))
    End While
    reader.Close()
End Using
If customerTable.ContainsKey("CACTU") Then
    For Each de As DictionaryEntry In customerTable
        If de.Key = "CACTU" Then
            Console.WriteLine(vbTab + "{0}" + vbTab + "{1}" + vbTab + _
                "{2}", de.GetHashCode, de.Key, de.Value)
        End If
    Next
End If
customerTable.Add("BBBB", "Clark ent.")
Console.WriteLine("------------------------------------------")
For Each de As DictionaryEntry In customerTable
    If CStr(de.Value).StartsWith("C") Then
        Console.WriteLine(vbTab + "{0}" + vbTab + "{1}" + vbTab + _
            "{2}", de.GetHashCode, de.Key, de.Value)
    End If
Next
```

Figure 9-12 shows the values of the keys, values, and hash codes.

```
Quick Console                                                              X
        2021566583      CACTU    Cactus Comidas para llevar                ▲
-----------------------------------------------
        2051197892      BBBB     Clark ent.
        2063402978      CHOPS    Chop-suey Chinese
        2021566583      CACTU    Cactus Comidas para llevar
        2035135871      CENTC    Centro comercial Moctezuma
        2028428723      CONSH    Consolidated Holdings
        2054861490      COMMI    Comércio Mineiro
```

Figure 9-12. *Hash table output*

The .NET Framework also provides specialized collections that implement specific functionality more efficiently than the Hashtable class. For example, a StringDictionary class provides better performance when the keys used in the collection are constrained as a string type. Another collection type is the SortedList, which is a hybrid between the ArrayList and the Hashtable. As items are added to or removed from the collection, the SortedList maintains a sort order based on the key. You can access items by their index, just as you can with an ArrayList. You can also access the items by their key, similar to working with a Hashtable. For a complete list of the various specialized collection classes provided by the .NET Framework, consult the documentation for the System.Collections and the System.Collections.Specialized namespaces.

Activity 9-2. Implementing Stacks, Queues, and Hash Tables

In this activity, you will become familiar with the following:

- Using stacks and queues

- Working with hash tables

Using Stacks and Queues

To create and populate a stack and queue, follow these steps:

1. Start VS. Select File ➤ New ➤ Project.

2. Choose a Windows Application project. Name the project Act9_2.

3. A default form is included in the project. Add controls to the form and change the property values, as listed in Table 9-3. Your completed form should look similar to Figure 9-13.

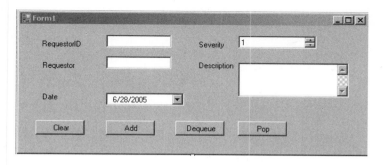

Figure 9-13. *The completed form for the stack and queue example*

Table 9-3. *Form and Control Properties*

Object	Property	Value
Label1	Text	RequestorID
Label2	Text	Requestor
Label3	Text	Date
Label4	Text	Severity
Label5	Text	Description
Textbox1	Name	txtID
Textbox2	Name	txtRequestor
Textbox3	Name	txtDescription
	Multiline	True
	ScrollBars	Vertical
DateTimePicker1	Name	dtpDate
	Format	Short
NumericUpDown1	Name	udSeverity
	Maximum	5
	Minimum	1
	Value	1
Button1	Name	btnClear
	Text	Clear
Button2	Name	btnAdd
	Text	Add
Button3	Name	btnDequeue
	Text	Dequeue
Button4	Name	btnPop
	Text	Pop

4. Select Project ➤ Add Class. Name the class Request.

5. Add the following code to the Request class. This class stores request information entered in the application.

```
Private _ID As Integer
Private _Requestor As String
Private _Severity As Integer
Private _Date As Date
Private _Description As String
Public Property ID() As Integer
    Get
        Return _ID
    End Get
    Set(ByVal value As Integer)
        _ID = value
    End Set
End Property
Public Property Requestor() As String
    Get
        Return _Requestor
    End Get
    Set(ByVal value As String)
        _Requestor = value
    End Set
End Property
Public Property Severity() As Integer
    Get
        Return _Severity
    End Get
    Set(ByVal value As Integer)
        _Severity = value
    End Set
End Property
Public Property [Date]() As Date
    Get
        Return _Date
    End Get
    Set(ByVal value As Date)
        _Date = value
    End Set
End Property
Public Property Description() As String
    Get
        Return _Description
    End Get
    Set(ByVal value As String)
        _Description = value
    End Set
End Property
```

6. Open `Form1` in the code editor and add a subprocedure to reset the entry controls:

```
Private Sub Reset()
    txtID.Text = String.Empty
    txtRequestor.Text = String.Empty
    udSeverity.Value = udSeverity.Minimum
    dtpDate.Value = Today
    txtDescription.Text = String.Empty
End Sub
```

7. Call the `Reset` procedure from the `btnClear` click event.

```
Private Sub btnClear_Click(ByVal sender As Object, _
        ByVal e As System.EventArgs) Handles btnClear.Click
        Reset()
End Sub
```

8. At the top of the `Form1` class code, declare and instantiate form-level variables of type `Queue` and Stack.

```
Private reqQueue As New Queue
Private reqStack As New Stack
```

9. In the `btnAdd` click event, add code to populate the queue and stack collections with request objects. Populate the request objects from values entered in the form.

```
Private Sub btnAdd_Click(ByVal sender As Object, _
    ByVal e As System.EventArgs) Handles btnAdd.Click
    Try
        Dim req As New Request
        req.ID = txtID.Text
        req.Requestor = txtRequestor.Text
        req.Severity = CInt(udSeverity.Value)
        req.Date = dtpDate.Value
        req.Description = txtDescription.Text
        reqQueue.Enqueue(req)
        reqStack.Push(req)
        Reset()
    Catch ex As Exception
        MessageBox.Show(ex.Message)
    End Try
End Sub
```

10. In the `btnDequeue` click event, add code to retrieve requests from the queue and populate the controls on the form.

```
Private Sub btnDequeue_Click(ByVal sender As Object, _
    ByVal e As System.EventArgs) Handles btnDequeue.Click
    Try
        Dim req As Request = reqQueue.Dequeue
        txtID.Text = req.ID
```

```
            txtRequestor.Text = req.Requestor
            udSeverity.Value = req.Severity
            dtpDate.Value = req.Date
            txtDescription.Text = req.Description
        Catch ex As Exception
            MessageBox.Show(ex.Message)
        End Try
    End Sub
```

11. In the `btnPop` click event, add code to retrieve requests from the stack and populate the controls on the form.

```
    Private Sub btnPop_Click(ByVal sender As System.Object, _
        ByVal e As System.EventArgs) Handles btnPop.Click
        Try
            Dim req As Request = reqStack.Pop
            txtID.Text = req.ID
            txtRequestor.Text = req.Requestor
            udSeverity.Value = req.Severity
            dtpDate.Value = req.Date
            txtDescription.Text = req.Description
        Catch ex As Exception
            MessageBox.Show(ex.Message)
        End Try
    End Sub
```

12. Select Debug ➤ Run. When the form launches, try adding and retrieving requests from the queue and stack. Notice the order in which objects are retrieved from the collections. When you're finished testing, stop the debugger.

Implementing a Hash Table Lookup

To implement a hash table lookup, follow these steps:

1. Open the `Form1` class code in the code editor.

2. At the top of the `Form1` class code, declare and instantiate a form-level variable of type `Hashtable`.

```
    Private lookUp As New Hashtable
```

3. In the `Form1` load event, add code to populate the hash table. The key represents the user ID, and the value represents the user name.

```
    Private Sub Form1_Load(ByVal sender As System.Object, _
        ByVal e As System.EventArgs) Handles MyBase.Load
        lookUp.Add("DRC", "Dan Clark")
        lookUp.Add("ACM", "Amy Mann")
        lookUp.Add("BXC", "Bob Smith")
    End Sub
```

4. In the `txtID` TextChanged event, add code to use the hash table to look up and populate the `txtRequest` text box depending on the value entered in the `txtID` text box.

```
Private Sub txtID_TextChanged(ByVal sender As Object, _
    ByVal e As System.EventArgs) Handles txtID.TextChanged
    If lookUp.ContainsKey(txtID.Text.ToUpper) Then
        txtRequestor.Text = lookUp.Item(txtID.Text.ToUpper)
    Else
        txtRequestor.Text = String.Empty
    End If
End Sub
```

5. Select Debug ➤ Run. When the form launches, experiment with it by entering user IDs in the `txtID` text box. You should see the `txtRequestor` text box automatically populate using the values stored in the hash table. When you are finished experimenting, stop the debugger and exit VS.

Using Strongly Typed Collections and Generics

With the exception of a few of the specialized collections strongly typed to hold strings, the collections provided by the .NET Framework are weakly typed. The items held by the collections are of type `Object`, and so they can be of any type, since all types derive from the `Object` type.

Weakly typed collections can cause performance and maintenance problems with your application. One problem is there are no inherent safeguards for limiting the types of objects stored in the collection. The same collection can hold any type of item, including dates, integers, or a custom type such as an employee object. If you build and expose a collection of integers, and inadvertently that collection gets passed a date, the chances are high that the code will fail at some point.

Fortunately, VB 2005 supports *generics*, and the .NET Framework provides generic-based collections in the `System.Collections.Generic` namespace. Generics offer the ability to define a class without specifying its type. The type is specified when the class is instantiated. Using a generic collection provides the advantages of type safety and performance of a strongly typed collection while also providing the code reuse associated with weakly typed collections.

The following code demonstrates creating a strongly typed collection of employees using the `Generic.List` class. Employee objects are added to the collection and then the employees in the collection are retrieved with the names written out to the console.

```
Dim emp1 As New employee(1, "Bob")
Dim emp2 As New employee(2, "Cathy")
Dim emp3 As New employee(3, "Alice")
Dim empCollection As New Generic.List(Of employee)
empCollection.Add(emp1)
empCollection.Add(emp2)
empCollection.Add(emp3)
For Each item As employee In empCollection
     Console.WriteLine(item.Name)
Next
```

There may be times when you need to extend the functionality of the collections provided by the .NET Framework. For example, you may need a collection of employee objects that offers the ability to sort the collection by either the employee ID number or the employee last name. You can implement this functionality by creating a custom employee collection that inherits from and extends the Generic.List class. The following code defines an employee collection class that implements a custom sorting of the collection. To implement sorting, you need to define a sorting class that implements the IComparer interface.

```
Public Class employeeCollection
    Inherits Generic.List(Of employee)

    Enum SortField
        ID
        Name
    End Enum
    Public Shadows Sub Sort(ByVal field As SortField)
        Select Case field
            Case SortField.ID
                MyBase.Sort(New IDComparer)
            Case SortField.Name
                MyBase.Sort(New NameComparer)
        End Select
    End Sub
    Private Class IDComparer
        Implements Generic.IComparer(Of employee)

        Public Function Compare(ByVal x As employee, _
            ByVal y As employee) As Integer _
            Implements System.Collections.Generic.IComparer(Of employee).Compare
            Return x.ID.CompareTo(y.ID)
        End Function
    End Class
    Private Class NameComparer
        Implements Generic.IComparer(Of employee)

        Public Function Compare(ByVal x As employee, _
            ByVal y As employee) As Integer _
            Implements System.Collections.Generic.IComparer(Of employee).Compare
            Return x.Name.CompareTo(y.Name)
        End Function
    End Class
End Class
```

The following code adds the three previous employees to the EmployeeCollection, sorts the collection by name, and writes the names out to the console.

```
Dim empCollection2 As New employeeCollection
empCollection2.Add(emp1)
empCollection2.Add(emp2)
empCollection2.Add(emp3)
empCollection2.Sort(employeeCollection.SortField.Name)
For Each item As employee In empCollection2
    Console.WriteLine(item.Name)
Next
```

Activity 9-3. Implementing and Extending Generic Collections

In this activity, you will become familiar with the following:

- Implementing a generic collection

- Creating a strongly typed collection

To create and populate a generic list, follow these steps:

1. Start VS. Select File ➤ New ➤ Project.

2. Choose a Console Application project. Name the project Act9_3.

3. Select Project ➤ Add Class. Name the class Request.

4. Add the following code to the Request class.

```
Public Class Request
    Private _Requestor As String
    Private _Priority As Integer
    Private _Date As Date
    Public Property Requestor() As String
        Get
            Return _Requestor
        End Get
        Set(ByVal value As String)
            _Requestor = value
        End Set
    End Property
    Public Property Priority() As Integer
        Get
            Return _Priority
        End Get
        Set(ByVal value As Integer)
            _Priority = value
        End Set
    End Property
    Public Property [Date]() As Date
```

```
        Get
            Return _Date
        End Get
        Set(ByVal value As Date)
            _Date = value
        End Set
    End Property
    Public Sub New(ByVal reqBy As String, _
        ByVal priorityLevel As Integer, ByVal reqDate As Date)
        Requestor = reqBy
        Priority = priorityLevel
        [Date] = reqDate
    End Sub
    Public Overrides Function ToString() As String
        Return Me.Requestor & "," & _
            Me.Priority.ToString & "," & Me.Date
    End Function
End Class
```

5. Open `Module1` in the code editor and add the following code to the `Sub Main` procedure. This code populates a generic list of type `Request` and displays the values in the console window.

```
Dim req1 As New Request("Dan", 2, "4/2/2005")
Dim req2 As New Request("Alice", 5, "2/2/2005")
Dim req3 As New Request("Bill", 4, "6/2/2005")
Dim reqColl As New Generic.List(Of Request)
reqColl.Add(req1)
reqColl.Add(req2)
reqColl.Add(req3)
For Each item As Request In reqColl
    Console.WriteLine(item.ToString)
Next
Console.ReadLine()
```

6. Select Debug ➤ Start to run the project. You should see a Quick Console window with the request information listed. After viewing the output, stop the debugger.

7. Select Project ➤ Add Class. Name the class `RequestCollection`.

8. Add the following code to the `RequestCollection` class. This class inherits from the `Generic.List` class and implements a custom sorting by request priority or date.

```
Public Class RequestCollection
    Inherits Generic.List(Of Request)
    Public Enum SortField
        Priority
        [Date]
    End Enum
```

```
    Public Shadows Sub Sort(ByVal field As SortField)
        Select Case field
            Case SortField.Priority
                MyBase.Sort(New PriorityComparer)
            Case SortField.Date
                MyBase.Sort(New DateComparer)
        End Select
    End Sub
    Private Class PriorityComparer
        Implements IComparer(Of Request)
        Public Function Compare(ByVal x As Request, _
          ByVal y As Request) As Integer _
          Implements System.Collections.Generic.IComparer(Of Request).Compare
            Return x.Priority.CompareTo(y.Priority)
        End Function
    End Class
    Private Class DateComparer
        Implements IComparer(Of Request)
        Public Function Compare(ByVal x As Request, _
          ByVal y As Request) As Integer _
          Implements System.Collections.Generic.IComparer(Of Request).Compare
            Return x.Date.CompareTo(y.Date)
        End Function
    End Class
End Class
```

9. Replace the existing code with the following code in the Sub Main procedure of Module1. This code populates a RequestCollection, sorts the collection, and displays the values in the console window.

```
Dim req1 As New Request("Dan", 2, "4/2/2005")
Dim req2 As New Request("Alice", 5, "2/2/2005")
Dim req3 As New Request("Bill", 4, "6/2/2005")
Dim reqColl As New RequestCollection
reqColl.Add(req1)
reqColl.Add(req2)
reqColl.Add(req3)
For Each item As Request In reqColl
    Console.WriteLine(item.ToString)
Next
reqColl.Sort(RequestCollection.SortField.Priority)
Console.WriteLine("******sorted by priority******")
For Each item As Request In reqColl
    Console.WriteLine(item.ToString)
```

```
Next
reqColl.Sort(RequestCollection.SortField.Date)
Console.WriteLine("******sorted by date*********")
For Each item As Request In reqColl
    Console.WriteLine(item.ToString)
Next
Console.ReadLine()
```

10. Select Debug ➤ Start to run the project. You should see the Quick Console window launched with the output shown in Figure 9-14. After viewing the output, stop the debugger and exit VS.

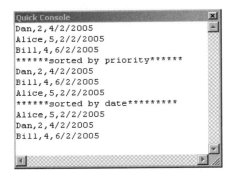

Figure 9-14. *Generic collection output*

Summary

In this chapter, you examined the various types of collections exposed by the .NET Framework. You learned how to work with arrays, array lists, hash tables, dictionaries, queues, stacks, and generic-based and strongly typed collections.

This chapter is the final chapter in a series that introduced you to the various OOP constructs such as classes, inheritance, and polymorphism as they are implemented in VB code. You should also have a firm understanding of how class structures, object collaboration, and collections are implemented in a VB application. You have been introduced to the VS IDE and practiced using it. You are now ready to put the pieces together and develop a working application.

The next chapter is the first in a series in which you will revisit the UML models you developed for the case study introduced in Chapter 4. You will transform these models into an application. In the process, you will investigate data access using ADO.NET, creating a Windows Forms-based GUI, creating a web form-based GUI, and using web services.

PART 3

Developing Applications with Visual Basic

CHAPTER 10

■■■

OSO Application Revisited: Implementing the Business Logic

During the past few chapters, you looked at the various object-oriented programming constructs such as classes, inheritance, and polymorphism as they are implemented in Visual Basic code. You have been introduced to and practiced using the VS integrated development environment. You should also have a firm understanding of how class structures and object collaboration are implemented in a Visual Basic application.

You are now ready to put the pieces together and develop a working application. In this chapter, you will revisit the office-supply ordering application you first started designing in Chapter 4. You are now ready to implement the business logic in Visual Basic code. Because most business applications involve working with and updating data in a backend database, you will first look at how the .NET Framework provides you with the functionality to work with relational data. Once you are familiar with working with relational data in the .NET Framework, you will construct and test the classes that will implement the business logic of the OSO application.

After reading this chapter, you should be familiar with the following:

- How to transition from the logical design phase to the physical design phase

- How to separate the application logic into distinct tiers

- How to establish a connection to a database using the Connection object

- How to use a Command object to execute SQL queries

- How to use a Command object to execute stored procedures

- How to retrieve records with the DataReader object

- How to populate DataTables and DataSets

- How to establish relationships between tables in a DataSet

- How to edit and update data in a DataSet

- DataSet population from an Extensible Markup Language structure

- DataSet persistence to an Extensible Markup Language structure

Revisiting Application Design

When designing applications, you can generally classify the design process into three distinct phases. The *conceptual design*, the first phase, constitutes the discovery phase of the process. The conceptual design phase involves a considerable amount of collaboration and communication between the users of the system and the system designers. The system designers must gain a complete understanding of the business processes that the proposed system will encompass. Using scenarios and use cases, the designers define the functional requirements of the system. A common understanding and agreement on system functionality and scope among the developers and users of the system is the required outcome of this phase.

The second phase of the design process is the *logical design*. During the logical design phase, you work out the details about the structure and organization of the system. This phase consists of the development and identification of the business objects and classes that will compose the system. UML class diagrams identify the system objects, for which you identify and document the attributes and behaviors. You also develop and document the structural interdependencies of these objects using the class diagrams. Using sequence and collaboration diagrams, you discover and identify the interactions and behavioral dependencies between the various system objects. The outcome of this phase, the application object model, is independent of any implementation-specific technology and deployment architecture.

The third phase of the design process is the *physical design*. During the physical design phase, you transform the application object model into an actual system. You evaluate and decide upon specific technologies and infrastructures, do cost analysis, and determine any constraints. Issues such as programmer experience and knowledge base, current implementation technologies, and legacy system integration will all influence your decisions during the physical design phase. You must also analyze security concerns, network infrastructure, and scalability requirements.

When designing a distributed application, you normally separate the logical architectural structure from the physical architectural structure. By separating the architectural structure in this way, you will find it much easier to maintain and update the application. You can make any physical architectural changes (to increase scalability, for example) with minimal impact. The logical architectural design of an application is separated into multiple tiers. Users interact with the *presentation tier*, which is responsible for presenting data to the user and providing a way for the user to initiate business service requests. The *business logic tier* encapsulates and implements the business logic of an application. It is responsible for performing calculations, processing data, and controlling application logic and sequencing. The *data tier* is responsible for managing the access to and storage of information that must be persisted and shared among various users and business processes.

One of the main functions of the business logic tier is retrieving and processing data. Before you implement the OSO application's business logic tier, you need to look more closely at how the .NET Framework provides the ability to retrieve and work with data structures. This functionality is encapsulated in a set of .NET namespaces commonly referred to as *ADO.NET*.

Introducing ADO.NET

A majority of applications developed for businesses need to interact with a data storage device. Data storage can occur in many different forms: for example, in a flat file system, as is the case with many traditional mainframe systems, or in a relational database management system, such as SQL Server, Oracle, or Sybase. You can also maintain data in a hierarchical textual file structure, as is the case with XML. To access and work with data in a consistent way across these various data stores, the .NET Framework provides a set of classes organized into the System.Data namespace. This collection of classes is known as ADO.NET.

Looking at the history of Microsoft's data access technologies reveals an evolution from a connected model to a disconnected one. When developing the traditional two-tier client-server applications prevalent in the 1980s and early 1990s, it was often more efficient to open a connection with the database, work with the data implementing server-side cursors, and close the connection when finished working with the data. The problem with this approach became apparent in the late 1990s as companies tried to evolve their data-driven applications from traditional two-tier client-server applications to multitier web-based models. It became apparent that opening and holding a connection open until processing was complete is not scalable. *Scalability* is the ability of an application to handle an increasing number of simultaneous clients without a noticeable degradation of performance.

Another problem with the traditional data access technologies developed during this time was the lack of interoperability. Systems with a high degree of interoperability can easily exchange data back and forth between one another regardless of the implementation technologies of the various systems. Traditional data access technologies rely on proprietary methods of data exchange. Using these techniques, it is hard for a system built using Microsoft technologies such as ADO (pre-.NET) and DCOM to exchange data with a system built using Java technologies such as JDBC and CORBA. The industry as a whole realized it was in the best interest of all parties to develop standards—such as SOAP and XML—for exchanging data between disparate systems. Microsoft has embraced these standards and has incorporated support of the standards into the .NET Framework.

Microsoft has designed ADO.NET to be highly scalable and interoperable. To achieve scalability, Microsoft has designed ADO.NET around a disconnected model. A connection is made to the database, the data and metadata are retrieved and cached locally, and the connection is closed. To achieve a high level of interpretability, Microsoft has embraced XML, which is based on open standards and is supported by many different segments of the software industry, as the main mechanism for transferring data. By exposing data natively as XML, it has become much easier to exchange data with components, applications, and business partners who may not be using Microsoft technologies. Transporting data using XML over HTTP also alleviates many of the problems associated with passing binary information between the various tiers of an application and through firewall security.

Working with Data Providers

To establish a connection and work with a specific data source such as SQL Server, you must work with the appropriate .NET provider classes. The SQL Server provider classes are located in the System.Data.SQLClient namespace. Other data providers exist, such as the OLEDB data provider classes located in the System.Data.OLEDB namespace. As time goes on, you can expect many more native providers will be added to the .NET Framework. Each of these providers implements a similar class structure used to work with the data source. Table 10-1 summarizes the main classes of the System.Data.SQLClient provider namespace.

Table 10-1. *Classes in the System.Data.SqlClient Namespace*

Class	Responsibility
SqlConnection	Establishes a connection and a unique session with the database
SqlCommand	Represents a Transact-SQL statement or stored procedure to execute at the database
SqlDataReader	Provides a means of reading a forward-only stream of rows from the database
SqlDataAdapter	Fills a DataSet and updates changes back to the database
SqlParameter	Represents a parameter used to pass information to and from stored procedures
SqlTransaction	Represents a Transact-SQL transaction to be made in the database
SqlError	Collects information relevant to a warning or error returned by the database server
SqlException	Defines the exception that is thrown when a warning or error is returned by the database server

A similar set of classes exists in the System.Data.OLEDB provider namespace. For example, instead of the SqlConnection class, you have an OleDbConnection class.

Establishing a Connection

The first step to retrieving data from a database is to establish a connection, which is done using a Connection object based on the type of provider being used. To establish a connection to a SQL Server, you instantiate a Connection object of type SqlConnection. You also need to provide the Connection object with a ConnectionString. The ConnectionString consists of a series of semicolon-delineated name-value pairs that provide information needed to connect to the database server. Some of the information commonly passed by the ConnectionString is the name of the server, the name of the database, and security information. The following code demonstrates a ConnectionString used to connect to a SQL Server database:

```
"Data Source=TestServer;Initial Catalog=Pubs;User ID=Dan;Password=training"
```

The attributes you need to provide through the ConnectionString are dependent on the data provider you are using. The following code demonstrates a ConnectionString used to connect to an Access database:

```
"Provider=Microsoft.Jet.OleDb.4.0;Data Source=D:\Data\Northwind.mdb"
```

■**Note** You also need to use a Connection object of type OleDbConnection.

The next step is to invoke the Open method of the Connection object. This will result in the Connection object loading the appropriate driver and opening a connection to the data source. Once the connection is open, you can work with the data. After you are done interacting with the database, it is important that you invoke the Close method of the Connection object, because when a `Connection` object falls out of scope or is garbage collected, the connection is not implicitly released. The following code demonstrates the process of opening a connection to the Pubs database in SQL Server, working with the data, and closing the connection.

```
Imports System.Data
Imports System.Data.SqlClient
Imports System.Windows.Forms
Public Class SqlData
    Public Sub MakeConnection()
        Dim oPubConnection As New SqlConnection
        Dim sConnString As String
        Try
            sConnString = "Data Source=drcsrv01;" & _
                "Initial Catalog=pubs;Integrated Security=True"
            oPubConnection.ConnectionString = sConnString
            oPubConnection.Open()
            MessageBox.Show(oPubConnection.State.ToString)
        Catch oEx As Exception
            MessageBox.Show(oEx.Message)
        Finally
            If Not oPubConnection Is Nothing Then
                oPubConnection.Close()
            End If
        End Try
    End Sub
End Class
```

Executing a Command

Once a database connection is established and opened, you can execute SQL statements against the database. A `Command` object stores and executes command statements against the database. You can use the `Command` object to execute any valid SQL statement understood by the data store. In the case of SQL Server, these can be Data Manipulation Language statements (`Select`, `Insert`, `Update`, and `Delete`), Data Definition Language statements (`Create`, `Alter`, and `Drop`), or Data Control Language statements (`Grant`, `Deny`, and `Revoke`). The `CommandText` property of the `Command` object holds the SQL statement that will be submitted. The `Command` object contains three methods for submitting the `CommandText` to the database depending on what is returned. If records are returned, as is the case when a `Select` statement is executed, then you can use the `ExecuteReader`. If a single value is returned—for example, the results of a `Select Count` aggregate function—you should use the `ExecuteScalar` method. When no records are returned from a query—for example, from an `Insert` statement—you should use the `ExecuteNonQuery` method. The following code demonstrates using a `Command` object to execute a SQL statement against the Pubs database that returns the number of employees.

```
Public Function CountEmployees() As Integer
    Dim oPubConnection As New SqlConnection
    Dim sConnString As String
    Dim oSqlCommand As SqlCommand
```

```
    Try
        sConnString = "Data Source=drcsrv01;Initial Catalog=pubs;" & _
                "Integrated Security=True"
        oPubConnection.ConnectionString = sConnString
        oPubConnection.Open()
        oSqlCommand = New SqlCommand()
        oSqlCommand.Connection = oPubConnection
        oSqlCommand.CommandText = "Select Count(emp_id) from employee"
        Return oSqlCommand.ExecuteScalar
    Catch oEx As Exception
        MessageBox.Show(oEx.Message)
    Finally
        If Not oPubConnection Is Nothing Then
            oPubConnection.Close()
        End If
    End Try
End Function
```

Using Stored Procedures

In many application designs, instead of executing a SQL statement directly, clients must execute *stored procedures*. Stored procedures are an excellent way to encapsulate the database logic, increase scalability, and enhance the security of multitiered applications. To execute a stored procedure, you use the Command object, setting the CommandType property of the Command object to StoredProcedure and the CommandText property to the name of the stored procedure. The following code executes a stored procedure that returns the number of employees in the Pubs database:

```
Public Overloads Function CountEmployees() As Integer
    Dim oPubConnection As New SqlConnection
    Dim sConnString As String
    Dim oSqlCommand As SqlCommand
    Try
        sConnString = "Data Source=drcsrv01;Initial Catalog=pubs;" & _
                "Integrated Security=True"
        oPubConnection.ConnectionString = sConnString
        oPubConnection.Open()
        oSqlCommand = New SqlCommand()
        oSqlCommand.Connection = oPubConnection
        oSqlCommand.CommandText = "GetEmployeeCount"
        oSqlCommand.CommandType = CommandType.StoredProcedure
        Return oSqlCommand.ExecuteScalar
    Catch oEx As Exception
            MessageBox.Show(oEx.Message)
    Finally
        If Not oPubConnection Is Nothing Then
            oPubConnection.Close()
        End If
    End Try
End Function
```

When executing a stored procedure, you often must supply input parameters. You may also need to retrieve the results of the stored procedure through output parameters. To work with parameters, you need to instantiate a parameter object of type SqlParameter and then add it to the Parameters collection of the Command object. When constructing the parameter you supply the name of the parameter and the SQL Server data type. For some data types, you also supply the size. If the parameter is an output, input-output, or return parameter, then you must indicate the parameter direction. The following example calls a stored procedure that accepts an input parameter of a letter. The procedure passes back a count of the employees whose last name starts with the letter. The count is returned in the form of an output parameter.

```
Public Overloads Function CountEmployees(ByVal LInitial As String) As Integer
    Dim oPubConnection As New SqlConnection
    Dim sConnString As String
    Dim oSqlCommand As SqlCommand
    Try
        sConnString = "Data Source=drcsrv01;Initial Catalog=pubs;" & _
            "Integrated Security=True"
        oPubConnection.ConnectionString = sConnString
        oPubConnection = New SqlConnection(sConnString)
        oPubConnection.Open()
        oSqlCommand = New SqlCommand()
        oSqlCommand.Connection = oPubConnection
        oSqlCommand.CommandText = "GetEmployeeCountbyLInitial"
        oSqlCommand.CommandType = CommandType.StoredProcedure
        Dim oInputParam As SqlParameter = _
            oSqlCommand.Parameters.Add("@LInitial", SqlDbType.Char, 1)
        oInputParam.Value = LInitial
        Dim oOutPutParam As SqlParameter = _
            oSqlCommand.Parameters.Add("@EmployeeCount", SqlDbType.Int)
        oOutPutParam.Direction = ParameterDirection.Output
        oSqlCommand.ExecuteNonQuery()
        Return oOutPutParam.Value
    Catch oEx As Exception
        MessageBox.Show(oEx.Message)
    Finally
        If Not oPubConnection Is Nothing Then
            oPubConnection.Close()
        End If
    End Try
End Function
```

Using the DataReader Object to Retrieve Data

A DataReader object accesses data through a forward-only, read-only stream. Oftentimes you will want to loop through a set of records and process the results sequentially without the overhead of maintaining the data in a cache. A good example of this would be loading a list or array with the values returned from the database. After declaring an object of type SqlDataReader, you instantiate it by invoking the ExecuteReader method of a Command object. The Read method of the DataReader object accesses the records returned. The Close method of the DataReader object is called after the records have been processed. The following code demonstrates using a DataReader object to retrieve a list of names and return it to the client:

```
Public Function ListNames() As ArrayList
    Dim oPubConnection As New SqlConnection
    Dim sConnString As String
    Dim oSqlCommand As SqlCommand
    Dim aNameArray As ArrayList
    Dim oDataReader As SqlDataReader
    Try
        sConnString = "Data Source=drcsrv01;Initial Catalog=pubs;" & _
                "Integrated Security=True"
        oPubConnection.ConnectionString = sConnString
        oPubConnection.Open()
        oSqlCommand = oPubConnection.CreateCommand
        oSqlCommand.CommandText = "Select lname from employee"
        oDataReader = oSqlCommand.ExecuteReader
        aNameArray = New ArrayList()
        Do Until oDataReader.Read = False
            aNameArray.Add(oDataReader("lname"))
        Loop
        oDataReader.Close()
        Return aNameArray
    Catch oEx As Exception
        MessageBox.Show(oEx.Message)
        Return Nothing
    Finally
        If Not oPubConnection Is Nothing Then
            oPubConnection.Close()
        End If
    End Try
End Function
```

Using the DataAdapter to Retrieve Data

In many cases, you need to retrieve a set of data from the database, work with the data, and return any updates to the data back to the database. In that case, you use a DataAdapter as a bridge between the data source and the in-memory cache of the data. This in-memory cache of data is contained in a DataSet, which is a major component of the ADO.NET architecture.

■**Note** The DataSet object is discussed in greater detail shortly in the section "Working with DataTables and DataSets."

To retrieve a set of data from a database, you instantiate a DataAdapter object. You set the SelectCommand property of the DataAdapter to an existing Command object. You then execute the Fill method, passing the name of a DataSet object to fill. Here you see how to use a DataAdapter to fill a DataSet and pass the DataSet back to the client:

```
Public Function GetEmployeeInfo() As DataSet
    Dim oPubConnection As New SqlConnection
    Dim sConnString As String
    Dim oSqlCommand As SqlCommand
    Dim oDataAdapter As SqlDataAdapter
    Try
        sConnString = "Data Source=drcsrv01;Initial Catalog=pubs;" & _
                "Integrated Security=True"
        oPubConnection.ConnectionString = sConnString
        oPubConnection.Open()
        oSqlCommand = oPubConnection.CreateCommand
        oSqlCommand.CommandText = _
                "Select emp_id,lname,Hire_Date from employee"
        oDataAdapter = New SqlDataAdapter()
        oDataAdapter.SelectCommand = oSqlCommand
        Dim dsEmployeeInfo As DataSet = New DataSet()
        oDataAdapter.Fill(dsEmployeeInfo)
        Return dsEmployeeInfo
    Catch oEx As Exception
        MessageBox.Show(oEx.Message)
        Return Nothing
    Finally
        If Not oPubConnection Is Nothing Then
            oPubConnection.Close()
        End If
    End Try
End Function
```

You may find that you need to retrieve a set of data by executing a stored procedure as opposed to passing in a SQL statement. The following code demonstrates executing a stored procedure that accepts an input parameter and returns a set of records. The records are loaded into a DataSet object and returned to the client.

```
Public Overloads Function GetEmployeeInfo(ByVal LInitial As String) As DataSet
    Dim oPubConnection As New SqlConnection
    Dim sConnString As String
    Dim oSqlCommand As SqlCommand
    Dim oDataAdapter As SqlDataAdapter
    Try
        sConnString = "Data Source=drcsrv01;Initial Catalog=pubs;" & _
                "Integrated Security=True"
        oPubConnection.ConnectionString = sConnString
        oPubConnection.Open()
```

```
        oSqlCommand = oPubConnection.CreateCommand
        oSqlCommand.CommandText = "GetEmployeeInfobyInitial"
        oSqlCommand.CommandType = CommandType.StoredProcedure
        Dim oInputParam As SqlParameter = _
            oSqlCommand.Parameters.Add("@LInitial", SqlDbType.Char, 1)
        oInputParam.Value = LInitial
        oDataAdapter = New SqlDataAdapter()
        oDataAdapter.SelectCommand = oSqlCommand
        Dim dsEmployeeInfo As DataSet = New DataSet()
        oDataAdapter.Fill(dsEmployeeInfo)
        Return dsEmployeeInfo
    Catch oEx As Exception
        MessageBox.Show(oEx.Message)
        Return Nothing
    Finally
        If Not oPubConnection Is Nothing Then
            oPubConnection.Close()
        End If
    End Try
End Function
```

Activity 10-1. Retrieving Data

In this activity, you will become familiar with the following:

- Establishing a connection to a SQL Server database

- Executing queries through a Command object

- Retrieving data with a DataReader object

- Executing a stored procedure using a Command object

■ **Note** For the activities in this chapter to work, you must have access to a SQL Server 2000 or higher database server with the Pubs and Northwind databases installed. You must be logged on under a Windows account that has been given the appropriate rights to these databases. You may have to alter the ConnectionString depending on your settings. For more information, refer to the "Software Requirements" section in the Introduction and Appendix C.

Creating a Connection and Executing SQL Queries

To create a connection and execute SQL queries, follow these steps:

1. Start VS. Select File ➤ New ➤ Project.

2. Choose Windows Application under the Visual Basic Projects folder. Rename the project to Act10_1 and click the OK button.

3. After the project opens, add a new class to the project named `Author`.

4. In the Solution Explorer window, right-click the `Act10_1` project node and select Add Reference. On the .NET tab of the Add Reference window, select both `System.Data` and `System.Data.SqlXml` by holding down the Ctrl key while clicking (see Figure 10-1). Click the OK button to add the references.

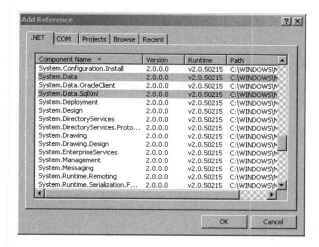

Figure 10-1. *Adding project references*

5. Open the `Author` class code in the code editor. Add the following `Imports` statement at the top of the file to import the `System.Data.SqlClient` and the `System.Data` namespaces:

```
Imports System.Data.SqlClient
Imports System.Data
```

6. Add this code to declare a private class-level variable of type `SQLConnection`:

```
Private cnPubs As SqlConnection
```

7. Create a class constructor that instantiates the `cnPubs` Connection object and set up the `ConnectionString` property:

```
Public Sub New()
    cnPubs = New SqlConnection()
    cnPubs.ConnectionString = _
        ("Integrated Security=True;Data Source=LocalHost;" & _
            "Initial Catalog=Pubs")
End Sub
```

8. Add a method to the class that will use a `Command` object to execute a query to count the number of authors in the authors table. Because you are only returning a single value, you will use the `ExecuteScalar` method of the `Command` object.

```
Public Function GetAuthorCount() As Integer
    Try
        Dim cmdAuthors As New SqlCommand()
        cmdAuthors.Connection = cnPubs
        cmdAuthors.CommandText = "Select count(*) from authors"
        cnPubs.Open()
        Return cmdAuthors.ExecuteScalar
    Catch ex As SqlException
        Debug.WriteLine(ex.Message)
    Finally
        cnPubs.Close()
    End Try
End Function
```

9. Add a button to Form1. Change the Name property of the button to btnCount and change the Text property to Get Count.

10. Add the following code to the button-click event procedure, which will execute the GetAuthorCount method defined in the Author class:

```
Dim oAuthor As New Author()
MessageBox.Show(oAuthor.GetAuthorCount.ToString)
```

11. Build the project and fix any errors. Once the project builds, run the project in debug mode and test the GetAuthorCount method.

Using the DataReader Object to Retrieve Records

To use the DataReader object to retrieve records, follow these steps:

1. Open the Author class code in the code editor.

2. Add a public function to the class definition called GetAuthorList that returns an ArrayList:

```
Public Function GetAuthorList() As ArrayList
End Function
```

3. Add the following code to create procedural scoped variables of type SqlCommand, SqlDataReader, and ArrayList:

```
Dim cmdAuthors As New SqlCommand()
Dim drAuthorList As SqlDataReader
Dim alAuthorsList As New ArrayList()
```

4. Add the following Try-Catch block, which executes a SQL Select statement to retrieve the authors' last names. A DataReader object then loops through the records and creates an array list that gets returned to the client.

```
Try
    cmdAuthors.Connection = cnPubs
    cmdAuthors.CommandText = "Select au_lname from authors"
    cnPubs.Open()
```

```
        drAuthorList = cmdAuthors.ExecuteReader
        Do While drAuthorList.Read = True
            alAuthorsList.Add(drAuthorList.GetString(0))
        Loop
Catch ex As SqlException
        Debug.WriteLine(ex.Message)
Finally
        cnPubs.Close()
End Try
Return alAuthorsList
```

5. Build the project and fix any errors.

6. Add a ListBox to Form1 and change the Name property to lstAuthors.

7. Open the Form1 class code in the code editor. In the left drop-down list, choose (Form1 Events). In the right drop-down list, choose Form1_Load.

8. Add the following code to the Form1_Load event procedure. This code calls the GetAuthorList of the Author class, which returns an ArrayList of author names. The elements of the ArrayList are then added to the lstAuthor.

```
Dim i As Integer
Dim oAuthor As New Author()
Dim alAuthorList As New ArrayList()
alAuthorList = oAuthor.GetAuthorList
For i = 0 To (alAuthorList.Count - 1)
    lstAuthors.Items.Add(alAuthorList.Item(i))
Next
```

9. Build the project and fix any errors.

10. Run the project and test to make sure the list fills when the form loads.

Executing a Stored Procedure Using a Command Object

To execute a stored procedure using a Command object, follow these steps:

1. Open the Author class code in the code editor.

2. Add a public function that overloads the GetAuthorList function by accepting an integer parameter named Royalty. This function will call the stored procedure byroyalty in the Pubs database. The procedure takes an integer input of royalty percentage and returns a list of author IDs with the percentage.

```
Public Function GetAuthorList(Royalty as Integer) As ArrayList
End Function
```

3. Add the following code to create procedural scoped variables of type SqlCommand, SqlDataReader, ArrayList, and SqlParameter:

```
Dim cmdAuthors As New SqlCommand()
Dim drAuthorList As SqlDataReader
Dim alAuthorsList As New ArrayList()
Dim parRoyalty As New SqlParameter()
```

4. Add the following `Try-Catch` block, which executes a stored procedure to retrieve the author IDs that have a certain royalty percentage. The royalty percentage is passed into the stored procedure by way of the `Parameter` collection. A `DataReader` object then loops through the records and creates an array list that gets returned to the client:

```
Try
    cmdAuthors.Connection = cnPubs
    cmdAuthors.CommandType = CommandType.StoredProcedure
    cmdAuthors.CommandText = "byroyalty"
    parRoyalty.ParameterName = "@percentage"
    parRoyalty.Direction = ParameterDirection.Input
    parRoyalty.SqlDbType = SqlDbType.Int
    parRoyalty.Value = Royalty
    cmdAuthors.Parameters.Add(parRoyalty)
    cnPubs.Open()
    drAuthorList = cmdAuthors.ExecuteReader
    Do While drAuthorList.Read = True
        alAuthorsList.Add(drAuthorList.GetString(0))
    Loop
Catch ex As SqlException
    Debug.WriteLine(ex.Message)
Finally
    cnPubs.Close()
End Try
Return alAuthorsList
```

5. Build the project and fix any errors.

6. Add a Button control to `Form1`. Change the `Name` property of the button to `btnRoyaltyList`. Change the `Text` property of the button to `Get Royalty List`.

7. Double-click `btnRoyaltyList` in the `Form1` designer window. The `btnRoyaltyList_Click` event procedure will display in the code editor window.

8. Add the following code to the `btnRoyaltyList_Click` event procedure. This code calls the overloaded `GetAuthorList` of the `Author` class, which returns an `ArrayList` of author IDs with a royalty percentage of 50. The elements of the `ArrayList` are then added to `lstAuthor`.

```
Dim oAuthor As New Author()
Dim alAuthorList As New ArrayList()
alAuthorList = oAuthor.GetAuthorList(50)
lstAuthors.Items.Clear()
For Each item As Object In alAuthorList
            lstAuthors.Items.Add(item)
Next
```

9. Build the project and fix any errors. Run the application in debug mode and test the code.

10. After testing, stop the debugger and exit VS.

Working with DataTables and DataSets

DataSets and DataTables are in-memory caches of data that provide a consistent relational programming model for working with data regardless of the data source. A DataTable represents one table of relational data and consists of columns, rows, and constraints. You can think of a DataSet as a minirelational database, including the data tables and the relational integrity constraints between the tables. You have several ways to create a DataTable/DataSet. The most obvious method is to populate a DataTable/DataSet from an existing relational database management system (RDBMS) such as a SQL Server database. As mentioned previously, a DataAdapter object provides the bridge between the RDBMS and the DataTable/DataSet. By using a DataAdapter object, the DataTable/DataSet is totally independent from the data source. Although you need to use a specific set of provider classes to load the DataTable/DataSet object, you work with a DataTable/DataSet with the same set of .NET Framework classes regardless of how the DataTable/DataSet was created and populated. The System.Data namespace contains the framework classes for working with DataTable/DataSet objects. Table 10-2 lists some of the main classes contained in the System.Data namespace.

Table 10-2. *The Main Members of the* System.Data *Namespace*

Class	Description
DataSet	Represents a collection of DataTable and DataRelation objects. Organizes an in-memory cache of relational data.
DataTable	Represents a collection of DataColumn, DataRow, and Constraint objects. Organizes records and fields related to a data entity.
DataColumn	Represents the schema of a column in a DataTable.
DataRow	Represents a row of data in a DataTable.
Constraint	Represents a constraint that can be enforced on DataColumn objects.
ForeignKeyConstraint	Enforces referential integrity of a parent/child relationship between two DataTable objects.
UniqueConstraint	Enforces uniqueness of a DataColumn or set of DataColumns. This is required to enforce referential integrity in a parent/child relationship.
DataRelation	Represents a parent/child relation between two DataTable objects.

Populating a DataTable from a SQL Server Database

To retrieve data from a database, you set up a connection with the database using a Connection object. After a connection is established, you create a Command object to retrieve the data from the database. If you are retrieving data from a single table or result set, you can populate and work with a DataTable directly without creating a DataSet object. The Load method of the DataTable fills the table with the contents of a DataReader object. This example code fills a DataTable with data from the publishers table of the Pubs database:

```
Public Function GetPubsTable() As DataTable
    Dim sConnString As String
    Dim dtPubs As New DataTable
    Try
        sConnString = "Data Source=drcsrv01;Initial Catalog=pubs;" & _
                "Integrated Security=True"
```

```
        Using oPubConnection As New SqlConnection(sConnString)
            oPubConnection.Open()
            'Create command to retrieve pub info
            Using oSqlCommPubs As New SqlCommand()
                oSqlCommPubs.Connection = oPubConnection
                oSqlCommPubs.CommandText = _
                  "Select pub_id,pub_name,city" & _
                  " from publishers"
                'Create Data reader for pub info
                Using oDataReaderPubs = oSqlCommPubs.ExecuteReader
                    'Fill Datatable with info
                    dtPubs.Load(oDataReaderPubs)
                    Return dtPubs
                End Using
            End Using
        End Using
    Catch oEx As Exception
        MessageBox.Show(oEx.Message)
        Return Nothing
    End Try
End Function
```

■**Note** By instantiating the objects in the proceeding code with the using statement, you do not need to close the Connection object. This is done automatically when the reference to the object is released at the End Using statement.

Populating a DataSet from a SQL Server Database

When you need to load data into multiple tables and maintain the referential integrity between the tables, you need to use the DataSet object as a container for the DataTables. To retrieve data from a database and fill the DataSet, you set up a connection with the database using a Connection object. After a connection is established, you create a Command object to retrieve the data from the database and then create a DataAdapter to fill the DataSet, setting the previously created Command object to the SelectCommand property of the DataAdapter. Create a separate DataAdapter for each DataTable. The final step is to fill the DataSet with the data by executing the Fill method of the DataAdapter. The following code demonstrates filling a DataSet with data from the publishers table and the titles table of the Pubs database:

```
Public Overloads Function GetBookInfo() As DataSet
    Dim sConnString As String
    Dim oSqlCommPubs As SqlCommand
    Dim oSqlCommTitles As SqlCommand
    Dim oDataAdapterPubs As SqlDataAdapter
    Dim oDataAdapterTitles As SqlDataAdapter
    Try
```

```vb
            sConnString = "Data Source=drcsrv01;Initial Catalog=pubs;" & _
                "Integrated Security=True"
            Using oPubConnection As New SqlConnection(sConnString)
                oPubConnection.Open()
                'Create command to retrieve pub info
                oSqlCommPubs = New SqlCommand()
                oSqlCommPubs.Connection = oPubConnection
                oSqlCommPubs.CommandText = _
                    "Select pub_id,pub_name from publishers"
                'Create Data Adapter for pub info
                oDataAdapterPubs = New SqlDataAdapter()
                oDataAdapterPubs.SelectCommand = oSqlCommPubs
                'Create command to retrieve title info
                oSqlCommTitles = New SqlCommand()
                oSqlCommTitles.Connection = oPubConnection
                oSqlCommTitles.CommandText = _
                    "Select pub_id,title,price,ytd_sales from titles"
                'Create Data Adapter for title info
                oDataAdapterTitles = New SqlDataAdapter()
                oDataAdapterTitles.SelectCommand = oSqlCommTitles
                'Create and fill a Data Set
                Dim dsBookInfo As DataSet = New DataSet()
                oDataAdapterPubs.Fill(dsBookInfo, "Publishers")
                oDataAdapterTitles.Fill(dsBookInfo, "Titles")
                Return dsBookInfo
            End Using
        Catch oEx As Exception
            MessageBox.Show(oEx.Message)
            return nothing
        End Try
End Function
```

Establishing Relationships Between Tables in a DataSet

In an RDBMS system, referential integrity between tables is enforced through a primary key and foreign key relationship. Using a DataRelation object, you can enforce data referential integrity between the tables in the DataSet. This object contains an array of DataColumn objects that define the common field(s) between the parent table and the child table used to establish the relation. Essentially, the field identified in the parent table is the primary key, and the field identified in the child table is the foreign key. When establishing a relationship, create two DataColumn objects for the common column in each table. Next, create a DataRelation object, pass a name for the DataRelation, and pass the DataColumn objects to the constructor of the DataRelation object. The final step is to add the DataRelation to the Relations collection of the DataSet object. This example code establishes a relationship between the publishers and the titles tables of the datBookInfo created in the previous section:

```vb
'create a DataRelation to link the two tables.
Dim drPub_Title As DataRelation
```

```
Dim dcPub_PubId As DataColumn
Dim dcTitle_PubId As DataColumn
'Get the parent and child columns of the two tables.
dcPub_PubId = dsBookInfo.Tables("Publishers").Columns("pub_id")
dcTitle_PubId = dsBookInfo.Tables("Titles").Columns("pub_id")
'Create the DataRelation and add it to the collection.
drPub_Title = New System.Data.DataRelation _
    ("PublishersToTitles", dcPub_PubId, dcTitle_PubId)
dsBookInfo.Relations.Add(drPub_Title)
```

Editing Data in the DataSet

Clients often need to be able to update a DataSet. They may need to add records, delete records, or update the information of an existing record. Because DataSet objects are disconnected by design, the changes made to the DataSet are not automatically propagated back to the database. They are held locally until the client is ready to replicate the changes back to the database. To replicate the changes, you invoke the Update method of the DataAdapter, which determines what changes have been made to the records and implements the appropriate SQL command (Update, Insert, or Delete) that has been defined to replicate the changes back to the database.

To demonstrate the process of updating a DataSet, construct an Author class that will pass a DataSet containing author information to a client when the GetData method is invoked. The Author class will accept a DataSet containing changes made to the author information and replicate the changes back to the Pubs database when its UpdateData method is invoked. The first step is to define the class and include an Imports statement for the referenced namespaces:

```
'Declare namespace references
Imports System.Data
Imports System.Data.SqlClient
Public Class Author
End Class
```

Define class-level variables for SQLConnection, SQLDataAdapter, and DataSet objects:

```
'Declare class level variables
Private m_oConn As SqlConnection
Private m_oDAPubs As SqlDataAdapter
Private m_oDSPubs As DataSet
```

In the class constructor, initialize a Connection object:

```
Public Sub New()
    Dim oSelCmd As SqlCommand
    Dim oUpdCmd As SqlCommand
    ' set up connection
    Dim sConnString As String
        sConnString = "Integrated Security=True;Data Source=LocalHost;" & _
                        "Initial Catalog=Pubs"
    m_oConn = New SqlConnection(sConnString)
```

Then create a SelectCommand object:

```
' set up the select command
Dim sSQL As String
sSQL = "Select au_id, au_lname, au_fname from authors"
oSelCmd = New SqlCommand(sSQL, m_oConn)
oSelCmd.CommandType = CommandType.Text
```

Next you create an Update command. The command text references parameters in the command's Parameters collection that will be created next:

```
'set up the update command
sSQL = "Update authors set au_lname = @au_lname," _
       & " au_fname = @au_fname where au_id = @au_id"
oUpdCmd = New SqlCommand(sSQL, m_oConn)
oUpdCmd.CommandType = CommandType.Text
```

A Parameter object is added to the Command object's Parameter collection for each Parameter in the Update statement. The Add method of the Parameters collection is passed information on the name of the Parameter, the SQL data type, size, and the source column of the DataSet:

```
oUpdCmd.Parameters.Add("@au_id", SqlDbType.VarChar, 11, "au_id")
oUpdCmd.Parameters.Add("@au_lname", SqlDbType.VarChar, 40, "au_lname")
oUpdCmd.Parameters.Add("@au_fname", SqlDbType.VarChar, 40, "au_fname")
```

The final step is to create and set up the DataAdapter object. Set the SelectCommand and UpdateCommand properties to the appropriate SQLCommand objects:

```
    'set up the data adapter
    m_oDAPubs = New SqlDataAdapter()
    m_oDAPubs.SelectCommand = oSelCmd
    m_oDAPubs.UpdateCommand = oUpdCmd
End Sub
```

Now that the SQLDataAdapter has been set up and created in the class constructor, the GetData and UpdateData methods will use the DataAdapter to get and update the data from the database:

```
Public Function GetData() As DataSet
    m_oDSPubs = New DataSet()
    m_oDAPubs.Fill(m_oDSPubs, "Authors")
    Return m_oDSPubs
End Function
Public Sub SaveData(ByVal DSChanges As DataSet)
    m_oDAPubs.Update(DSChanges, "Authors")
End Sub
```

In a similar fashion, you could implement the InsertCommand and the DeleteCommand properties of the DataAdapter to allow clients to insert new records or delete records in the database.

> **Note** For simple updates to a single table in the data source, the .NET Framework provides a `CommandBuilder` class to automate the creation of the `InsertCommand`, `UpdateCommand`, and `DeleteCommand` properties of the `DataAdapter`.

Converting Between Relational DataSet Objects and Hierarchical XML Files

One of the most powerful features of ADO.NET is its tight integration with XML. By default, when an ADO.NET `DataSet` is transferred from a client to a server (or vice versa), it is persisted in XML structures. The ability to load XML files into a relational `DataSet` structure and to persist relational `DataSet` objects as XML structures is fundamental to the .NET Framework. The `DataSet` class includes the `ReadXML` method to load an existing XML document into a `DataSet` object. The following function reads author data from an existing XML file and returns it to the client in the form of a `DataSet`:

```
Public Function LoadDataFromXML() As DataSet
    Dim ds As DataSet = New DataSet()
    ds.ReadXml("c:\Authors.xml", XmlReadMode.ReadSchema)
    Return ds
End Function
```

You can just as easily persist a `DataSet` to an XML file by using the `WriteXml` method of the `DataSet` class. The following method accepts a `DataSet` from the client and writes the data and the schema of the `DataSet` to a file:

```
Public Sub SaveDataAsXML(ByVal ds As DataSet)
    ds.WriteXml("c:\Authors.xml", XmlWriteMode.WriteSchema)
End Sub
```

> **Note** The `DataTable` also contains the `ReadXml` and `WriteXml` methods, which are useful for persisting single table result sets to and from an XML file or text stream.

Activity 10-2. Working with DataSet Objects

In this activity, you will become familiar with the following:

- Populating a `DataSet` from a SQL Server database

- Editing data in a `DataSet`

- Updating changes from the `DataSet` to the database

- Establishing relationships between tables in a `DataSet`

Populating a DataSet from a SQL Server Database

To populate a DataSet from a SQL Server database, follow these steps:

1. Start VS. Select File ➤ New ➤ Project.

2. Choose Windows Application under the Visual Basic Projects folder. Rename the project to Act10_2 and click the OK button.

3. After the project opens, add a new class to the project named Author.

4. In the Solution Explorer window, right-click the Act10_2 project node and select Add Reference. On the .Net tab of the Add Reference window, select System.Data, System.Xml, and System.Data.SqlXml.

5. Open the Author class code in the code editor. Add the following Imports statement at the top of the file to import the System.Data.SqlClient and the System.Data namespaces:

```
Imports System.Data.SqlClient
Imports System.Data
```

6. Add the following code to declare private class level variables of type SQLConnection, SqlDataAdapter, and DataSet:

```
Private cnPubs As SqlConnection
Private daPubs As SqlDataAdapter
Private dsPubs As DataSet
```

7. Create a class constructor that instantiates the cnPubs Connection object and set up the ConnectionString property:

```
Public Sub New()
    cnPubs = New SqlConnection()
    cnPubs.ConnectionString = _
      ("Integrated Security=True;Data Source=LocalHost;" & _
        "Initial Catalog=Pubs")
End Sub
```

8. Add the following code to set up a SqlCommand object that will execute a select query to retrieve author information:

```
Dim strSQL As String
Dim oSelCmd As SqlCommand
strSQL = "Select au_id, au_lname, au_fname from authors"
oSelCmd = New SqlCommand(strSQL, cnPubs)
```

9. Add the following code to instantiate the DataAdapter and set its SelectCommand property to the SqlCommand object created in step 8:

```
    daPubs = New SqlDataAdapter()
    daPubs.SelectCommand = oSelCmd
```

10. Create a method of the Author class called GetData that will use the DataAdapter object to fill the DataSet and return it to the client:

```
Public Function GetData() As DataSet
    dsPubs = New DataSet()
    daPubs.Fill(dsPubs, "Authors")
    Return dsPubs
End Function
```

11. Build the project and fix any errors.

12. Add the controls listed in Table 10-3 to Form1 and set the properties as shown.

Table 10-3. *Form1 Controls*

Control	Property	Value
DataGridView	Name	dgvAuthors
	AllowUserToAddRows	False
	AllowUserToDeleteRows	False
Button	Name	btnGetData
	Text	Get Data
Button	Name	btnUpdate
	Text	Update

13. Add a System.Data imports statement at the top of the Form1 class code file. Declare a class-level DataSet object after the class declaration.

```
Imports System.Data
Public Class Form1
    Private m_dsPubs As DataSet
```

14. Add the following code to the btnGetData click event procedure, which will execute the GetData method defined in the Author class. The DataSet returned by the method is passed to the class-level DataSet object m_dsPubs.

```
Dim oAuthor As Author = New Author()
m_dsPubs = oAuthor.GetData
dgvAuthors.DataSource = m_dsPubs.Tables("Authors")
```

15. Build the project and fix any errors. Once the project builds, run the project in debug mode and test the GetData method. After testing, stop the debugger.

Editing and Updating a DataSet to a SQL Server Database

To edit and update a DataSet to a SQL Server database, follow these steps:

1. Open the Author class code in the code editor.

2. At the end of the class constructor (in other words, Sub New), add code to set up a SqlCommand object that will execute an Update query to update author information:

```
Dim cmdUpdate As SqlCommand
strSQL = "Update authors set au_lname = @au_lname, au_fname = " _
            & "@au_fname where au_id = @au_id"
cmdUpdate = New SqlCommand(strSQL, cnPubs)
```

3. Add code to include the update parameters in the Parameters collection of the SqlCommand object created in step 2:

```
cmdUpdate.Parameters.Add _
    ("@au_id", SqlDbType.VarChar, 11, "au_id")
cmdUpdate.Parameters.Add _
    ("@au_lname", SqlDbType.VarChar, 40, "au_lname")
cmdUpdate.Parameters.Add _
    ("@au_fname", SqlDbType.VarChar, 40, "au_fname")
```

4. Add code to set the DataAdapter object's Update Command property to the SqlCommand object created in step 2:

```
    daPubs.UpdateCommand = cmdUpdate
```

5. Create a method of the Author class called UpdateData that will use the Update method of the DataAdapter object to pass updates made to the DataSet to the Pubs database:

```
Public Function UpdateData(ByVal DSChanged As DataSet) As Boolean
    Try
        daPubs.Update(DSChanged, "Authors")
        Return True
    Catch ex As Exception
        Return False
    End Try
End Function
```

6. Build the project and fix any errors.

7. Open the Form1 class code in the code editor.

8. Add the following code to the btnUpdate click event procedure, which will execute the UpdateData method defined in the Author class. By using the GetChanges method of the DataSet object, only data that has changed is passed for updating:

```
Dim oAuthor As Author = New Author()
If m_dsPubs Is Nothing Then Exit Sub
MessageBox.Show(oAuthor.UpdateData(m_dsPubs.GetChanges))
```

9. Build the project and fix any errors. Once the project builds, run the project in debug mode and test the Update method. First, click the Get Data button. Change the last name of several authors and click the Update button. Click the Get Data button again to retrieve the changed values back from the database. After testing, stop the debugger.

Establishing Relationships Between Tables in a DataSet

To establish relationships between tables in a DataSet, follow these steps:

1. Add a new class named Orders to the project.

2. Open the Orders class code in the code editor.

3. Add the following `Imports` statement at the top of the file to import the `System.Data.SqlClient` and the `System.Data` namespaces:

```
Imports System.Data.SqlClient
Imports System.Data
```

4. Add the following code to declare private class-level variables of type `SQLConnection`, `SqlDataAdapter`, and `DataSet`:

```
Private cnNWind As SqlConnection
Private daCustomers As SqlDataAdapter
Private daOrders As SqlDataAdapter
Private dsOrders As DataSet
```

5. Create a class constructor that instantiates the `cnNWind` `Connection` object and set up the `ConnectionString` property:

```
Public Sub New()
    cnNWind = New SqlConnection()
    cnNWind.ConnectionString = _
            ("Integrated Security=True;Data Source=LocalHost;" & _
            "Initial Catalog=Northwind")
End Sub
```

6. Add the following code to set up a `SqlCommand` object that will execute a `Select` query to retrieve customer information:

```
Dim cmdSelect As SqlCommand
Dim strSQL As String
strSQL = "Select CustomerID, CompanyName from Customers"
cmdSelect = New SqlCommand(strSQL, cnNWind)
```

7. Add the following code to instantiate the `DataAdapter` and set its `SelectCommand` property to the `SqlCommand` object created in step 6:

```
daCustomers = New SqlDataAdapter()
daCustomers.SelectCommand = cmdSelect
```

8. Repeat steps 6 and 7 to add code to set up a `DataAdapter` to retrieve order info:

```
        strSQL = "Select OrderID, CustomerID, OrderDate from Orders"
        cmdSelect = New SqlCommand(strSQL, cnNWind)
        daOrders = New SqlDataAdapter()
        daOrders.SelectCommand = cmdSelect
```

9. Create a method of the `Orders` class called `GetData` that will use the `DataAdapter` objects to fill the `DataSet`, establish a table relation, and return the `DataSet` to the client:

```
Public Function GetData() As DataSet
    dsOrders = New DataSet()
    daCustomers.Fill(dsOrders, "Customers")
    daOrders.Fill(dsOrders, "Orders")
```

```
    Dim drOrders As New DataRelation("CustomersOrders", _
          dsOrders.Tables("Customers").Columns("CustomerID"), _
          dsOrders.Tables("Orders").Columns("CustomerID"))
    dsOrders.Relations.Add(drOrders)
    Return dsOrders
End Function
```

10. Build the project and fix any errors.

11. Add a second form to the project. Add the controls listed in Table 10-4 to Form2 and set the properties as shown.

Table 10-4. *Form2 Controls*

Control	Property	Value
DataGridView	Name	dgvCustomers
DataGridView	Name	dgvOrders
BindingSource	Name	bsCustomers
BindingSource	Name	bsOrders

12. Add the following declaration to the top of the Form2 class code. This code creates a class-level DataSet object.

```
Private dsOrders As System.Data.DataSet
```

13. Add the following code to the Form2_Load event procedure, which will execute the GetData method defined in the Orders class. The DataSet returned by the method is passed to the class-level DataSet object dsOrders.

```
        Dim oOrders As New Orders
        dsOrders = oOrders.GetData
```

14. Add the following code to the Form2_Load event procedure, which sets the BindingSource of dvgCustomers to the customer table and the BindingSource of the dgvOrders to the DataRelation between the customers and orders tables:

```
        dgvCustomers.DataSource = bsCustomers
        dgvOrders.DataSource = bsOrders
        bsCustomers.DataSource = dsOrders
        bsCustomers.DataMember = "Customers"
        bsOrders.DataSource = bsCustomers
        bsOrders.DataMember = "CustomersOrders"
```

15. Build the project and fix any errors.

16. Change the startup object of the project to Form2. Run the project in debug mode. When you select a row in the customers grid, the orders grid displays the orders associated to that customer.

17. After testing, stop the debugger and exit VS.

Building the OSO Application's Business Logic Tier

Now that you are familiar with the System.Data and the System.Data.SQLClient namespaces, you are ready to build the OSO application's business logic tier. First let's review the OSO application's class diagram that you created in Chapter 4, presented here in Figure 10-2.

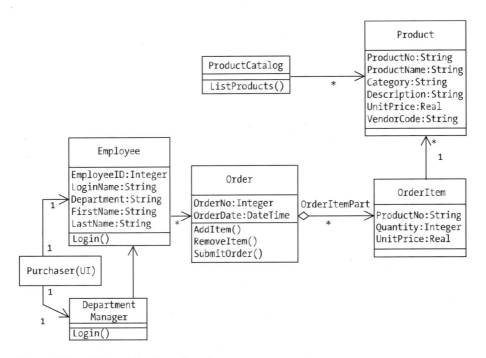

Figure 10-2. *OSO application class diagram*

You also must review the structure of the database that will comprise the data tier of the OSO application. Figure 10-3 shows the database diagram for the OSO application. This database will be implemented in a SQL Server database.

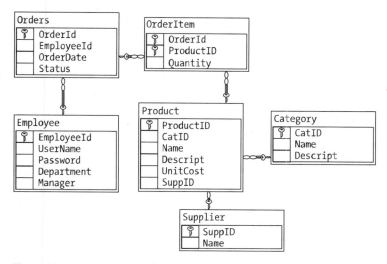

Figure 10-3. *OSO application database diagram*

The first class you are going to construct is the ProductCatalog class, the purpose of which is to encapsulate the functionality of retrieving a listing of the available products in the database. You also want the ability to view the products based on the category to which they belong. The information you need is in two database tables: the catalog table and the products table. These two tables are related through the CatID field. When a client requests the product catalog information, a DataSet will be created and returned to the client. This service will be provided in the ProductCatalog class's GetProductInfo method, as shown here:

```
'/// Retrieves information on product categories and products
'/// Returns information as a dataset object
Imports System.Data.SqlClient
Public Class ProductCatalog
    Private m_conn As SqlConnection
    Private m_dsProducts As New DataSet()

    Public Function GetProductInfo() As DataSet
        Try
            'Get the Category info
            Dim strSQL As String = _
              "select CatID, Name, Descript from Category"
            Dim cmdSelCategory As SqlCommand = _
              New SqlCommand(strSQL, m_conn)
            Dim daCategory As SqlDataAdapter = _
              New SqlDataAdapter(cmdSelCategory)
            daCatagory.Fill(m_dsProducts, "Category")
            'Get the product info
            strSQL = _
```

```
                "Select ProductID,CatID,Name," & _
                "Descript,UnitCost from Product"
                Dim cmdSelProductInfo As SqlCommand = _
                    New SqlCommand(strSQL, m_conn)
                Dim daProductInfo As SqlDataAdapter = _
                    New SqlDataAdapter(cmdSelProductInfo)
                daProductInfo.Fill(m_dsProducts, "Product")
                'Set up the table relation
                Dim drCat_Prod As New DataRelation _
                    ("drCat_Prod", _
                    m_dsProducts.Tables("Category").Columns("CatID"), _
                    m_dsProducts.Tables("Product").Columns("CatID"))
                m_dsProducts.Relations.Add(drCat_Prod)
            Catch ex As Exception
                Debug.WriteLine(ex.ToString)
            End Try
            Return m_dsProducts
        End Function
        Public Sub New ()
            m_conn = New SqlConnection()
            m_conn.ConnectionString = "Integrated Security=True;" & _
                "Data Source=LocalHost;Initial Catalog=OfficeSupply"
        End Sub
    End Class
```

The next class you need to construct is the OrderItem class, shown in the following code, which will hold information pertaining to an order item of an order. The quantity, product ID, and price will be exposed as read/write properties. The subtotal of the order item will be calculated and exposed as a read-only property of the class.

```
'/// Used to hold line item information for orders.
'/// toString method has been overriden to provide order
'/// item info in an XML structure.
Public Class OrderItem
    Private m_ProductID As String
    Private m_Quantity As Integer
    Private m_UnitPrice As Double
    Private m_SubTotal As Double

    Public Property ProductID() As String
        Get
            Return m_ProductID
        End Get
        Set(ByVal Value As String)
            Value = m_ProductID
        End Set
    End Property
    Public Property Quantity() As Integer
```

```vbnet
        Get
            Return m_Quantity
        End Get
        Set(ByVal Value As Integer)
            m_Quantity = Value
        End Set
    End Property
    Public Property UnitPrice() As Double
        Get
            Return m_UnitPrice
        End Get
        Set(ByVal Value As Double)
            m_UnitPrice = Value
        End Set
    End Property
    Public ReadOnly Property SubTotal() As Double
        Get
            Return m_SubTotal
        End Get
    End Property

    Public Sub New(ByVal ProductID As String, _
        ByVal UnitPrice As Double, ByVal Quantity As Integer)

        m_ProductID = ProductID.Trim
        m_UnitPrice = UnitPrice
        m_Quantity = Quantity
        m_SubTotal = m_UnitPrice * m_Quantity
End Sub
    Public Overrides Function toString() As String
        Dim xml As String
        xml = "<OrderItem"
        xml &= " ProductID='" & m_ProductID & "'"
        xml &= " Quantity='" & m_Quantity & "'"
        xml &= " />"
        Return xml
    End Function
End Class
```

An `Order` class will encapsulate the process of adding items to an order and removing items from an order. Order items will be held in a generic `List` object. The `Generic List` class is part of the `System.Collections.Generic` namespace and provides the functionality for working with a list of strongly typed objects. The list of order items is exposed to clients through a read-only property that returns a list of `OrderItem` objects, as you see in the following example:

```vbnet
'/// Used to process orders.
'/// Items can be added or removed.
'/// The total cost of the order is calculated.
'/// When the order is placed it is sent as XML
```

```vbnet
'/// to the dbOrder class for processing.
Public Class Order
    Private m_alOrderItems As New Generic.List(Of OrderItem)
    Public ReadOnly Property OrderItems() As _
      Generic.List(Of OrderItem)
        Get
            Return m_alOrderItems
        End Get
    End Property
    Public Sub AddItem(ByVal Value As OrderItem)
        Dim oItem As OrderItem
        For Each oItem In m_alOrderItems
            If oItem.ProductID = Value.ProductID Then
                oItem.Quantity += Value.Quantity
                Exit Sub
            End If
        Next
        m_alOrderItems.Add(Value)
    End Sub
    Public Sub RemoveItem(ByVal ProductID As String)
        Dim oItem As OrderItem
        For Each oItem In m_alOrderItems
            If oItem.ProductID = ProductID Then
                m_alOrderItems.Remove(oItem)
                Exit Sub
            End If
        Next
    End Sub
    Public Function GetOrderTotal() As Double
        If m_alOrderItems.Count = 0 Then
            Return 0.0
        Else
            Dim oItem As OrderItem
            Dim total As Double
            For Each oItem In m_alOrderItems
                total += oItem.SubTotal
            Next
            Return total
        End If
    End Function
    Public Function PlaceOrder(ByVal EmployeeID As Integer) As Integer
        Dim xmlOrder As String
        xmlOrder = "<Order EmployeeID='" & EmployeeID.ToString & "'>"
        Dim oItem As OrderItem
        For Each oItem In m_alOrderItems
            xmlOrder &= oItem.ToString
        Next
        xmlOrder &= "</Order>"
```

```
        Dim odbOrder As New dbOrder()
        Return odbOrder.PlaceOrder(xmlOrder)
    End Function
End Class
```

When a client is ready to submit an order, the PlaceOrder method of the Order class will be called. The client will pass the employee ID into the method and receive an order number as a return value. The PlaceOrder method of the Order class will pass the order information in the form of an XML string to the dbOrder class for processing. This example demonstrates the creation of a separate class to process the order information and pass it into data storage, which will enable you to more effectively decouple the data tier from the business logic tier. The dbOrder class contains the PlaceOrder method that receives an XML order string from the Order class and passes it into a stored procedure in the SQL Server database. The stored procedure updates the database and passes back the order number. This order number is then returned to the Order class, which in turn passes it back to the client. Following is the code used to define the dbOrder class:

```
'/// Persists order data to the database.
'/// Uses the up_PlaceOrder stored procedure
Imports System.Data.SqlClient
Public Class dbOrder
    Public Function PlaceOrder(ByVal xmlOrder As String) As Integer
        Dim cn As SqlConnection = New SqlConnection()
        cn.ConnectionString = _
            "Integrated Security=True;Data Source=localhost;" & _
            "Initial Catalog=OfficeSupply"
        Try
            Dim cmd As SqlCommand = cn.CreateCommand()
            cmd.CommandType = CommandType.StoredProcedure
            cmd.CommandText = "up_PlaceOrder"

            Dim inParameter As New SqlParameter()
            inParameter.ParameterName = "@xmlOrder"
            inParameter.Value = xmlOrder
            inParameter.DbType = DbType.String
            inParameter.Direction = ParameterDirection.Input
            cmd.Parameters.Add(inParameter)

            Dim ReturnParameter As New SqlParameter()
            ReturnParameter.ParameterName = "@OrderID"
            ReturnParameter.Direction = ParameterDirection.ReturnValue
            cmd.Parameters.Add(ReturnParameter)

            Dim intOrderNo As Integer
            cn.Open()
            cmd.ExecuteNonQuery()
            cn.Close()
            intOrderNo = cmd.Parameters("@OrderID").Value
```

```
            Return intOrderNo
        Catch ex As Exception
            Debug.WriteLine(ex.ToString)
        End Try
    End Function
End Class
```

The final class that you need to construct is the Employee class, shown in the following code. This class will encapsulate the process of verifying an employee before an order can be placed. The Login method of the Employee class will verify the login credentials of an employee attempting to submit a purchase order. Once an employee has been verified, the Login method will return the EmployeeID to the client.

```
'/// Used to verify employees and provide the employee
'/// id so employees can place an order.
Imports System.Data.SqlClient
Public Class Employee
    Private m_LoginAttempt As Integer
    Public Function Login(ByVal UserName As String, _
        ByVal Password As String) As Integer
        Dim conn As SqlConnection = New SqlConnection()
        Try
            conn.ConnectionString = "Integrated Security=True;" & _
                "Data Source=LocalHost;Initial Catalog=OfficeSupply"
            conn.Open()
            Dim comm As SqlCommand = New SqlCommand()
            Dim userID As Integer
            comm.Connection = conn
            comm.CommandText = "Select EmployeeID from Employee" & _
                " where UserName='" _
                & UserName & "' and Password='" & Password & "'"
            userID = comm.ExecuteScalar()
            If userID > 0 Then
                Return userID
            Else
                m_LoginAttempt += 1
                If m_LoginAttempt >= 3 Then
                    Throw New Exception("Too many invalid attemps!")
                End If
                Return -1
            End If
        Catch ex As Exception
            Debug.WriteLine(ex.ToString)
        Finally
            conn.Close()
        End Try
    End Function
End Class
```

Now that you have created the business logic classes for this part of the application, you should revise the class diagram to more accurately reflect the classes developed up to this point. It is important to remember that the purpose of the class diagram is to help you plan the development of the classes and the relationships between those classes. As you develop and test the classes in the implementation phase, it is natural and almost inevitable that the class structure of the application will evolve. Figure 10-4 represents the current class structure of the OSO application's business logic tier.

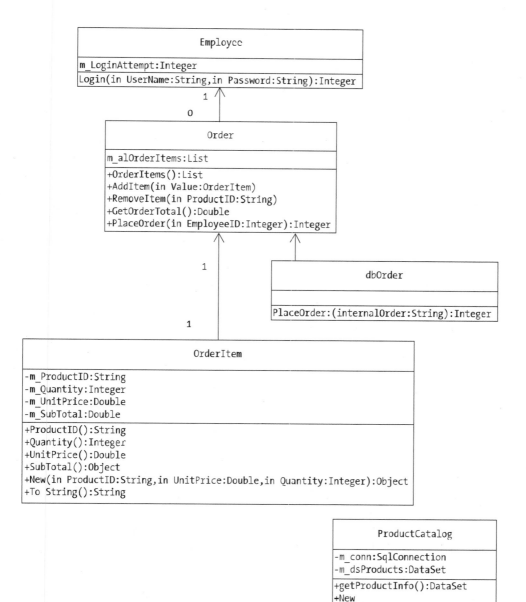

Figure 10-4. *OSO business logic class diagram*

Activity 10-3. Reviewing and Testing the OSO Application's Business Logic Tier

In this activity, you will become familiar with the following:

- Reviewing the OSO application's business logic class structure

- Testing the OSO application's business logic

■**Note** In order to complete this activity, it is assumed that you have downloaded and installed OSO database and code files. Refer to Appendix C for instruction on completing this.

Testing and Reviewing the OSO Application Business Logic

To test the OSO application business logic, follow these steps:

1. Select File ➤ Open ➤ Project.

2. Navigate to the OSOBusTier folder and open it.

3. Select the OSOBusTier solution file and click Open. The project contains the OSO business logic classes and a form that you will use to test the classes.

4. Add the controls listed in Table 10-5 to Form1 and set the properties as shown.

Table 10-5. *Form1 Control Property Settings*

Control	Property	Value
Label	Text	UserName
TextBox	Name	txtUserName
	Text	[blank]
Label	Text	Password
TextBox	Name	txtPassword
	Text	[blank]
Button	Name	btnLogin
	Text	Login

5. Add the following code to the btnLogin click event procedure. This will execute the Login method defined in the Employee class and display the EmployeeID passed back in a message box.

```
Dim oEmployee As New Employee()
MessageBox.Show(oEmployee.Login(txtUserName.Text,txtPassword.Text).ToString)
```

6. Build the project and fix any errors.

7. Run the project in debug mode. To test the Login method, enter a user name of jsmith and a password of js. After logging, a message box containing an Employee ID of 2 should be displayed.

8. After testing, stop the debugger.

9. Add the additional controls in Table 10-6 to Form1 and set the properties as shown.

Table 10-6. *Additional Form1 Control Property Settings*

Control	Property	Value
DataGridView	Name	dgvCategories
DataGridView	Name	dgvProducts
BindingSource	Name	bsCategories
BindingSource	Name	bsProducts
Button	Name	btnGetProducts
	Text	Get Products

10. Add the following code to the btnGetProducts click event procedure. This will execute the GetProductInfo method defined in the ProductCatalog class and display the DataSet passed back in the grids.

```
Dim oProducts As New ProductCatalog()
dgvCategories.DataSource = bsCategories
dgvProducts.DataSource = bsProducts
bsCategories.DataSource = oProducts.getProductInfo
bsCategories.DataMember = "Category"
bsProducts.DataSource = bsCategories
bsProducts.DataMember = "drCat_Prod"
```

11. Build the project and fix any errors.

12. Run the project in debug mode. Click the Get Product button. The grids should populate with the category and product information as shown in Figure 10-5.

13. After testing, stop the debugger.

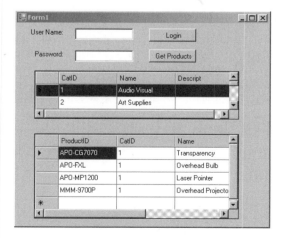

Figure 10-5. *Displaying products*

Testing the Order Class

To test the Order class, follow these steps:

1. Add a Button control to Form1. Change the Name property to btnTestOrder and the Text property to Test Order.

2. Add the following code to the btnTestOrder click event procedure. This code will create an order and add order items. A message box will display the order items in the order as an XML node. Another message box will display the total cost of the order. A final message box will display the order number of the order returned from the database when the order is placed:

```
Dim oOrder As New Order()
oOrder.AddItem(New OrderItem("ACM-10414", 3.79, 2))
oOrder.AddItem(New OrderItem("ACM-10414", 3.79, 4))
oOrder.AddItem(New OrderItem("OIC-5000", 1.99, 2))
oOrder.AddItem(New OrderItem("MMM-6200", 3.9, 2))

Dim i As Integer
For i = 0 To oOrder.OrderItems.Count - 1
    MessageBox.Show(oOrder.OrderItems.Item(i).ToString)
Next

MessageBox.Show(oOrder.GetOrderTotal.ToString)
MessageBox.Show(oOrder.PlaceOrder(1).ToString)
```

3. Build the project and fix any errors.

4. Run the project in debug mode. Click the Test Order button. A series of message boxes should be displayed showing the order information described in step 2.

5. After testing, stop the debugger and close VS.

Summary

This chapter is the first in a series aimed at introducing you to building the various tiers of an OOP application. To implement the application's business logic, you learned about ADO.NET. You looked at the various classes that make up the System.Data.SqlClient namespace. These classes retrieve and update data stored in a SQL Server database. You also examined the System.Data namespace classes that work with disconnected data.

In the next chapter, you will look at implementing the interface tier of an application through traditional Windows Forms. Along the way, you will take a closer look at the classes and namespaces of the .NET Framework used to implement rich Windows Forms-based user interfaces.

CHAPTER 11

■■■

Developing Windows Applications

In the previous chapter, you looked at developing the business logic layer of an application. To implement the business logic, you worked with the classes contained in the System.Data namespace. These classes retrieve and work with relational data, which is a common requirement of many business applications. You are now ready to look at how users will interact with your application. Users interact with an application through the user interface layer. This layer in turn interacts with the business logic layer, which in turn interacts with the data storage layer. This chapter covers building a "traditional" user interface consisting of Windows Forms. In the next chapter, you will look at creating a Web interface for an application.

After reading this chapter, you should be familiar with the following:

- How to work with forms and controls

- The inheritance hierarchy of forms and controls

- How to respond to form and control events

- Base and derived forms construction

- How to work with and create modal dialog forms

- Data binding controls contained in a Windows Form

Windows Forms Fundamentals

Forms are objects with a visual interface that are painted on the screen to provide users the ability to interact with programs. Just like most objects you work with in object-oriented languages, forms expose properties, methods, and events. The form's properties define the appearance of the form; for example, a form's BackColor property determines the background color of the form. The methods of a form define its behaviors; for example, a form object has a Hide method that causes its visual interface to be hidden from the user. The form's events define interactions with the user (or other objects); for example, the MouseDown event could initiate an action when the user clicks the right mouse button on the form.

Controls are components with visual interfaces that provide users with a way to interact with the program. A form is a special type of control, called a *container control*, which hosts other controls. You can place many different types of controls on Windows Forms. Some common controls used on forms are TextBoxes, Labels, OptionButtons, ListBoxes, and CheckBoxes, just to name a few. In addition to the controls provided by the .NET Framework, you can also create your own custom controls or purchase controls from third-party vendors.

Understanding Windows Forms Inheritance Hierarchy

If you trace the inheritance chain of form classes, you can see that the Form class you create in a Windows application inherits from the Form class, which is part of the System.Windows.Forms namespace. This class defines the common functionality required by all Windows Forms. For example, the class defines the form's FormBorderStyle property, which determines how the outer edge of the form appears. One of the methods defined in the System.Windows.Forms.Form, the Activate method, brings the form to the front if it is contained in the active application, or it flashes the window caption if the application is not the active application. A MenuStart event is defined in the System.Windows.Forms.Form class. This event is raised when the user clicks any menu item in the form's menu.

If you trace the inheritance chain of Windows Forms further, you discover that the Form class inherits functionality from the ContainerControl class, which provides management functionality for controls that function as a container for other controls. The ContainerControl class inherits from the ScrollableControl class, which provides support for autoscrolling behavior. The ScrollableControl class inherits from the Control class, which provides the basic functionality required by classes that display information to the user. Although tracing this hierarchy is not necessary to add and use Windows Forms (or controls, which have a similar hierarchy) in your application, it is beneficial to understand this hierarchy exists and how the forms you construct gain their built-in functionality. Figure 11-1 shows the hierarchical chain of a Windows Form as represented in the Class View window of VS. Figure 11-2 illustrates the hierarchical chain of a TextBox control, as represented in the Object Browser window of VS.

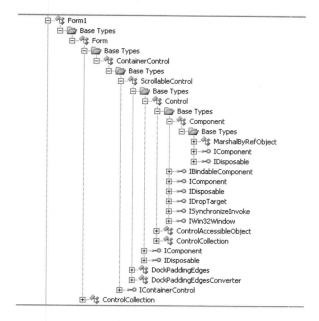

Figure 11-1. *Windows Form hierarchy*

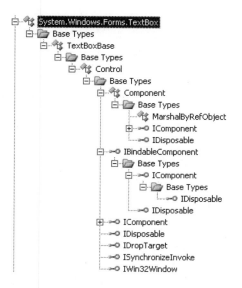

Figure 11-2. *TextBox control hierarchy*

Using the VS Form Designer

Although it is quite possible to create your forms entirely through code using a text editor, you will probably find this process quite tedious and not a very productive use of your time. Thankfully, the VS IDE includes an excellent visual form designer. Using the designer, you can drag and drop controls onto the form from the Toolbox and set control properties using the Properties window. Figure 11-3 shows a form in the VS designer.

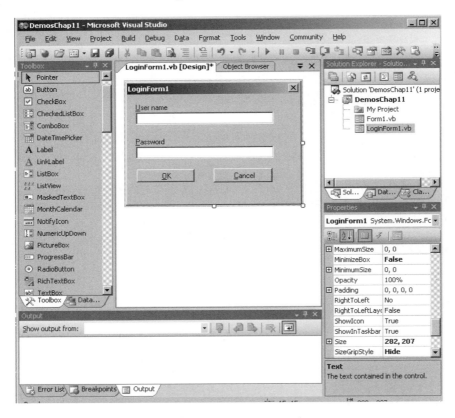

Figure 11-3. *VS form designer*

Clicking the Show All Files button at the top of the Solution Explorer window reveals a *FormName*.Designer.vb file for each form in the project. This file defines a partial class containing Windows form designer-generated code. This partial class contains the code needed to construct and manage the controls contained on the form. Although it is generally not a good idea to alter the code contained in this file directly, it is beneficial to look at the code to gain an understanding of what the code is doing.

The first part of the code in the file declares a partial class for the form and inherits from the Form base class.

```
<Global.Microsoft.VisualBasic.CompilerServices.DesignerGenerated()> _
Partial Public Class LoginForm1
    Inherits System.Windows.Forms.Form
```

The partial class contains two procedures—InitializeComponent and Dispose. Just above the InitializeComponent subprocedure, a container object is declared. The container object keeps track of the various components added to the form. It encapsulates the functionality for adding, removing, and retrieving components. Prior to the container object declaration, the various component objects (controls) added to the form are declared:

```
Friend WithEvents UsernameLabel As System.Windows.Forms.Label
Friend WithEvents PasswordLabel As System.Windows.Forms.Label
Friend WithEvents UsernameTextBox As System.Windows.Forms.TextBox
Friend WithEvents PasswordTextBox As System.Windows.Forms.TextBox
Friend WithEvents OK As System.Windows.Forms.Button
Friend WithEvents Cancel As System.Windows.Forms.Button


'Required by the Windows Form Designer
Private components As System.ComponentModel.IContainer
```

Because these declarations are made outside of any procedure blocks, they have class-level scope. The Friend keyword makes these controls accessible from anywhere within the current application or assembly. The WithEvents keyword allows these controls to raise events. After the control declarations, the InitializeComponent subprocedure instantiates the various components. A call to the SuspendLayout method of the form halts the layout of the controls until the initial properties have been set. The initial properties of the controls are then set (the ones you set in the designer's Properties window), and the controls are added to the control collection of the form. The final step of the InitializeComponent subprocedure is a call to the ResumeLayout method to resume laying out the form. The following code shows the complete InitalizeComponent subprocedure.

```
<System.Diagnostics.DebuggerStepThrough()> _
Private Sub InitializeComponent()
    Me.UsernameLabel = New System.Windows.Forms.Label
    Me.PasswordLabel = New System.Windows.Forms.Label
    Me.UsernameTextBox = New System.Windows.Forms.TextBox
    Me.PasswordTextBox = New System.Windows.Forms.TextBox
    Me.OK = New System.Windows.Forms.Button
    Me.Cancel = New System.Windows.Forms.Button
    Me.SuspendLayout()
    '
    'UsernameLabel
    '
    Me.UsernameLabel.Location = New System.Drawing.Point(12, 9)
    Me.UsernameLabel.Name = ""UsernameLabel"
    Me.UsernameLabel.Size = New System.Drawing.Size(220, 23)
    Me.UsernameLabel.TabIndex = 0
    Me.UsernameLabel.Text = "&User name"
    Me.UsernameLabel.TextAlign = _
      System.Drawing.ContentAlignment.MiddleLeft
    '
    'PasswordLabel
    '
```

```vb
Me.PasswordLabel.Location = New System.Drawing.Point(12, 66)
Me.PasswordLabel.Name = "PasswordLabel"
Me.PasswordLabel.Size = New System.Drawing.Size(220, 23)
Me.PasswordLabel.TabIndex = 2
Me.PasswordLabel.Text = "&Password"
Me.PasswordLabel.TextAlign = _
 System.Drawing.ContentAlignment.MiddleLeft
'
'UsernameTextBox
'
Me.UsernameTextBox.Location = New System.Drawing.Point(14, 29)
Me.UsernameTextBox.Name = "UsernameTextBox"
Me.UsernameTextBox.Size = New System.Drawing.Size(220, 20)
Me.UsernameTextBox.TabIndex = 1
'
'PasswordTextBox
'
Me.PasswordTextBox.Location = New System.Drawing.Point(14, 86)
Me.PasswordTextBox.Name = "PasswordTextBox"
Me.PasswordTextBox.PasswordChar = _
 Global.Microsoft.VisualBasic.ChrW(42)
Me.PasswordTextBox.Size = New System.Drawing.Size(220, 20)
Me.PasswordTextBox.TabIndex = 3
'
'OK
'
Me.OK.Location = New System.Drawing.Point(14, 123)
Me.OK.Name = "OK"
Me.OK.Size = New System.Drawing.Size(94, 23)
Me.OK.TabIndex = 4
Me.OK.Text = "&OK"
'
'Cancel
'
Me.Cancel.DialogResult = _
 System.Windows.Forms.DialogResult.Cancel
Me.Cancel.Location = New System.Drawing.Point(138, 123)
Me.Cancel.Name = "Cancel"
Me.Cancel.Size = New System.Drawing.Size(94, 23)
Me.Cancel.TabIndex = 5
Me.Cancel.Text = "&Cancel"
'
'LoginForm1
'
Me.AcceptButton = Me.OK
Me.AutoScaleDimensions = New System.Drawing.SizeF(6.0!, 13.0!)
Me.AutoScaleMode = System.Windows.Forms.AutoScaleMode.Font
Me.CancelButton = Me.Cancel
```

```
    Me.ClientSize = New System.Drawing.Size(276, 182)
    Me.Controls.Add(Me.Cancel)
    Me.Controls.Add(Me.OK)
    Me.Controls.Add(Me.PasswordTextBox)
    Me.Controls.Add(Me.UsernameTextBox)
    Me.Controls.Add(Me.PasswordLabel)
    Me.Controls.Add(Me.UsernameLabel)
    Me.FormBorderStyle = _
     System.Windows.Forms.FormBorderStyle.FixedDialog
    Me.MaximizeBox = False
    Me.MinimizeBox = False
    Me.Name = "LoginForm1"
    Me.SizeGripStyle = System.Windows.Forms.SizeGripStyle.Hide
    Me.StartPosition = _
     System.Windows.Forms.FormStartPosition.CenterParent
    Me.Text = "LoginForm1"
    Me.ResumeLayout(False)
    Me.PerformLayout()

End Sub
```

The `Dispose` procedure calls the `Dispose` method of the components object, which in turn loops through the controls in the container collection and calls the `Dispose` method of the controls. Once the controls have been properly disposed, a call is made to the form's base class so that the required cleanup code can be processed up through the form inheritance chain:

```
<System.Diagnostics.DebuggerNonUserCode()> _
Protected Overloads Overrides Sub Dispose(ByVal disposing As Boolean)
    If disposing Then
        If Not (components Is Nothing) Then
            components.Dispose()
        End If
    End If
    MyBase.Dispose(disposing)
End Sub
```

Handling Windows Form and Control Events

Windows graphical user interface (GUI) programs are based on an event-driven model. *Events* are actions initiated by a user or the system—for example, a user clicking a button or a `SqlConnection` object issuing a `StateChange` event. Event-driven applications execute code in response to the various events that occur. To respond to an event, you define an *event handler* that will execute when an event occurs. The .NET Framework uses delegation to bind an event, with the event handler procedures written to respond to the event. A delegation object maintains an invocation list of methods that have subscribed to receive notification when the event occurs. When an event occurs—for example, a button is clicked—the control will raise the event by invoking the delegate for the event, which in turn will call the event handler methods that have subscribed to receive the event notification. Although this sounds complicated, the framework classes do most of the work for you.

Adding Form Event Handlers

The easiest way to add a form event handler is to use the drop-down list boxes at the top of the code editor. In the left drop-down box, choose the (*FormName* Events) option, as shown in Figure 11-4. In the right drop-down list, select the event you want to handle, as shown in Figure 11-5. As you can see from the list, you can respond to many different form events. Part of your education is to investigate these various events to determine when they fire, what information they pass to the method handlers, and any dependencies they may have on other events.

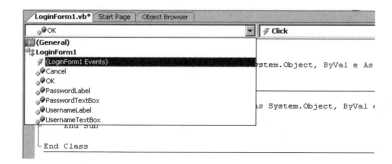

Figure 11-4. *Choosing a control*

Figure 11-5. *Choosing an event*

After choosing the form event, the code editor inserts an event handler method. The following code shows the event handler method inserted for the Form_Load event. When the form displays for the first time, the Form_Load event occurs.

```
Private Sub LoginForm1_Load(ByVal sender As Object, _
    ByVal e As System.EventArgs) Handles Me.Load

End Sub
```

By convention, the name of the event handler method is the name of the object issuing the event followed by an underscore character (_) and the name of the event. The actual name of the event handler, however, is unimportant. The Handles keyword adds this method to the invocation list of the event's delegation object.

All event handlers must provide two parameters that are passed to the method when the event is fired. The first parameter is the sender, which represents the object that initiated the event. The second parameter, of type System.EventArgs, is an object used to pass any information specific to a particular event. For example, the MouseDown event passes information on which button was clicked and the coordinates of the mouse cursor when it was clicked. The following code demonstrates checking which button was pressed in a form's MouseDown event handler:

```
Private Sub LoginForm1_MouseDown(ByVal sender As Object, _
    ByVal e As System.Windows.Forms.MouseEventArgs) _
    Handles Me.MouseDown
        If e.Button = MouseButtons.Right Then
            'implementation code goes here
        End If
End Sub
```

Adding Control Event Handlers

You add control event handlers the same way you add form event handlers, by using the drop-down lists at the top of the code editor. The left drop-down list selects the control, and the right drop-down list selects the event to handle. Figure 11-6 demonstrates adding an event handler for a button click event.

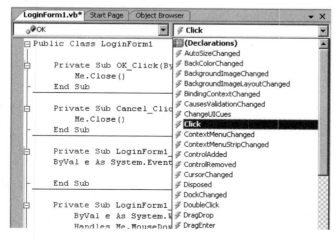

Figure 11-6. *Adding a button click event handler*

Because the .NET Framework uses delegates for event notification, you can handle multiple events with the same method. The only requirement is that the events being handled have the same signatures. For example, you could handle a button click event and a menu click event with the same event handler, but you could not handle a button click event and a button KeyPress event using the same method. The following code demonstrates handling the MouseHover event of a Label and a TextBox using the same handler method. The sender parameter is interrogated to determine which control fired the event.

```
Private Sub UsernameLabel_MouseHover(ByVal sender As Object, _
    ByVal e As System.EventArgs) _
    Handles UsernameLabel.MouseHover, UsernameTextBox.MouseHover

    If sender.Name = "UsernameLabel" Then
        MessageBox.Show(sender.GetType.AssemblyQualifiedName)
    ElseIf sender.Name = "UsernameTextBox" Then
        MessageBox.Show(sender.GetType.Name)
    End If
End Sub
```

In the following activity, you will investigate working with forms and controls by constructing a simple menu viewer application that will allow users to load and view memo documents.

Activity 11-1. Working with Forms and Controls

In this activity, you will become familiar with the following:

- Creating a Windows Form-based GUI application

- Working with Menu, StatusStrip, and Dialog controls

- Working with Control events

Creating the Memo Viewer Interface

To create the memo viewer interface, follow these steps:

1. Start VS. Select File ➤ New ➤ Project.

2. Choose a Windows Application under the Visual Basic Projects folder. Rename the project to Act11_1 and click the OK button.

3. Add the controls to Form1 and set the properties as listed in Table 11-1. The MenuStrip and StatusStrip controls show up in the component tray below the form.

Table 11-1. *Memo Viewer Interface Form and Control Properties*

Control	Property	Value
Form1	Name	frmMemoViewer
	Text	Memo Viewer
MenuStrip1	Name	msMainMenu
	Text	[Empty]
StatusStrip1	Name	ssViewer
	Text	[Empty]
RichTextBox1	Name	rtbMemo
	Text	[Empty]
	Dock	Fill (click in center)
	ReadOnly	True

Note It is easier to add all the controls to the form before setting the Dock property of the RichTextBox.

4. To create a ToolStripMenuItem, click the msMainMenu in the component tray. Type File in the Type Here box located at the top of the form (see Figure 11-7), and then press the Enter key. Click back on the File menu, and in the Properties window, change the Name property to miFile. Complete the menu items for the form as indicated in Table 11-2.

Figure 11-7. *Creating a menu item*

Table 11-2. *Memo Viewer Interface Menu Items*

Name	Text	Top Menu
miFile	File	
miOpen	Open	miFile
miClose	Close	miFile
miExit	Exit	miFile
miSave	Save	miFile
miNew	New	miFile
miView	View	
miStatusStrip	StatusStrip	miView

5. Using the Properties window, change the `Checked` and `CheckOnClick` properties of the miStatusStrip control to `True`. Change the `Enabled` property of the miSave and miNew controls to `False`.

6. Click the ssViewer control in the component tray. Click the `Items` property located in the Properties window. Click again on the ellipses that are presented. This will display the items collection editor.

7. Clicking the Add button will add a ToolStripStatusLabel to the collection and present the properties for this control. Add two ToolStripStatusLabels and set the properties as shown in Figure 11-8 and listed in Table 11-3.

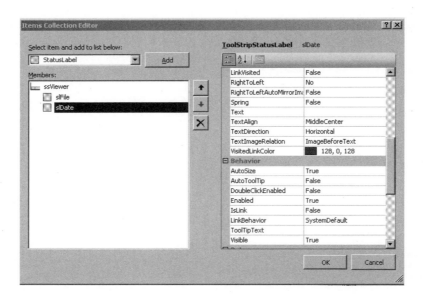

Figure 11-8. *Editing ToolStrip items*

Table 11-3. *ToolStripStatusLabel Properties*

Panel	Property	Value
ToolStripStatusLabel1	Name	slFile
	Text	[Empty]
	Spring	True
ToolStripStatusLabel2	Name	slDate
	Text	[Empty]

8. Close the items collection editor.

9. Add an OpenFileDialog control to the form. This control shows up in the component tray below the form. Change the property values as shown in Table 11-4.

Table 11-4. *OpenFileDialog Properties*

Property	Value
Name	ofdMemoViewer
Filter	memo files | *.memo
InitialDirectory	c:\Memos\
Title	Open Memo Files

10. To display the code editor for the frmMemoViewer form, right-click the frmMemoViewer node in the Solution Explorer window and select View Code. In the left drop-down list, choose the (frmMemoViewer Events) option. In the right drop-down list, select Load. Add the following code to display a message and the date in the StatusStrip control:

```
ssViewer.Items(0).Text = "Ready to load file..."
ssViewer.Items(1).Text = System.DateTime.Today.ToShortDateString
```

11. Build the solution and fix any errors.

12. Select Debug ➤ Start. When the form displays, the StatusStrip control should contain the text added in step 10 and today's date. After testing, stop the debugger.

Coding the Menu Click Events

To code the menu click events, follow these steps:

1. Switch to the code editor for the frmMemoViewer form. In the left drop-down list, choose miOpen. In the right drop-down list, select Click event. Add the following code to open a memo file and load it into the rtbMemo control:

```
ofdMemoViewer.ShowDialog()
rtbMemo.LoadFile(ofdMemoViewer.FileName, RichTextBoxStreamType.PlainText)
ssViewer.Items(0).Text = ofdMemoViewer.FileName
```

2. Add the following code to the miClose click event procedure to clear the rtbMemo control and reset the text in the first panel of the status bar:

```
rtbMemo.Clear()
ssViewer.Items(0).Text = "Ready to load file ..."
```

3. Add the following code to a miExit click event procedure to close the form:

```
Me.Close()
```

4. Add the following code to a miStatusStrip click event procedure to toggle the visibility of the status bar:

```
ssViewer.Visible = miStatusStrip.Checked
```

5. Build the solution and fix any errors.

6. Create a Memos folder on the C drive. Using Notepad, create a text file containing a test message. Save the file to the Memos folder. Using Windows Explorer, rename the file to Test.memo.

7. Select Debug ➤ Start. Test the application by loading the Test.memo file. Try changing the memo message. You should not be able to because the rtbMemo control was set to read-only. After viewing the file, close it using the Close menu. Toggle the visibility of the status bar using the StatusBar menu located under the View menu. Exit the application using the Exit menu.

8. After testing the application, exit VS.

Working with Form-Based Inheritance

Because forms are classes in the .NET Framework, you can create your own base forms to encapsulate standard functionality in your applications. Derived forms can then inherit from the base form and gain access to this built-in functionality or override it if necessary. Derived forms inherit not only the methods of the base form, but also the visual aspects as well. This can be handy when creating forms for an application that needs to convey a common look-and-feel experience to the users.

Creating the base form is no different from creating a regular form. Simply add a form to the project and place the controls on the form. Set the required properties and add any methods needed. Once the controls and methods have been set up, you need to determine how derived forms can access and alter the control properties and methods of the base form. You must mark any methods that can be overridden by derived forms as overridable. You can alter the access modifiers of the controls to restrict how they can be altered in the derived form. Table 11-5 summarizes the various modifiers and the implication of each. By default, most controls added to a form are designated with the Friend modifier.

Table 11-5. *Access Modifiers of the Base Form*

Modifier	Implication on Inherited Form
Public	Control may be resized and moved. All other classes can modify the properties.
Protected	Control may be resized and moved. Derived forms can modify the properties.
Friend	Control cannot be resized and moved. All classes within the same assembly can modify the properties.
Private	Control cannot be resized and moved. Only the base form can modify the properties.

Figure 11-9 demonstrates the effect the access modifier has on the derived implementation of a control. The Label controls marked as `Public` and `Protected` can be resized and moved as indicated by the sizing handles on the borders. The labels marked as `Private` and `Friend` cannot be resized or moved as indicated by the absence of the resizing handles and the lock icons.

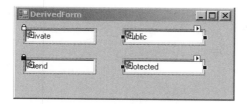

Figure 11-9. *Control access on the derived form*

Working with the event handlers of the inherited controls on the derived form can be a little tricky. The following base form class code creates a private event handler for the `MouseHover` event of a private control:

```
Private Sub lblPrivate_MouseHover(ByVal sender As Object, _
            ByVal e As System.EventArgs) Handles lblPrivate.MouseHover
    MessageBox.Show("Hello from Base")
End Sub
```

When you hover over the control in the derived form, you get the message "Hello from Base."

Even though the control was declared as private, you can still override its `MouseHover` event implementation in the derived class. If you declare the event procedure as `Public Overridable` in the base class and create an `Overrides` procedure in the derived class, hovering over the control in the derived form reveals the overridden message "Hello from Derived":

```
'Base class code
Public Overridable Sub lblPrivate_MouseHover(ByVal sender As Object, _
        ByVal e As System.EventArgs) Handles lblPrivate.MouseHover
        MessageBox.Show("Hello from Base")
End Sub
'Derived class code
Public Overrides Sub lblPrivate_MouseHover(ByVal sender As Object, _
        ByVal e As System.EventArgs)
    MessageBox.Show("Hello from Derived")
End Sub
```

The key to this working is the event handler was defined in the base form and marked as being overridable. Without doing this, the derived form would not have access to the private inherited control's events.

When a control on the base form is marked as Public or Protected, a derived form can create event handlers for the controls even if the base form does not. The following code demonstrates creating an event handler for an inherited control marked as protected:

```
'Derived class code
Private Sub lblProtected_MouseHover(ByVal sender As Object, _
    ByVal e As System.EventArgs) Handles lblProtected.MouseHover
    MessageBox.Show("Hello from derived")
End Sub
```

The final scenario you will look at is what happens when you handle the event in both the derived class and the base class. When you do this, you are actually creating two separate event handlers for the same event (this is referred to as *multicasting*):

```
'Base class code
Private Sub lblProtected_MouseHover(ByVal sender As Object, _
    ByVal e As System.EventArgs) Handles lblProtected.MouseHover
    MessageBox.Show("Hello from Base")
End Sub
'Derived class code
Private Sub lblProtected_MouseHover(ByVal sender As Object, _
    ByVal e As System.EventArgs) Handles lblProtected.MouseHover
MessageBox.Show("Hello from derived")
End Sub
```

When the mouse is hovered over the label in the derived form, both event handler methods are executed.

Creating and Using Dialog Boxes

Dialog boxes are special forms often used in Windows Form-based GUI applications. A *dialog box* displays information or retrieves information from the user of the application. The difference between a normal form and a dialog box is that a dialog box is displayed modally. A *modal form* prevents the user from performing other tasks within the application until the dialog box has been dismissed. When you start a new project in VS, you are presented with a New Project dialog box, as shown in Figure 11-10. You can also use dialog boxes to present the user with critical information and query them for a response. If you try to run an application in debug mode and a build error is encountered, the VS IDE presents you with a dialog box asking whether you want to continue (see Figure 11-11).

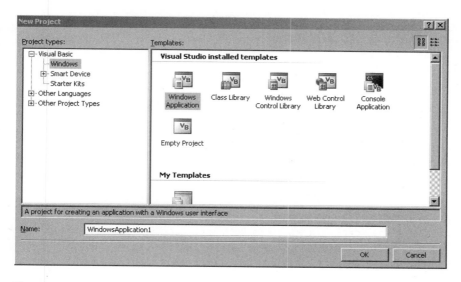

Figure 11-10. *The New Project dialog box*

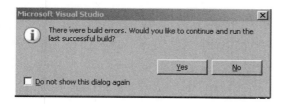

Figure 11-11. *Displaying critical information using a dialog box*

Presenting a MessageBox to the User

The dialog box shown in Figure 11-11 is a special predefined type called a *MessageBox*. The MessageBox class is part of the System.Windows.Forms namespace. The MessageBox class can display a standard Windows message dialog box. To display a MessageBox to the user, you call the shared Show method of the MessageBox class as you have been doing in many of the examples:

```
MessageBox.Show("File Saved")
```

The Show method is overloaded so that you can optionally show a MessageBox icon, show a title, change the buttons displayed, set the default button, and indicate the form to display it in front of. The only required setting is the text message that will be displayed on the form. Figure 11-12 shows the MessageBox displayed by the previous code.

Figure 11-12. *A basic MessageBox*

The following code calls the Show method using all the parameters. Figure 11-13 shows the resulting MessageBox that gets displayed. For more information on the various parameters and settings available, look up the MessageBox class in the help file.

```
MessageBox.Show(Me, "Are you sure you want to quit?", _
          "Closing Application", MessageBoxButtons.OKCancel, _
          MessageBoxIcon.Warning, MessageBoxDefaultButton.Button2, _
          MessageBoxOptions.RightAlign)
```

Figure 11-13. *A more complex MessageBox*

Retrieving the MessageBox Dialog Box Result

Many times you will use a MessageBox to query for a response to a question. The user indicates the response by clicking the corresponding button. The result is passed back as the return value of the MessageBox.Show method in the form of a DialogResult enumeration. The following code demonstrates capturing the dialog box result and canceling the closing of the form depending on the result:

```
Private Sub Form1_Closing(ByVal sender As Object, _
        ByVal e As System.ComponentModel.CancelEventArgs) _
    Handles MyBase.Closing
    Dim mbResult As DialogResult
    mbResult = MessageBox.Show("Are you sure you want to quit?", _
        "Closing Application", MessageBoxButtons.OKCancel, _
        MessageBoxIcon.Warning, MessageBoxDefaultButton.Button2)
    If mbResult = DialogResult.Cancel Then
        e.Cancel = True
    End If
End Sub
```

Creating a Custom Dialog Box

One of the most exciting features about the .NET Framework is its extensibility. Although there are many types of dialog boxes, you can use "right-out-of-the-box" ones for such things as printing, saving files, and loading files, just to name a few. You can also build your own custom dialog boxes. The first step in creating a custom dialog box is to add a Windows Form to the application. Next, add any controls needed to interact with the user. Figure 11-14 shows a dialog box created to verify a user's identity. The border style has been set to FixedDialog, and the ControlBox, MaximizeBox, and MinimizeBox properties have been set to false. To determine which button a user clicked to dismiss the form, the DialogResult property of the buttons on the form are set to the appropriate DialogResult enumeration. This DialogResult enumeration gets passed back to the parent form when the button is clicked. For example, the DialogResult property of the Login button in Figure 11-14 has been set to OK.

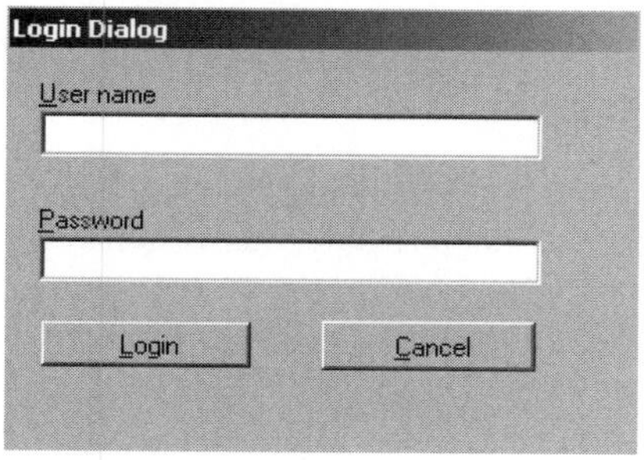

Figure 11-14. *A custom dialog box*

To display the dialog box, the ShowDialog method of the form is called. This method will display the dialog box modally, which means the user cannot interact with any other forms until the dialog box has been dismissed. Once the user clicks a button to dismiss the form, the form becomes hidden, and the DialogResult enumeration is passed back to the parent form. The following code demonstrates the process of showing the Login dialog box and inspecting the DialogResult that is returned:

```
Dim dlgLogin As New LoginDialog()
Dim mbResult As DialogResult
mbResult = dlgLogin.ShowDialog()
If mbResult = DialogResult.OK Then
     'verification code here
Else
     MessageBox.Show("You could not be verified.")
End If
dlgLogin.Dispose()
```

When the user dismisses a form that has been shown as a dialog box, it is hidden, not closed. Because of this behavior, you need to call the Dispose method of the form when you no longer need an instance of it, as demonstrated by the last line of the code block shown previously. Because the dialog box is hidden when control returns to the calling form, you can interrogate the properties of the controls to retrieve the information the user entered. The following code demonstrates passing user information to the Verify method of an Employee class:

```
Dim dlgLogin As New LoginDialog()
Dim mbResult As DialogResult
Dim oEmployee As New Employee()
Dim bVerify As Boolean
mbResult = dlgLogin.ShowDialog()
If mbResult = DialogResult.OK Then
    bVerify = oEmployee.Verify (dlgLogin.txtUserName.Text, _
                    dlgLogin.txtPassword.Text)
Else
    MessageBox.Show("You could not be verified.")
End If
dlgLogin.Dispose()
```

Another way of retrieving the user information from the dialog box is to create a class or structure to hold the information and expose it as a property of the dialog form. The following code creates a LoginInfo structure, which is used to pass the information back to the parent form:

```
Public Structure LoginInfo
    Public UserName As String
    Public Password As String
End Structure
```

Next, a property of the dialog form of type LoginInfo is created to hold the user's information:

```
Public ReadOnly Property dlgInfo() As LoginInfo
    Get
        Dim UserInfo As LoginInfo
        UserInfo.UserName = txtUserName.Text
        UserInfo.Password = txtPassword.Text
        Return UserInfo
    End Get
End Property
```

When the user dismisses the dialog box, this property is interrogated to retrieve the dialog information:

```
Dim dlgLogin As New LoginDialog()
Dim mbResult As DialogResult
Dim oEmployee As New Employee()
Dim bVerify As Boolean
Dim dlgInfo As LoginInfo
mbResult = dlgLogin.ShowDialog()
```

```
If mbResult = DialogResult.OK Then
    dlgInfo = dlgLogin.dlgInfo
    bVerify = oEmployee.Verify(dlgInfo.UserName, dlgInfo.Password)
Else
    MessageBox.Show("You could not be verified.")
End If
dlgLogin.Dispose()
```

Activity 11-2. Working with Form Inheritance and Dialog Boxes in a Windows Form-Based GUI

In this activity, you will become familiar with the following:

- Implementing form-based inheritance

- Using MessageBox dialog boxes

- Creating custom dialog boxes and retrieving user information

Creating an Inherited Form

To create an inherited form, follow these steps:

1. Start VS. Select File ➤ Open ➤ Project.

2. Navigate to the Act11_1.sln file and click the Open button.

3. Right-click the project node in the Solution Explorer. From the context menu, choose Add ➤ New Item. In the Add New Item dialog box, select the Inherited Form template. Change the name of the form to frmMemoEditor and click Open. You will be presented with the Inheritance Picker dialog box, as shown in Figure 11-15.

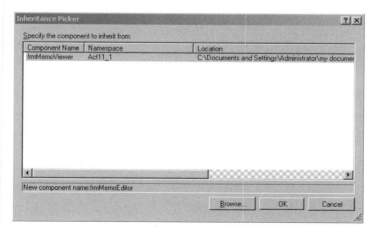

Figure 11-15. *Inheritance Picker dialog box*

4. In the Inheritance Picker dialog box, select the `frmMemoViewer` form and click OK.

5. Double-click the `frmMemoEditor` node in the Solution Explorer to open the form in the form designer. Select the form in the Properties window. Notice that you can change the properties of the form. This is because the base form class was declared with the `Public` modifier. Change the `Text` property of the form to `Memo Editor`.

6. Select the rtbMemo control in the Property Editor window. Notice that you cannot change the properties of rtbMemo control. This is because the rtbMemo control is declared with the `Friend` modifier in the base class.

7. Double-click the frmMemoViewer node in the Solution Explorer to open the form in the form design editor. Select the rtbMemo control in the Property Editor window. Change the `Modifiers` property of the rtbMemo control to `Protected`. Also change the `Modifiers` property of the miSave and miNew controls to `Protected`.

8. Select View ➤ Error List. Notice that the Error List window displays a message stating that the project needs to be rebuilt. This must be done so that the designer can reflect the changes in the inherited `frmMemoEditor` form. Rebuild the solution.

9. Close and reopen the `frmMemoEditor` in the Form Design Editor. Select the rtbMemo control in the Property Editor window. Notice that you now have access to the properties of the control. Change the `ReadOnly` property to `False`.

10. Switch to the code editor for `frmMemoEditor`. In the right drop-down list, select the (frmMemoEditor Events) option, and in the left drop-down list, select the Load event. Add the following code, to enable the New and Save menu items:

```
miSave.Enabled = True
miNew.Enabled = True
```

11. Build the solution and fix any errors.

12. Open the My Project folder in the Solution Explorer. Change the startup object to `frmMemoEditor`.

13. Select Debug ➤ Start. Test the application by loading the `Test.memo` file. Try changing the memo message. You should now be able to because the rtbMemo control's `ReadOnly` property was overriden and changed to `False`. After viewing the file, close it using the Close menu. Toggle the visibility of the status strip using the StatusStrip menu located under the View menu. Exit the application using the Exit menu.

Adding an Application Closing Dialog Box

To add a dialog box that closes the application, follow these steps:

1. Switch to the code editor for `frmMemoViewer`. In the left drop-down list, select miOpen, and in the right drop-down list, select the Click event. Change the name of the event handler method and the access modifier as shown in the following code. You will override this method in the inherited `frmMemoEditor` class:

```
Public Overridable Sub OpenMemo(ByVal sender As Object, _
        ByVal e As System.EventArgs) Handles miOpen.Click
```

2. Switch to the code editor for frmMemoEditor. Add an OpenMemo method that overrides the base class's OpenMemo method. Call the base class's OpenMemo method and change the rtbMemo's Modified property back to False. This was set to True by the initial file load.

```
Public Overrides Sub OpenMemo(ByVal sender As Object, ByVal e As
System.EventArgs)
    MyBase.OpenMemo(sender, e)
    rtbMemo.Modified = False
End Sub
```

3. In the code editor for frmMemoEditor, use the left drop-down list to select the (frmMemoEditor Events) option. In the right drop-down list, select the FormClosing event. Add the following code to the event handler method. This code checks whether there are unsaved changes and aborts the event by changing the Cancel event argument to True:

```
If rtbMemo.Modified Then
    MessageBox.Show("You must save changes before closing.")
    e.Cancel = True
End If
```

4. Build the solution and fix any build errors.

5. Select Debug ➤ Start. Test the application by loading the Test.memo file. Do not make any changes, but click the menu Exit. The application should close.

6. Repeat step 5, but add some text to the memo. This time you will get the message and the closing will be canceled. After testing, switch back to the VS IDE and stop the debugger.

7. Alter the code in the frmMemoEditor_FormClosing event handler method to give the user the option of closing without saving:

```
If rtbMemo.Modified Then
    Dim Response As DialogResult
    Response = MessageBox.Show _
        ("You have unsaved changes. Exit without saving?", _
        "Closing Application", MessageBoxButtons.YesNo, _
        MessageBoxIcon.Warning)
    If Response = DialogResult.No Then
        e.Cancel = True
    End If
End If
```

8. Select Debug ➤ Start. Test the application by loading the Test.memo file. Do not make any changes, but click the menu Exit. The application should close.

9. Repeat step 8, but add some text to the memo. This time you will get a MessageBox dialog box giving you the option to cancel closing the application. After testing, stop the debugger and exit VS.

Data Binding in Windows Form-Based GUIs

Once you have retrieved the data from the business logic tier, you must present it to the user. The user may need to read through the data, edit the data, add records, or delete records. Many of the controls placed on a form can display the data to the user. The choice of what control to use often depends on the data type, what kind of data manipulation is required, and the interface design. Some common controls used to present data are TextBoxes, DataGrids, Labels, ListBoxes, CheckBoxes, and Calendars. When different fields of a data source are presented to the user in different controls (for example, a first name TextBox and last name TextBox), it is important that the controls remain synchronized to show the same record.

The .NET Framework encapsulates much of the complexity of synchronizing controls to a data source through a process called *data binding*. A BindingSource component is responsible for managing the interaction between the controls on the form and the data source. The BindingSource handles any necessary interaction with the data such as navigating, sorting, filtering, and updating.

Once a BindingSource is established, controls on the form bind their properties to the BindingSource through their DataBindings collection. The following code demonstrates connecting a BindingSource (bsCustomers) to the Customers table of a dataset returned from the GetData method of an Orders object. The Text property of a label control is then bound to the CompanyName field through the DataBindings collection.

```
Dim oOrders As New Orders
bsCustomers.DataSource = oOrders.GetData
bsCustomers.DataMember = "Customers"
Label1.DataBindings.Add("Text", bsCustomers, "CompanyName")
```

The following code uses the BindingSource to move to the next record. All controls bound to the BindingSource will update accordingly.

```
bsCustomers.MoveNext()
```

As you can see, binding to a data source and moving through records is fairly painless using the .NET Framework. An interesting point to note is that although the previous code uses a DataSet object as the DataSource, in the .NET Framework you can bind to any object that implements the IList interface. This opens up the possibility of binding to arrays, collections, and custom business objects as well.

Controls such as Labels and TextBoxes are *simple-bound controls*, which are limited to displaying one record of the data source at a time. Controls such as the DataGridView, ListBox, and ComboBox support complex data binding. Complex binding is the ability to bind and display more than one record at a time. To bind a listbox, set the DataSource property to the BindingSource. The DisplayMember and ValueMember properties are then set to fields contained in the DataSource.

```
ListBox1.DataSource = bsCustomers
ListBox1.DisplayMember = "CompanyName"
ListBox1.ValueMember = "CustomerID"
```

Since a DataGridView can display all the fields exposed by the BindingSource, all you need to do is set the DataSource property to the BindingSource.

```
DataGridView1.DataSource = bsCustomers
```

Activity 11-3. Binding Controls in a Windows Form

In this activity, you will become familiar with the following:

- Working with simple-bound controls

- Employing complex binding

- Binding to a business object

Implementing Simple Bound Controls

To implement simple-bound controls, follow these steps:

1. Start VS. Select File ➤ Open ➤ Project.

2. Navigate to the Act11_3Starter.sln file and click Open. This project contains a PubDB class that encapsulates the functionality of retrieving records from the Publisher database in SQL Server.

3. View the code for the GetBookInfo method of the PubDB class. This method returns a DataSet object containing book information. You will implement simple-binding using this DataSet.

4. Add the following controls to Form1 and set the properties as listed in Table 11-6. The completed form should look similar to Figure 11-16.

Table 11-6. *Form1 and Control Property Values*

Control	Property	Value
Form1	Name	frmBookInfo
	Text	Book Information
TextBox1	Name	txtTitle
	Text	[Empty]
TextBox2	Name	txtSales
	Text	[Empty]
DateTimePicker1	Name	dtpPubDate
	Format	Short
Button1	Name	btnNext
	Text	Next
Button2	Name	btnPrevious
	Text	Prev

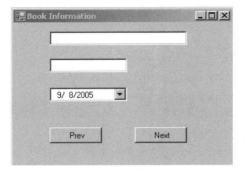

Figure 11-16. *The completed book info form*

5. Switch to the code editor for the `frmBookInfo` class. Declare a class-level variable to hold a `DataSet` and a BindingSource for the controls.

```
Private dsBookInfo As DataSet
Private bsBookInfo As New BindingSource
```

6. Create a subprocedure called `BindControls`. This procedure will call the `GetBookInfo` method and store the `DataSet` returned in a class-level `DataSet` variable. After retrieving the `DataSet`, the controls are bound to their related column in the `DataSet` through the BindingSource object.

```
Private Sub BindControls()
    Dim oPubDB As New PubDB()
    dsBookInfo = oPubDB.GetBookInfo
    bsBookInfo.DataSource = dsBookInfo
    bsBookInfo.DataMember = "Books"
    txtTitle.DataBindings.Add("Text", bsBookInfo, "title")
    txtSales.DataBindings.Add("Text", bsBookInfo, "ytd_Sales")
    dtpPubDate.DataBindings.Add("Value", bsBookInfo, "pubdate")
End Sub
```

7. Create a `Form_Load` event handler that calls the `BindControls` method:

```
Private Sub frmBookInfo_Load(ByVal sender As Object, _
          ByVal e As System.EventArgs) Handles MyBase.Load
    BindControls()
End Sub
```

8. Change the startup object of the project to the `frmBookInfo` class.

9. Press the F5 key to run the project in the debugger. After the form loads, you should see the values for the first book record in the controls.

10. After testing, stop the debugger.

11. Switch to the code editor for the `frmBookInfo` class. Add the following button click event handler methods to implement the ability to move through the records:

```
Private Sub btnPrevious_Click(ByVal sender As Object, _
        ByVal e As System.EventArgs) Handles btnPrevious.Click
    bsBookInfo.MovePrevious()
End Sub

Private Sub btnNext_Click(ByVal sender As Object, _
        ByVal e As System.EventArgs) Handles btnNext.Click
    bsBookInfo.MoveNext()
End Sub
```

12. Press the F5 key to run the project in the debugger. After the form loads, test the Next and Prev buttons.

13. After testing, stop the debugger.

Implementing Complex-Bound Controls

To implement complex-bound controls, follow these steps:

1. Add a second form to the project named frmPubBookInfo. Add the following controls to the form and set the properties as listed in Table 11-7. The completed form should look similar to Figure 11-17.

Table 11-7. *frmPubBookInfo Form and Control Property Values*

Control	Property	Value
Form	Name	frmPubBookInfo
	Text	Publisher-Book Information
ComboBox1	Name	cboPubInfo
	DropDownStyle	DropDownList
	Text	[Empty]
DataGridView1	Name	dgvBookInfo
	ReadOnly	True

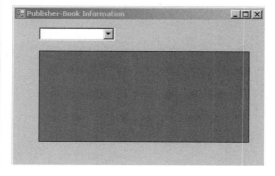

Figure 11-17. *The completed pub book info form*

2. View the code for the GetPubBookInfo method of the PubDB class. This method calls two methods: one that returns a DataSet containing publisher information, and one that returns a DataSet containing book information. The two DataSet objects are merged together, and a DataRelation is added that relates publishers to the books they publish. The merged DataSet is returned to the caller. You will use this to create a master/detail display.

3. Switch to the code editor for the frmPubInfo class. Declare a class-level variable to hold a DataSet and a BindingSource object to bind the controls.

```
Private dsPubBookInfo As DataSet
Private bsPubBookInfo As New BindingSource
```

4. Create a subprocedure called BindControls. This procedure will call the GetPubBookInfo method and store the DataSet returned in a class-level DataSet variable. The ComboBox control's and DataGrid control's DataSource properties are set to the BindingSource. The DisplayMember and ValueMember properties are then set to the appropriate column objects. The DataMember property of the DataGridView is set to the DataRelation that relates the book information to the publisher information:

```
Private Sub BindControls()
    Dim oPubDB As New PubDB()
    dsPubBookInfo = oPubDB.GetPubBookInfo
    bsPubBookInfo.DataSource = dsPubBookInfo
    bsPubBookInfo.DataMember = "Publishers"
    cboPubInfo.DataSource = bsPubBookInfo
    cboPubInfo.ValueMember = "pub_id"
    cboPubInfo.DisplayMember = "pub_name"
    dgvBookInfo.DataSource = bsPubBookInfo
    dgvBookInfo.DataMember = "PubBookKey"
End Sub
```

5. Create a Form_Load event handler that calls the BindControls method:

```
Private Sub frmPubBookInfo_Load(ByVal sender As Object, _
            ByVal e As System.EventArgs) Handles MyBase.Load
    BindControls()
End Sub
```

6. Change the startup object of the project to the frmPubBookInfo class.

7. Press the F5 key to run the project in the debugger. After the form loads, you should see publisher names in the ComboBox and the related books displayed in the DataGrid. Choosing a different publisher in the ComboBox should automatically update the DataGrid with the related book information.

8. After testing, stop the debugger.

Binding to a Business Object

The project contains a PubBO class that creates a collection of Publisher objects and fills them with data retrieved from the database. To bind controls to this collection, follow these steps:

1. Add a third form to the project named frmPubCollection. Add the following controls to the form and set the properties as listed in Table 11-8.

Table 11-8. *frmPubCollection Form and Control Property Values*

Control	Property	Value
Form	Name	frmPubCollection
	Text	Publisher Collection Information
TextBox1	Name	txtPubID
	Text	[Empty]
TextBox2	Name	txtPubName
	Text	[Empty]
Button1	Name	btnNext
	Text	Next
Button2	Name	btnPrevious
	Text	Prev

2. View the code for the Load method of the PubBO class. This populates a collection of Publisher objects.

3. Switch to the code editor for the frmPubInfo class. Declare a class-level variable to hold a DataSet and a BindingSource object to bind the controls.

```
Private bsPubCollection As New BindingSource
```

4. Create a sub procedure called BindControls. This procedure will create a collection of publisher objects and attach it to the BindingSource. The Text properties of the TextBoxes are bound to the properties of the Publishers objects.

```
Private Sub BindControls()
    Dim oPubBO As New PubBO()
    oPubBO.Load()
    bsPubCollection.DataSource = oPubBO
    txtPubID.DataBindings.Add("Text", bsPubCollection, "ID")
    txtPubName.DataBindings.Add("Text", bsPubCollection, "Name")
End Sub
```

5. Create a Form_Load event handler that calls the BindControls method:

```
Private Sub frmPubBookInfo_Load(ByVal sender As Object, _
            ByVal e As System.EventArgs) Handles MyBase.Load
    BindControls()
End Sub
```

6. Change the startup object of the project to the frmPubCollection class.

7. Press the F5 key to run the project in the debugger. After the form loads, you should see the values for the first publisher's record in the controls.

8. After testing, stop the debugger.

9. Switch to the code editor for the frmPubCollection class. Add the following button-click event handler methods to implement the ability to move through the records:

```
Private Sub btnPrevious_Click(ByVal sender As Object, _
        ByVal e As System.EventArgs) Handles btnPrevious.Click
    bsPubCollection.MovePrevious()
End Sub

Private Sub btnNext_Click(ByVal sender As Object, _
        ByVal e As System.EventArgs) Handles btnNext.Click
    bsPubCollection.MoveNext()
End Sub
```

10. Press the F5 key to run the project in the debugger. After the form loads, test the Next and Prev buttons.

11. After testing, stop the debugger.

Creating the OSO Application's Windows Form-Based GUI

In the following sections, you will review the design and code used to build the Windows Form-based GUI for the OSO application. After reviewing the design and code, you will add the forms (which have been prebuilt for you) to the OSO business logic application project and test the user interface.

Displaying Products

The first goal of the user interface is to present information about the products that can be ordered. The product information is presented in a DataGridView control. The user will view products in a particular category by selecting the category in a ComboBox control. Figure 11-18 shows the OSO order form with the controls added. The properties of the form and controls have been set to the values shown in Table 11-9.

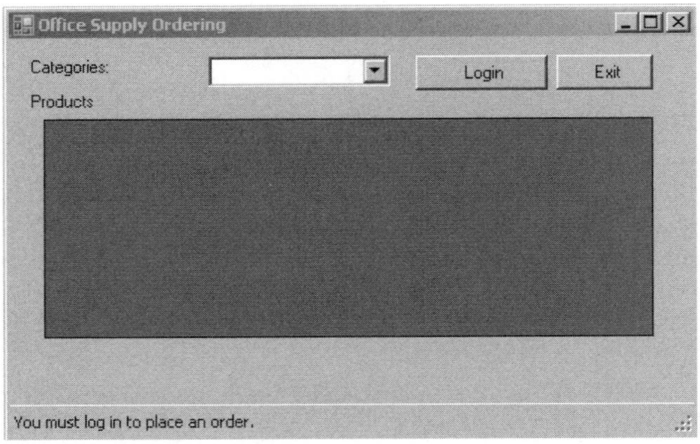

Figure 11-18. *The OSO order form*

Table 11-9. *Order Form and Control Property Values*

Control	Property	Value
Form	Name	frmOrder
	Text	Office Supply Ordering
ComboBox	Name	cboProductCategories
	DropDownStyle	DropDownList
DataGridView	Name	dgvProducts
	ReadOnly	True
	SelectionMode	FullRowSelect
	MultiSelect	False
Label	Text	Categories:
Label	Text	Products:
Button	Name	btnExit
	Text	Exit
Button	Name	btnLogin
	Text	Login
StatusStrip	Name	ssOSO
ToolStripStatusLabel	Name	ssMsg
	Text	You must log in to place an order.

You place the following code at the top of the form class after the Inherits statement. These variables have class-level scope and will be used in the various methods of the form.

```
Private EmployeeID As Integer
Private dsProdCat As DataSet
Private bsProdCat As New BindingSource
Private oOrder As Order
Private oOrderItemDlg As New dlgOrderItem()
Private oLoginDlg As New dlgLogin()
```

A Form_Load event handler creates an instance of the ProductCatalog class and uses its GetProductInfo method to load a local DataSet object. This DataSet is used as the DataSource for the BindingSource of the ComboBox and the DataGridView. The DisplayMember property of the ComboBox is set to the Name column of the Category table contained in the DataSet. The DataMember property of the DataGridView is set to the relation drCat_Prod, which has been defined in the DataSet. By setting the DataMember to the relation, when the user selects a category in the ComboBox, the DataGridView will display the related products.

```
Private Sub frmOrder_Load(ByVal sender As Object, _
        ByVal e As System.EventArgs) Handles MyBase.Load
    Dim oProdCat As New ProductCatalog()
    dsProdCat = oProdCat.getProductInfo
    bsProdCat.DataSource = dsProdCat
    bsProdCat.DataMember = "Category"
```

```
    cboProductCategories.DataSource = bsProdCat
    cboProductCategories.DisplayMember = "Name"

    dgvProducts.DataSource = bsProdCat
    dgvProducts.DataMember = "drCat_Prod"
End Sub
```

The controls for implementing the ordering functionality are placed in a Panel control, which is enabled after the user has logged in. Figure 11-19 shows the order form with the order Panel control added. The properties of the panel and controls have been set to the values in Table 11-10.

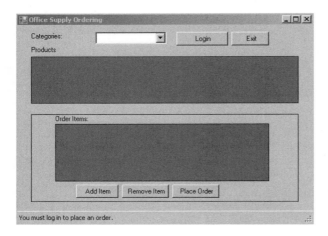

Figure 11-19. *The order Panel control*

Table 11-10. *Order Panel and Control Property Values*

Control	Property	Value
Panel	Name	pnlOrder
	BorderStyle	FixedSingle
	Enabled	False
DataGridView	Name	dgvOrders
	ReadOnly	True
	SelectionMode	FullRowSelect
	MultiSelect	False
Label	Text	OrderItems:
Button	Name	btnAddItem
	Text	Add Item
Button	Name	btnRemoveItem
	Text	Remove Item
Button	Name	btnPlaceOrder
	Text	Place Order

Validating Employees

To implement the employee login functionality, the user is presented with a custom dialog form (see Figure 11-20). The properties of the form and controls have been set to the values in Table 11-11.

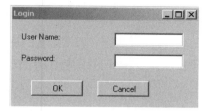

Figure 11-20. *The login dialog form*

Table 11-11. *Login Form and Control Property Values*

Control	Property	Value
Form	Name	dlgLogin
	FormBorderStyle	FixedDialog
	Text	Login
	StartPosition	CenterParent
Label	Name	Label1
	Text	User Name:
Label	Name	Label2
	Text	Password:
TextBox	Name	txtName
	Text	[Blank]
TextBox	Name	txtPassword
	Text	[Blank]
	PasswordChr	*
Button	Name	btnOK
	Text	OK
	DialogResult	OK
Button	Name	btnCancel
	Text	Cancel
	DialogResult	Cancel

The btnLogin_Click event handler displays the Login dialog form and checks the result returned. If the user presses the OK button, then the Login method of the Employee object is called for verification. If the employee is validated, a new instance of the Order class is created and the order controls are enabled. The following code is the complete btnLogin_Click event handler.

```
Private Sub btnLogin_Click(ByVal sender As System.Object, _
            ByVal e As System.EventArgs) Handles btnLogin.Click
    Dim oEmployee As New Employee()
    Dim strUserName As String
    Dim strPassword As String

    If oLoginDlg.ShowDialog(Me) = DialogResult.OK Then
        strUserName = oLoginDlg.txtName.Text
        strPassword = oLoginDlg.txtPassword.Text
        EmployeeID = oEmployee.Login(strUserName, strPassword)
        If EmployeeID > 0 Then
            ssMsg.Text = _
              "You are logged in as employee number " & EmployeeID
            pnlOrder.Enabled = True
            oOrder = New Order()
        Else
            MessageBox.Show _
              ("You could not be verified. Please try again.")
            pnlOrder.Enabled = False
        End If
    End If
End Sub
```

Adding Order Items

When a user clicks the Add Item button, the user is presented with an Order Item dialog box
containing the selected product information. The user then selects the item quantity and clicks
the OK button to add the order item to the order. The Order Item grid is bound to the OrderItem
property of the Order object, which contains an array of OrderItem objects. The following is the
complete btnAddItem_Click event handler code.

```
Private Sub btnAddItem_Click(ByVal sender As Object, _
            ByVal e As System.EventArgs) Handles btnAddItem.Click
    Dim strProdID As String
    Dim dblUnitPrice As Double
    Dim intQuantity As Integer
    Dim selectedRow As DataGridViewRow
    selectedRow = dgvProducts.SelectedRows(0)
    strProdID = CStr(selectedRow.Cells(0).Value)
    dblUnitPrice = CDbl(selectedRow.Cells(4).Value)
    oOrderItemDlg.txtProductID.Text = strProdID
    oOrderItemDlg.txtUnitPrice.Text = dblUnitPrice.ToString
    If oOrderItemDlg.ShowDialog(Me) = DialogResult.OK Then
        intQuantity = oOrderItemDlg.nupQuantity.Value
        oOrder.AddItem _
          (New OrderItem(strProdID, dblUnitPrice,intQuantity))
        Dim bsOrderItems As New BindingSource
```

```
        bsOrderItems.DataSource = oOrder
        bsOrderItems.DataMember = "OrderItems"
        dgvOrders.DataSource = bsOrderItems
End Sub
```

Figure 11-21 shows the Order Item dialog form. The properties of the form and controls have been set to the values shown in Table 11-12.

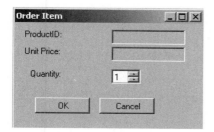

Figure 11-21. *The Order Item dialog form*

Table 11-12. *Order Item Dialog Form and Control Properties*

Control	Property	Value
Form	Name	dlgOrderItem
	FormBorderStyle	FixedDialog
	Text	Order Item
	StartPosition	CenterParent
Label	Name	Label1
	Text	ProductID:
Label	Name	Label2
	Text	Unit Price:
Label	Name	Label3
	Text	Quantity:
TextBox	Name	txtProductID
Control	Property	Value
	Text	[Blank]
	ReadOnly	True
TextBox	Name	txtUnitPrice
	Text	[Blank]
	ReadOnly	True
NumericUpDown	Name	nupQuantity
	Minimum	1
	Maximum	5

(Continued)

Table 11-12. *Continued*

Control	Property	Value
Button	Name	btnOK
	Text	OK
	DialogResult	OK
Button	Name	btnCancel
	Text	Cancel
	DialogResult	Cancel

Removing Items

When a user clicks the Remove Item button, the following event handler passes the ProductID of the item to the RemoveItem method of the Order object. This method removes the OrderItem from the OrderItem array:

```
Private Sub btnRemoveItem_Click(ByVal sender As Object, _
        ByVal e As System.EventArgs) Handles btnRemoveItem.Click
    Dim strProdID As String
    Dim selectedRow As DataGridViewRow
    selectedRow = dgvOrders.SelectedRows(0)
    strProdID = CStr(selectedRow.Cells(1).Value)
    oOrder.RemoveItem(strProdID)
    Dim bsOrderItems As New BindingSource
    bsOrderItems.DataSource = oOrder
    bsOrderItems.DataMember = "OrderItems"
    dgvOrders.DataSource = bsOrderItems
End Sub
```

Placing an Order

When a user is ready to place an order, the btnPlaceOrder_click event handler runs. This method calls the PlaceOrder method of the Order object and displays the OrderNumber returned to the user:

```
Private Sub btnPlaceOrder_Click(ByVal sender As System.Object, _
        ByVal e As System.EventArgs) Handles btnPlaceOrder.Click
    Dim intOrderNumber As Integer
    intOrderNumber = oOrder.PlaceOrder(EmployeeID)
    ssMsg.Text = "The order has been placed. The order number is " _
        & intOrderNumber
End Sub
```

Activity 11-4. Testing the OSO Windows GUI

To test the OSO Windows GUI, follow these steps:

1. Start VS. Select File ➤ Open ➤ Project.

2. Navigate to the OSOBusTier folder and open it.

3. Select the `OSOBusTier` solution file and click Open. The project contains the OSO business logic classes and the test form that you used to test the classes in Chapter 10.

4. Select the project node in the Solution Explorer. Right-click and select Add ➤ Add Existing Item. Navigate to the OSOGUIForms folder and select the `dlgLogin.vb`, `dlgLogin.Designer.vb`, `dlgOrderItem.vb`, `dlgOrderItem.Designer.vb`, `frmOrder.vb`, and the `frmOrder.Designer.vb` files, and click Open.

5. Change the project startup object to `frmOrder`. Press the F5 key to launch the debugger. Verify that the product information is updated in the grid when the category is changed in the ComboBox.

6. Click the Login button and enter a username of `jsmith` and a password of `js`. You should be validated as an employee. Add some items to the order. Place the order and note the `OrderID` value is returned.

7. After testing the OSO Windows GUI, stop the debugger and exit VS.

Summary

In this chapter, you looked at implementing the interface tier of an application. You implemented the user interface through a traditional Windows Forms-based application front end. Along the way, you took a closer look at the classes and namespaces of the .NET Framework used to implement rich Windows Forms-based user interfaces. In the next chapter, you will revisit implementing the UI tier of a .NET application. Instead of implementing the GUI using Windows Forms, you will implement the GUI as an ASP.NET application using Web Forms. Along the way, you will take a closer look at the namespaces available for creating Web-based GUI applications and the techniques involved in implementing the classes contained in these namespaces.

CHAPTER 12

■ ■ ■

Developing Web Applications

In the previous chapter, you looked at developing a "traditional" Windows Form-based graphical user interface (GUI). Although a Windows Form-based interface gives a programmer the ability to easily build an extremely rich user interface, including advanced control functionality, enhanced graphics capabilities, and visual inheritance, it is not always practical to assume users will be able to access your programs through a Windows-based interface. With the proliferation of intranets, the Internet, and mobile devices, many applications need to allow users the ability to access the interface through a variety of browsers. This chapter covers building a Web-based user interface consisting of Web Forms that can be rendered in any HTML-compliant browser. If you experience a sense of *déjà vu* while reading this chapter, it is by design. Microsoft has implemented Web Form interface design and programming using an object model that is remarkably similar to the one used to design and program Windows Form-based interface.

After reading this chapter, you should be familiar with the following:

- How to work with Web Forms and controls

- The inheritance hierarchy of Web Forms and controls

- How to respond to Web Form and control events

- Data binding controls contained in a Web Form

Web Form Fundamentals

An ASP.NET web page contains one or more Web Forms. A Web Form acts as a container for controls with a visual interface for interacting with users of the application. The advantage of a Web Form over a traditional Windows Form is its ability to allow users to interact with programs remotely through any HTML-compliant browser. A Web application can expose its services to a variety of different client configurations using different operating systems and browsers.

A web page consists of two parts: the visual interface and the programming logic. The visual interface consists of a text file containing HTML markup tags, include files, processing directives, and client-side scripting blocks. This text file is given the default extension of .aspx and is referred to as a *page*. It is this page that acts as a container for the text and controls that will be displayed in the browser. Figure 12-1 shows the .aspx file for a Web Form containing a TextBox control, a Button control, and a Label control. When the web page is compiled, the code is combined into a new class file dynamically. This file is then compiled into a new class that inherits from the System.Web.UI.Page class. It is this class code that executes when the .aspx page is requested.

Figure 12-1. *Code contained in the .aspx file*

Looking at the page directive at the top of the page reveals the second piece of the Web Form, which is referred to as the *code-behind file* and is indicated by the .aspx.vb extension. The code-behind file contains a partial class file in which code is placed to handle any necessary events exposed by the page or controls contained within the page. The following class code is contained in the code-behind file linked to the .aspx file of Figure 12-1:

```
Partial Class _Default
    Inherits System.Web.UI.Page

    Protected Sub txtName_TextChanged(ByVal sender As Object, _
      ByVal e As System.EventArgs) Handles txtName.TextChanged

    End Sub

    Protected Sub Page_Load(ByVal sender As Object, _
      ByVal e As System.EventArgs) Handles Me.Load

    End Sub
End Class
```

When a browser requests the Web Form, the page file and the code-behind file combine, along with a partial class generated for the .aspx file, and compile into a single executable Page class file. It is this Page class that intercepts and processes incoming requests. After processing the incoming request, the Page class dynamically creates and sends an HTML response stream back to the browser. Because the Page class is compiled code, execution is much faster than technologies that rely on interpreting script. The Internet Information Services (IIS) Web server is also able to cache the execution code in memory to further increase performance.

Web Server Control Fundamentals

The .NET Framework provides a set of Web server controls specifically for hosting within a Web Form. Developers work with these various controls using the familiar object model associated with Windows Form controls. The types of Web server controls available include common form controls such as a TextBox, Label, and Button, as well as more complex controls such as a GridView and a Calendar. The Web server controls abstract out the HTML coding from the developer. When the Page class sends the response stream to the browser, the Web server control is rendered on the page using the appropriate HTML. The HTML sent to the browser depends on such factors as the browser type and the control settings that have been made.

The following code is used to place a TextBox Web server control in the Web Form:

```
<asp:TextBox ID=""txtName" runat="server" BorderStyle="Dashed"
    ForeColor="#0000C0"></asp:TextBox>
```

The control is then rendered in Internet Explorer (IE) 6.0 as the following HTML code:

```
<input name="txtName" type="text" id="txtName"
style="color:#0000C0;border-style:Dashed;" /></td>
```

If the TextMode property of the TextBox control is set to MultiLine, the code in the web page is altered to reflect the property setting:

```
<asp:TextBox ID="txtName" runat="server" BorderStyle="Dashed" ForeColor="#0000C0"
 TextMode="MultiLine"></asp:TextBox>
```

Although the change in the code for the Web server control was minimal, the HTML code rendered to the browser changes to a completely different HTML control:

```
<textarea name="txtName" rows="0" cols="0" id="txtName"
style="color:#0000C0;border-style:Dashed;"></textarea>
```

Web Forms and Web server controls offer Web programmers many advantages, including a familiar event-driven object model, automatic browser detection with dynamic rendering, data binding capabilities, and automatic control state maintenance, just to name a few.

Understanding Web Page and Web Server Control Inheritance Hierarchy

At the top of the web page interface code contained in the .aspx file is the following page directive:

```
<%@ Page Language="VB" AutoEventWireup="false"
    CodeFile="Default.aspx.vb" Inherits="_Default" %>
```

This code reveals that the web page interface code inherits from the `_Default` code-behind class located in the `Default.aspx.vb` file. The code-behind class in turn inherits from the `Page` class located in the `System.Web.UI` namespace:

```
Partial Class _Default
    Inherits System.Web.UI.Page
```

The `Page` class exposes important functionality needed to program a Web application and interact with the Web server. For example, it enables access to the `Application`, `Session`, `Response`, and `Request` objects. The `Application` object enables sharing of global information across multiple sessions and requests within the Web application. The `Request` object enables the reading of values sent by a client during a Web request. The `Page` class also exposes functionality such as working with `Postback` events initiated by client script, initiating page-level validation, and registration of hidden fields required by server controls.

If you trace the inheritance chain of the web page further, you discover that the `Page` class inherits functionality from the `TemplateControl` class. This class adds support for loading user controls, which are custom controls commonly created to partition and reuse user interface (UI) functionality in several web pages. User controls are created in `.ascx` files and are hosted by the web pages. Along with managing the user controls inserted into a web page, the `TemplateControl` class adds transactional support and error handling functionality to the `Page` class.

The `TemplateControl` class inherits from the `Control` class. The `Control` class exposes much of the functionality needed by all server controls. This class includes important properties such as the `ID` and `Page` properties. The former of these gets and sets the programmatic identifier of a control, and the latter gets a reference to the `Page` object that contains the control. The `Control` class exposes methods for rendering the HTML code for the control and any child controls. There are methods for handling and raising events such as the `Load`, `Unload`, and `PreRender` events. The `Control` class also exposes the functionality needed to add data binding support to Web server controls. Figure 12-2 shows the hierarchy chain of the `Page` class in the Object Browser.

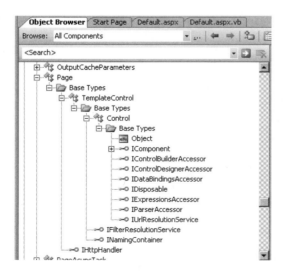

Figure 12-2. *Hierarchy chain of the Page class*

Tracing the hierarchy chain of a Web server control—for example, a TextBox control—reveals that they also gain much of their functionality from the Control class. When you place a TextBox server control on a Web Form, at runtime it instantiates an object instance of the TextBox class, which is part of the System.Web.UI.WebControls namespace. This class exposes properties, methods, and events needed by a TextBox. For example, it defines such properties as the Text, ReadOnly, and Wrap properties. The TextBox class also adds functionality for raising and handling the TextChanged event.

All Web server control classes inherit common functionality from the WebControl class. The WebControl class provides properties that control the look of the control when it gets rendered in the browser. For example, the ForeColor, Backcolor, Height, and Width properties are defined in the WebControl class. It also defines properties that control the behavior of the control such as the Enabled and TabIndex properties. The WebControl class inherits from the Control class discussed previously. Figure 12-3 shows the hierarchy chain of a TextBox Web server control in the Object Browser.

Figure 12-3. *Hierarchy chain of a TextBox control*

Using the VS Web Page Designer

The VS IDE includes an excellent Web Page Designer, which makes designing web pages similar to designing traditional Windows Forms. Using the designer, you can drag and drop controls onto the web page from the Toolbox and set control properties using the Properties window. Figure 12-4 shows a web page being designed in VS.

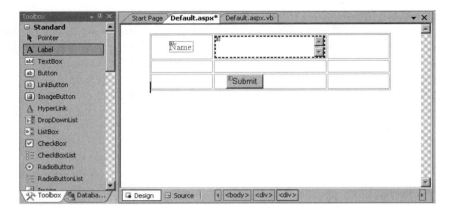

Figure 12-4. *VS Web Page Designer*

Unlike the Windows Form Designer, the Web Page Designer contains two tabs at the bottom of the window—a Design tab and a Source tab. These tabs switch the view in the window from a visual representation of the web page (Design) to the HTML code (Source). The Source view shows the tag markup code used to render the page and allows you to insert client-side script into the page. Figure 12-5 shows a web page displayed in the Source view of the designer.

```
Client Objects & Events                          (No Events)

    <%@ Page Language="VB" AutoEventWireup="false" CodeFile="Default.aspx.vb" Inherits="

    <!DOCTYPE html PUBLIC "-//W3C//DTD XHTML 1.1//EN" "http://www.w3.org/TR/xhtml11/DTD/x

  <html xmlns="http://www.w3.org/1999/xhtml" >
  <head runat="server">
      <title>Untitled Page</title>
  </head>
  <body>
      <form id="form1" runat="server">
      <div>
        <div style="text-align: center">
            <table>
              <tr>
                <td style="width: 100px">
                    <asp:Label ID="Label1" runat="server" Text="Name:" ForeColor=
                <td style="width: 100px">
                    <asp:TextBox ID="txtName" runat="server" BorderStyle="Dashed"
                <td style="width: 100px">
                </td>
              </tr>
              <tr>
                <td style="width: 100px">
                </td>
```

Design | Source   <html> <body> <form#form1> <div> <div> <table> <tr> <td>

Figure 12-5. *VS Web Page Designer in the Source view*

As mentioned previously, the code-behind page contains the code for handling events and adding methods that will be executed on the server before the page is rendered or when it gets posted back to the server. You use the code editor to add the server-side processing code to the web page class. Figure 12-6 shows the code editor displaying the code for a web page class. Looking at the web page class code in the code-behind file reveals a code structure similar to the code in a Windows Form class.

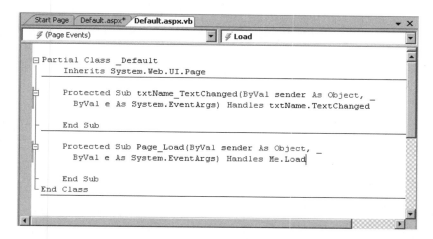

Figure 12-6. *Code editor displaying the code-behind file*

Handling Web Page, Form, and Control Events

Just like their Windows GUI counterparts, Web controls interact with users based on an event-driven model. When an event occurs on the client—for example, a button click—the event information is captured on the client and the information is transmitted to the server via an HTTP post. On the server, the event information is intercepted by an event delegate object, which in turn informs any event handler methods that have subscribed to the invocation list. Although this sounds complicated, the .NET Framework classes abstract and encapsulate most of the process from you.

Adding Page and Server Control Event Handlers

The easiest way to add a web page event handler is to use the drop-down list boxes at the top of the code editor. In the left drop-down box, choose the (Page Events) option. In the right drop-down list, select the event you want to handle, as shown in Figure 12-7.

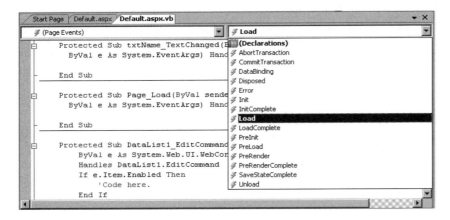

Figure 12-7. *Adding a Page event handler*

Because of the overhead of handling events through postbacks requiring a roundtrip from the browser to the server, only a limited set of events are exposed by Web Forms and server controls. Events that can occur frequently, such as mouse movement and key press events, are not supported through server-side event handlers. (These events are supported through client-side event handlers written in script.)

After choosing the Page event, the code editor inserts an event handler method. The following code shows the event handler method inserted for the Page_Load event:

```
Protected Sub Page_Load(ByVal sender As Object, _
     ByVal e As System.EventArgs) Handles Me.Load
        If IsPostBack Then
            Session("UserName") = txtName.Text
        End If
End Sub
```

The Page_Load event occurs at the beginning of a page request after the controls in the Page have been initialized. This event is often used to read data from and load data into the server controls. The IsPostBack Page property is interrogated to determine whether the page is being viewed for the first time or in response to a Postback event.

You can add Web server control event handlers in a similar fashion. Select the control in the left drop-down list and the event to handle in the right drop-down list, as shown in Figure 12-8.

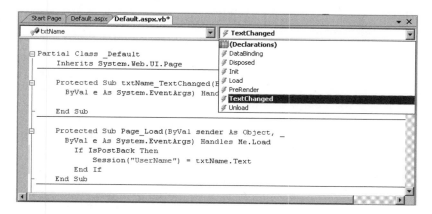

Figure 12-8. *Adding a control event handler*

By convention, the name of the event handler method is the name of the object issuing the event followed by an underscore character and the name of the event (which is similar to Windows Form event handling). The actual name of the event handler, however, is unimportant. It is the handles keyword that adds this method to the invocation list of the event's delegation object.

All event handlers must provide two parameters that will be passed to the method when the event is fired. The first parameter is the sender, which represents the object that initiated the event. The second parameter, e of type System.EventArgs, is an object used to pass any information specific to a particular event. For example, the EditCommand event is raised when the Edit button for an item in a DataList control is clicked. The event argument e passes information about the item being edited in the DataList control. The following code checks to see whether the item selected in the DataList is enabled:

```vb
Private Sub DataList1_EditCommand(ByVal source As Object, _
    ByVal e As System.Web.UI.WebControls.DataListCommandEventArgs) _
    Handles DataList1.EditCommand
    If e.Item.Enabled Then
        'code here
    End If
End Sub
```

Server-Side Event Processing

Because of the overhead of raising events on the browser and handling them on the server, the .NET Framework supports two types of events for server controls. Postback events will cause the immediate posting back of the event to the server for processing. The button-click event is an example of a Postback event. Nonpostback events do not get immediately posted back to the server for processing. Instead, the event message is cached locally until a Postback event occurs. The server then processes the cached events, after which the Postback event is processed. The TextChanged event of a TextBox control and the CheckedChanged event of the CheckBox control are examples of nonpostback events. You can override this behavior by setting the AutoPostBack property of the control to True, in which case the event will cause an immediate postback to the server.

Table 12-1 summarizes the common page processing events that occur when a page is requested or posted back to the browser.

Table 12-1. *Web Page Processing Events*

Event	Typical Uses
Page_Init	The ASP.NET Framework uses this event to restore control properties and post back data.
Page_Load	Performs initial data binding. Reads and updates control properties when postback occurs.
Nonpostback Change events	Any nonpostback change events are processed. The processing does not reflect the order that they occurred in the browser.
Postback Change event	The event that caused the postback is processed.
Page_Unload	Performs any cleanup code. Closes files and database connections. Discards object instances.

Understanding Application and Session Events

Along with the Page and control events, the .NET Framework provides the ability to intercept and respond to events raised when a Web session starts or ends. A Web session starts when a user requests a page from the application and ends when the session is abandoned or times out. In addition to the session events, the .NET Framework exposes several application-level events. Application_Start occurs the first time anyone requests a page in the Web application. Application_BeginRequest occurs when any page or service is requested. Corresponding events fire when ending requests, authenticating users, raising errors, and stopping the application. The session-level and application-level event handlers are placed in the Global.asax page using a script block. Figure 12-9 shows the Global.asax in the code editor.

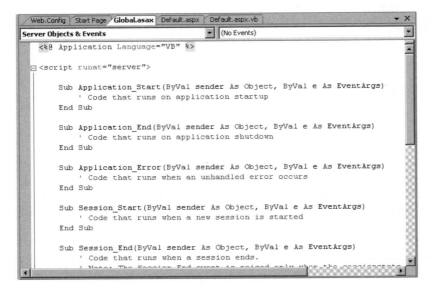

Figure 12-9. *The Global.asax file open in the code editor*

When the application begins, the Global.asax compiles into a dynamically generated class that derives from the HttpApplication base class. This class exposes and defines the methods, properties, and events common to all application objects within an ASP.NET application. A detailed explanation of HttpApplication is beyond the scope of this book. For more information, see the HttpApplication object in the help files.

Activity 12-1. Working with Web Pages and Server Controls

In this activity you will become familiar with the following:

- Creating a Web Form-based GUI application

- Working with page and server control events

Creating the Web Application

To create the web application, follow these steps:

1. Start VS. Select File ➤ New Web Site.

2. Choose an ASP.NET Web Site. Change the name of the web site at the end of the location path to Act12_1. By default, web sites are stored in a folder under the path My Documents\ Visual Studio 2005\WebSites. Figure 12-10 shows the New Web Site dialog box for creating a Web Site or Service.

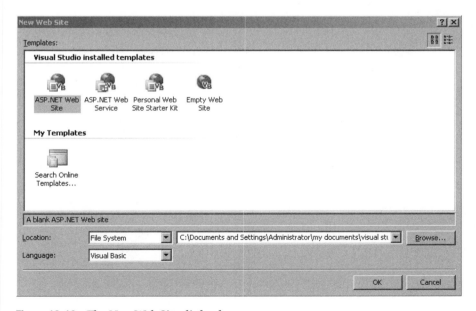

Figure 12-10. *The New Web Site dialog box*

3. Click the OK button in the New Web Site dialog box.

4. After the web site and default files are created, right-click the `Default.aspx` node in the Solution Explorer window and select View Designer. The Toolbox displays the various ASP.NET server controls that can be hosted on the web page, as you see in Figure 12-11.

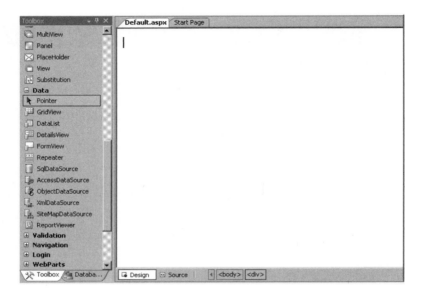

Figure 12-11. *The Web Page Designer Toolbox*

5. Select LayOut ➤ Position ➤ Auto-Position options. In the Options dialog box, change the Positioning Options to Absolutely Positioned as shown in Figure 12-12. This will allow you to position the controls on the page by dragging them with the mouse.

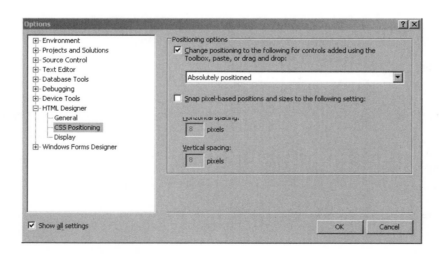

Figure 12-12. *The Options dialog box*

6. Add the controls (located under the Standard tab in the Toolbox) listed in Table 12-2 to the web page and set the properties of the controls using the Properties window. Figure 12-13 shows the completed page in the Web Page Designer.

Table 12-2. *Web Control Properties*

Control	Property	Value
Label	id	lblMessage
	Text	Hello Stranger
	Font-Size	X-Large
Label	id	Label1
	Text	Enter your name:
TextBox	id	txtName
	Text	[Blank]
Button	id	btnSubmit
	Text	Submit

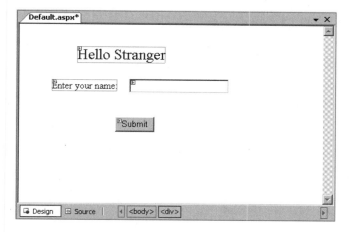

Figure 12-13. *The Completed web page*

7. Click the Source tab at the bottom of the Web Page Designer. The tags used to render the page are displayed in the designer. Notice the various ASP.NET controls you added to the form contain an asp prefix. They also contain a runat server attribute.

8. Press F5 to launch the page in the debugger. A warning dialog box asks if you want to enable debugging (see Figure 12-14). Enable debugging and click OK. When the page launches, enter your name in the TextBox and click the Submit button. The page will post to the server and redisplay in your browser. Because ASP.NET controls maintain their view state by default, your name still displays in the TextBox after the postback.

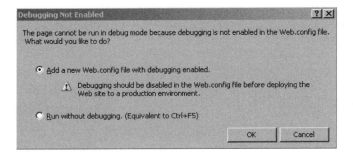

Figure 12-14. *The warning dialog box*

9. In the browser, choose View ➤ Source. The source code for the page is displayed in Notepad. Notice that the ASP.NET controls render using standard HTML tags. A hidden control named __VIEWSTATE tracks the view state information of the controls on the form.

10. Close the browser window and Notepad.

Creating Server-Side Control Event Handlers

To create server-side control event handlers, follow these steps:

1. In the Solution Explorer, select the Default.aspx node. At the top of window, click the View Code button to display the code-behind class for the page.

2. Using the drop-down lists at the top of the code editor, add a Page_Load event handler method. In this event handler procedure, check to see whether the page request is the result of a postback. If it is, change the lblMessage text to say hello using the text contained in the txtName control.

```
Private Sub Page_Load(ByVal sender As System.Object, _
        ByVal e As System.EventArgs) Handles Me.Load
    If IsPostBack Then
        lblMessage.Text = "Hello " & txtName.Text
    End If
End Sub
```

3. Press F5 to launch the page in debug mode. When the page displays in the browser, enter your name and click the Submit button. Verify that the page redisplays with your name included in the Hello... message. After testing, close the browser.

4. Switch to the code editor for the Default page. Remove the code in the Page_Load event handler. In the left drop-down list at the top of the code editor, select the btnSubmit control. In the right drop-down list, select the Click event.

5. Add the following code to display the user's name in the message to the btnSubmit_Click event procedure:

```
Private Sub btnSubmit_Click(ByVal sender As Object, _
    ByVal e As System.EventArgs)  Handles btnSubmit.Click
        lblMessage.Text = "Hello " & txtName.Text
End Sub
```

6. Add the following code to display an abort message and clear the txtName text to the btnCancel_Click event procedure:

```
Private Sub btnCancel_Click(ByVal sender As Object, _
    ByVal e As  System.EventArgs) Handles btnCancel.Click
        lblMessage.Text = "Login Canceled"
        txtName.Text = ""
End Sub
```

7. Press F5 to launch the page in debug mode. When the page is displayed in the browser, enter your name and click the Submit button. Verify that the page displays with your name included in the Hello... message. Now click the Cancel button. Verify that the page redisplays with the cancel message and the text in the txtName control is cleared. After testing, close the browser.

Creating Nonpostback Server Control Events

To create nonpostback server control events, follow these steps:

1. Switch to the Page Designer for the Default page. Add a RadioButtonList control to the page. Change the ID property to rblFontColor. Click the Items collection in the Properties window to display the ListItem Collection Editor dialog box. Add a Black item and a Red item to the list as shown in Figure 12-15.

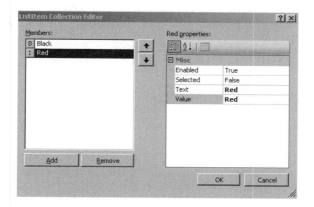

Figure 12-15. *The ListItem Collection Editor dialog box*

2. Switch to the code editor for the Default page. In the left drop-down list at the top of the code editor, select the rblFontColor control. In the right drop-down list, select the SelectedIndexChanged event. Add the following code to change the font color of the lblMessage control in the event handler:

```
Private Sub rblFontColor_SelectedIndexChanged(ByVal sender As Object, _
    ByVal e As System.EventArgs) Handles rblFontColor.SelectedIndexChanged
        If rblFontColor.SelectedItem.Text = "Red" Then
            lblMessage.ForeColor = System.Drawing.Color.Red
        Else
            lblMessage.ForeColor = System.Drawing.Color.Black
        End If
End Sub
```

3. Press F5 to launch the page in debug mode. When the page displays in the browser, click the Red radio button. Notice that the event does not cause a postback to occur. This event will queue until an `AutoPostBack` event triggers a postback.

4. Enter your name in the txtName control and click the Submit button. When the postback is processed, both the `SelectedIndexChanged` event of `rblFontColor` and the `Click` event of the Submit button are processed. After testing, close the browser.

5. Exit VS.

■Note This chapter has explored only server-side event handling. If the browser supports client-side scripting and Dynamic HTML, you can add code to `.aspx` pages to take advantage of the client-side processing capabilities.

Storing and Sharing State in a Web Application

Web applications use a stateless protocol (HTTP) to communicate between the browser and the server. In most Web applications, however, some sort of state maintenance needs to exist during a user's session. Traditionally, maintaining state efficiently has been challenging for Web programmers. To help alleviate the challenge of state management, the .NET Framework provides several options to manage state on both the client and the server.

Maintaining View State

One type of state management that needs to occur in a Web application is the preservation of control property values when a form posts back to the client. Because a web page is re-created and destroyed each time the page is requested, any changes to a control made by the client are lost when the page is posted back. For example, any information entered into a TextBox control would be lost when posted back. To overcome this type of state loss, the server controls have a `ViewState` property, which provides a dictionary object used to retain the value of the control between postbacks. When a page is processed, the current state of the page and the controls are hashed into a string and saved as a hidden field on the page. During a postback, the values are retrieved and restored when the controls are initialized for rendering of the page back to the browser. The following code shows the ViewState hidden control that gets rendered to the browser:

```
<input type="hidden" name="__VIEWSTATE"
value="dDw1Njg2NjE2ODY7O2w8XNOMTowOz4+upC3lZ6nNLX/ShtpGHJAmi8mpH4=" />
```

Using Cookies

You can use *cookies* to store small amounts of data in a text file located on the client device. The `HttpResponse` class's `Cookie` property provides access to the `Cookies` collection, which contains cookies transmitted by the client to the server in the `Cookies` header. This collection contains cookies originally generated on the server and transmitted to the client in the `Set-Cookie` header. Because the browser can only send cookie data to the server that originally created the cookie, and cookie information can be encrypted before being sent to the browser, it is a fairly secure way of maintaining user data. A common use for cookies is to send a user identity token to the client that can be retrieved the next time the user visits the site. This token is then used to retrieve client-specific information from a database. The use of cookies is a good way to maintain client state between visits to the site. In the following code, a Cookie object is first created to hold the date and time of the user's visit and then added to the Cookies collection and sent to the browser:

```
Dim VisitDate As New HttpCookie("VisitDate")
Dim CurrentDate As Date = Date.Today
VisitDate.Value = CurrentDate.ToShortDateString
VisitDate.Expires = CurrentDate.AddMonths(1)
Response.Cookies.Add(VisitDate)
```

Maintaining Session and Application State

Another type of state management often needed in Web applications is session state. *Session state* is the ability to maintain information pertinent to users as they request the various pages within a Web application. Session state is maintained on the server and is provided by an object instance of the HttpSessionState class. This class provides access to session state values and session-level settings for the Web application. Session state values are stored in a key-value dictionary structure only accessible by the current browser session. The following code uses the Session object to store a validated attribute for the current user in a session key-value pair. The intrinsic Session object exposes an object instance of the HttpSessionState class:

```
Sub btnLogin_Click(ByVal Sender As Object, ByVal E As EventArgs) _
  Handles btnLogin.Click
    Dim EmployeeId As Integer
    Dim oEmployee As New Employee()
    'Attempt to Validate User Credentials
    EmployeeId = oEmployee.Login(txtUserName.Value, txtPassword.Value)

    If EmployeeId > 0 Then
        Session("isValid") = True
    Else ' Login failed
        Session("isValid") = False
        spnInfo.InnerHtml = "Login Failed!"
    End If
End Sub
```

Although session state is scoped on a per-session basis, there are times a Web application needs to share a state among all sessions in the application. You can achieve this globally scoped state using an object instance of the HttpApplicationState class. The application state is stored in a key-value dictionary structure similar to the session state, except that it is available to all sessions and from all forms in the application. The first time a client requests any URL resource from the Web application, a single instance of an HttpApplicationState class is created, which is exposed through the intrinsic Application object. The following code uses the Application object to store a connection string attribute for a SqlConnection object:

```
Dim PubsConnectionString As String
PubsConnectionString = "Integrated Security=SSPI;Initial Catalog=pubs;" _
      & "Data Source=localhost"
Application("PubsConnectionString") = PubsConnectionString
```

■**Note** Application state can also be stored in a cache using the Cache class in the System.Web.Caching namespace.

Data Binding Web Controls

Just as with traditional Windows Form-based GUIs, programs developed using a Web Form-based GUI need to interact with data. Users of business applications need to view, query, and update data held in a backend data store. The .NET Framework exposes the functionality needed to implement data binding in Web Forms. Although the end result of data binding in Web Forms and Windows Forms looks similar, the mechanisms for achieving the data binding are not.

You can use two types of data binding in Web Forms: simple binding or complex binding. Controls such as the TextBox, Label, and CheckBox are used for simple binding and display one value from one record at a time. Controls such as the Repeater, DataList, and GridView use complex binding to display multiple fields of multiple records at the same time. Because of the nature of the Web, it is often not practical to use simple data binding to bind fields to a data source and then loop through the records using command buttons (see Figure 12-16).

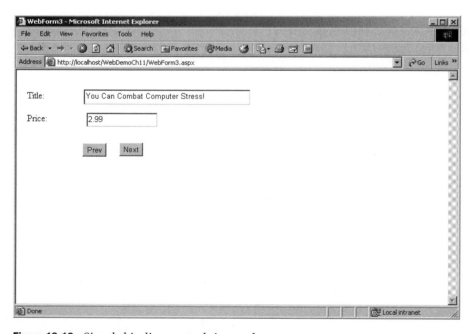

Figure 12-16. *Simple binding controls in a web page*

In this scenario, moving between records would cause a Postback event to occur. During this postback, the data source needs to be regenerated, which is not an efficient way to view data over a Web connection.

Multivalue Data Binding

The GridView, DataList, and Repeater Web server controls have been specially designed to efficiently perform data binding. The GridView control displays the records of a data source as an HTML table. To bind data for display in the GridView, the DataSource property is set to a DataSource object. The DataSource object abstracts the underlying attributes of the data structure, providing a common interface for the various data sources. Table 12-3 lists the types of DataSources provided by the .NET Framework.

Table 12-3. *DataSource Types in the .NET Framework*

DataSource	Use
AccessDataSource	Interacts with data held in an Access database
SqlDataSource	Specifies database products that have a corresponding ADO.NET database provider
ObjectDataSource	Indicates objects that support the IEnumerable interface
XmlDataSource	Specifies data stored in XML files
SiteMapDataSource	Binds to a site map XML file

The ObjectDataSource can bind to any object instance method that returns a type that supports the IEnumerable interface, such as a DataTable, DataView, DataRow, ArrayList, DataReader, Collection, or an ArrayList. This is useful when you need to bind to the business objects defined in the application. The following code demonstrates binding a GridView to an ObjectDataSource. The SelectMethod of the ObjectDataSource is set to the GetAuthors method of the Author business object.

```
<asp:GridView ID="GridView1" runat="server" AutoGenerateColumns="True"
        DataSourceID="odsAuthors" Style="z-index: 100; left: 7px;
            position: absolute; top: 8px">
 </asp:GridView>
 <asp:ObjectDataSource ID="odsAuthors" runat="server"
            SelectMethod="GetAuthors" TypeName="DALDemo.Author">
 </asp:ObjectDataSource>
```

The GetAuthors method returns a DataSet containing author information, as you can see in the code that follows:

```
Public Function GetAuthors() As DataSet
    Try
        Using cnPubs As New SqlConnection()
            cnPubs.ConnectionString = _
              ("Integrated Security=True;Data Source=LocalHost;" & _
               "Initial Catalog=Pubs")
            Dim strSQL As String
```

```
            Dim oSelCmd As SqlCommand
            strSQL = "Select au_id, au_lname, au_fname from authors"
            oSelCmd = New SqlCommand(strSQL, cnPubs)
            daPubs = New SqlDataAdapter()
            daPubs.SelectCommand = oSelCmd
            dsPubs = New DataSet()
            daPubs.Fill(dsPubs, "Authors")
            Return dsPubs
        End Using
    Catch ex As Exception
        Return Nothing
    End Try
End Function
```

Figure 12-17 shows the GridView displayed in IE 6.0. The ObjectDataSource automatically handles creating an instance of the object before the call to the SelectMethod and destruction of the object after the call.

au_id	au_lname	au_fname
648-92-1872	Blotchet-Halls	KD
409-56-7008	Blue	Abraham
238-95-7766	Clark	Cheryl
722-51-5454	DeFrance	Michel
712-45-1867	del Castillo	Innes
427-17-2319	Dull	Ann
213-46-8915	Green	Marjorie
527-72-3246	Greene	Morningstar
472-27-2349	Gringlesby	Burt
846-92-7186	Hunter	Sheryl
756-30-7391	Karsen	Livia
486-29-1786	Locksley	Charlene
724-80-9391	MacFeather	Stearns
893-72-1158	McBadden	Heather
267-41-2394	O'Leary	Michael
807-91-6654	Panteley	Sylvia
998-72-3567	Ringer	Albert
899-46-2035	Ringer	Anne
341-22-1782	Smith	Meander
274-80-9391	Straight	Dean
724-08-9931	Stringer	Dirk
172-32-1176	White	User 2
672-71-3249	Yokomoto	Akiko

Figure 12-17. *Binding a GridView control*

The appearance of the GridView control is highly customizable; you have the ability to change the color, font, and alignment of the rows. You can add a header and footer to the GridView as well as control the appearance of alternating and selected rows in the grid. Figure 12-18 shows the same GridView displayed in Figure 12-17 with custom formatting applied.

au_id	au_lname	au_fname
648-92-1872	Blotchet-Halls	KD
409-56-7008	Blue	Abraham
238-95-7766	Clark	Cheryl
722-51-5454	DeFrance	Michel
712-45-1867	del Castillo	Innes
427-17-2319	Dull	Ann
213-46-8915	Green	Marjorie
527-72-3246	Greene	Morningstar
472-27-2349	Gringlesby	Burt
846-92-7186	Hunter	Sheryl

1 2 3

Figure 12-18. *Formating applied to a GridView control*

Updating Data in a GridView Control

To allow users to update data in the GridView control, the object you are binding to must implement an update method. The UpdateMethod property of the ObjectDataSource is set to the method. The AutoGenerateEditButton property of the GridView control is set to True. The following code demonstrates creating an editable GridView control bound to the Author business object.

```
<asp:GridView ID="GridView1" runat="server" AutoGenerateColumns="False"
    AutoGenerateEditButton="True" DataKeyNames="au_id" DataSourceID="odsAuthors"
    Style="z-index: 100; left: 195px; position: absolute; top: 17px">
        <Columns>
            <asp:BoundField DataField="au_id" ReadOnly="True" HeaderText="ID" />
            <asp:BoundField DataField="au_lname" HeaderText="Last Name" />
            <asp:BoundField DataField="au_fname" HeaderText="First Name" />
        </Columns>
</asp:GridView>
<asp:ObjectDataSource ID="odsAuthors" runat="server" SelectMethod="GetAuthors"
    TypeName="DALDemo.Author" UpdateMethod="UpdateAuthor">
</asp:ObjectDataSource>
```

The UpdateAuthor method that follows is used to update the data. Figure 12-19 shows the grid in edit mode.

```
Public Sub UpdateAuthor(ByVal original_au_id As String, _
    ByVal au_lname As String, ByVal au_fname As String)
```

```
        Try
            Using cnPubs As New SqlConnection()
                cnPubs.ConnectionString = _
                  ("Integrated Security=True;Data Source=LocalHost;" & _
                   "Initial Catalog=Pubs")
                Dim strSQL As String
                Dim cmdUpdate As SqlCommand
                strSQL = "Update authors set au_lname = @au_lname, au_fname = " _
                                    & "@au_fname where au_id = @au_id"
                cmdUpdate = New SqlCommand(strSQL, cnPubs)
                cmdUpdate.Parameters.AddWithValue("@au_id", original_au_id)
                cmdUpdate.Parameters.AddWithValue("@au_lname", au_lname)
                cmdUpdate.Parameters.AddWithValue("@au_fname", au_fname)
                cnPubs.Open()
                cmdUpdate.ExecuteNonQuery()
                cnPubs.Close()
            End Using
        Catch ex As Exception
            'Error handler code
        End Try
    End Sub
```

	ID	Last Name	First Name
Edit	648-92-1872	Blotchet-Halls	KD
Edit	409-56-7008	Blue	Aqua
Update Cancel	238-95-7766	Clark	Cheryl
Edit	722-51-5454	DeFrance	Michel
Edit	712-45-1867	del Castillo	Innes
Edit	427-17-2319	Dull	Ann
Edit	213-46-8915	Green	Marjorie
Edit	527-72-3246	Greene	Morningstar
Edit	472-27-2349	Gringlesby	Burt
Edit	846-92-7186	Hunter	Sheryl

Figure 12-19. *GridView in edit mode*

When the user clicks the Update button, the ObjectDataSource calls the update method and passes the parameters from the GridView control. The GridView control automatically creates the parameters from the updatable BoundFields. It also passes in any parameters defined in the DataKeyNames property. These parameters are tagged as original to indicate that they are the unedited versions of the column. The ObjectDataSource and GridView controls support inserting and deleting data using a similar process.

Activity 12-2. Binding a GridView Control

In this activity, you will become familiar with the following:

- Investigating data binding to a GridView control
- Implementing data updating using a GridView control

Displaying Data in an ASP.NET GridView Control

To display data in an ASP.NET GridView control, follow these steps:

1. Start VS. Select File ➤ Open ➤ Project.

2. Navigate to the `Act12_1.sln` file and click Open.

3. Right-click the `Act12_1` project node in the Solution Explorer. In the pop-up menu that appears, choose Add New Item. Add a new class to the project called `dbAuthorInfo` that will encapsulate the retrieval of author information from the Pubs database. You will get a dialog box asking whether you want to add the class to the `App_Code` folder, as shown in Figure 12-20. Click the Yes button.

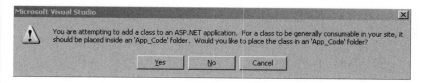

Figure 12-20. *Adding a class to the App_Code folder*

4. Add an Imports statement at the top of the class file to import the `System.Data` namespace.

```
Imports System.Data

Public Class dbAuthorInfo

End Class
```

5. Add the following function to the class that returns a `DataSet` to the client containing author information. Select Build ➤ Build Solution.

```
Public Function GetAuthorInfo() As DataSet
    Dim cn As New SqlClient.SqlConnection _
            ("Integrated Security=True;Data Source=LocalHost;" & _
                "Initial Catalog=Pubs")
    Dim da As New SqlClient.SqlDataAdapter _
            ("Select au_id, au_lname, au_fname, contract from authors", cn)
    Dim ds As New DataSet()
    da.Fill(ds, "Authors")
    Return ds
End Function
```

6. Right-click the `Act12_1` project node in the Solution Explorer window. In the pop-up menu that appears, choose Add New Item. In the Add New Item dialog box, select the Web Form template. Name the Web Form `AuthorInfo.aspx` and click Add. Using the Web Page Designer, add an ObjectDataSource control to the form from the Data tab of the Toolbox. Select Configure DataSource from the ObjectDataSource Tasks pop-up menu.

7. In the Configure DataSource dialog box, select the `dbAuthorInfo` class as the business object as shown in Figure 12-21 and click Next.

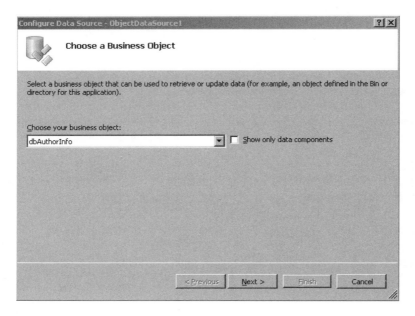

Figure 12-21. *Configuring a DataSource*

8. On the Select tab, choose the `GetAuthorInfo` method as shown in Figure 12-22 and click Finish.

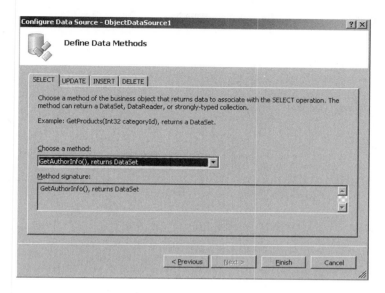

Figure 12-22. *Choosing the select method*

9. Add a GridView control to the form from the Data tab of the Toolbox. Select ObjectDataSource1 as the DataSource in the GridView Tasks pop-up menu (see Figure 12-23).

Figure 12-23. *GridView Tasks pop-up menu*

10. Select the Source tab at the bottom of the Web Page Designer. Review the following code, which was inserted by the designer:

```
<asp:ObjectDataSource ID="ObjectDataSource1" runat="server"
     SelectMethod="GetAuthorInfo" TypeName="dbAuthorInfo">
</asp:ObjectDataSource>

<asp:GridView ID="GridView1" runat="server" DataSourceID="ObjectDataSource1"
    Style="z-index: 100; left: 15px; position: absolute; top: 1px">
</asp:GridView>
```

11. Right-click the `AuthorInfo.aspx` node in the Solution Explorer and choose Set as Start Page.

12. Press the F5 key to run the project in the debugger. After the page loads in the browser, you should see the author information displayed in an HTML table like the one in Figure 12-24.

au_id	au_lname	au_fname	contract
172-32-1176	White	User 2	☑
213-46-8915	Green	Marjorie	☑
238-95-7766	Clark	Dan	☑
267-41-2394	O'Leary	Michael	☑
274-80-9391	Straight	Dean	☑
341-22-1782	Smith	Meander	☐
409-56-7008	Blue	Aqua	☑
427-17-2319	Dull	Ann	☑
472-27-2349	Gringlesby	Burt	☑
486-29-1786	Locksley	Charlene	☑
527-72-3246	Greene	Morningstar	☐
648-92-1872	Blotchet-Halls	KD	☑
672-71-3249	Yokomoto	Akiko	☑
712-45-1867	del Castillo	Innes	☑
722-51-5454	DeFrance	Michel	☑
724-08-9931	Stringer	Dirk	☐
724-80-9391	MacFeather	Stearns	☑
756-30-7391	Karsen	Livia	☑

Figure 12-24. *Displaying author information*

13. After testing, close the browser.

Updating Data Using the ASP.NET GridView Control

To update data using the ASP.NET GridView control, follow these steps:

1. Right-click the `AuthorInfo.aspx` node in the Solution Explorer and choose View Designer.

2. Select GridView1 in the drop-down list at the top of the Properties window. In the Columns property, click the ellipsis (...) to launch the Fields dialog box, shown in Figure 12-25.

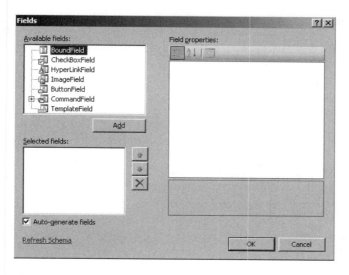

Figure 12-25. *The Fields dialog box*

3. Uncheck the Auto-Generate Fields checkbox.

4. Expand the `CommandField` node in the Available Fields list. Select the Edit, Update, Cancel field and add it to the Selected Fields list as shown in Figure 12-26.

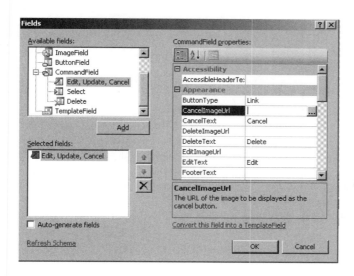

Figure 12-26. *Adding fields*

5. In the Available Fields list, select the `BoundField` node and add it to the Selected Fields list. Set the `BoundField` properties to the values in Table 12-4.

Table 12-4. *BoundField Property Values*

Property	Value
HeaderText	Author ID
DataField	au_id
ReadOnly	True

6. Repeat step 5 to add another BoundField with the properties in Table 12-5.

Table 12-5. *The Next BoundField Property Values*

Property	Value
HeaderText	Last Name
DataField	au_lname
ReadOnly	False

7. Close the Fields editor in the Properties window. Enter a value of au_id for the DataKeyNames property of GridView1.

8. Double-click the dbAuthorInfo.vb node in the Solution Explorer to bring up the code editor. Add the following method to update author information and build the solution:

```
Public Sub UpdateAuthor(ByVal original_au_id As String, _
    ByVal au_lname As String)
  Try
      Using cnPubs As New SqlClient.SqlConnection()
          cnPubs.ConnectionString = _
            ("Integrated Security=True;Data Source=LocalHost;" & _
             "Initial Catalog=Pubs")
          Dim strSQL As String
          Dim cmdUpdate As SqlClient.SqlCommand
          strSQL = "Update authors set au_lname = @au_lname" _
                              & " where au_id = @au_id"
          cmdUpdate = New SqlClient.SqlCommand(strSQL, cnPubs)
          cmdUpdate.Parameters.AddWithValue("@au_id", original_au_id)
          cmdUpdate.Parameters.AddWithValue("@au_lname", au_lname)
          cnPubs.Open()
          cmdUpdate.ExecuteNonQuery()
          cnPubs.Close()
      End Using
  Catch ex As Exception
      'Error handler code
  End Try
End Sub
```

9. In the Properties window, select the ObjectDataSource1 control in the top drop-down list. Enter a value of `UpdateAuthor` for the `UpdateMethod` property.

10. Press F5 to view the page in the browser. You should see the grid with Edit buttons displayed in the first column. Click the Edit button. Change the last name value and click Update. After testing, close the browser.

Creating the OSO Application's Web-Based GUI

Now that you have a basic understanding of how Web Forms and server controls are used to construct a Web-based GUI, you are ready to review the user interface for the OSO application.

Displaying Products

The first goal of the user interface is to present information about the products that can be ordered. The product information is presented in a DataGrid Web server control. The user will view products in a particular category by selecting that category in a DropDownList server control. `OrderForm.aspx` hosts the Web Form and server controls.

The properties of the server controls are set as shown in Table 12-6.

Table 12-6. *Server Control Property Values*

Control	Property	Value
ObjectDataSource	id	odsCategories
	TypeName	ProductCatalog
	SelectMethod	GetCategories
ObjectDataSource	id	odsProducts
	TypeName	ProductCatalog
	SelectMethod	GetProducts
	SelectParameters	
	Name	CatID
	ControlID	ddlCategories
	PropertyName	SelectedValue
	Type	int32
DropDownList	id	ddlCategories
	AutoPostBack	True
	runat	server
GridView	id	dgvProducts
	runat	server
	DataSourceID	odsProducts
	AutoGenerateColumns	False

Table 12-7 shows the properties to which the DataGrid columns are set.

Table 12-7. *Column Property Values*

Column	Property	Value
0	Type	CommandField
	ButtonType	Link
	SelectText	Add To Order
	ShowSelectButton	True
1	Type	BoundField
	DataField	ProductID
	HeaderText	Product ID
2	Type	BoundField
	DataField	Name
	HeaderText	Name
3	Type	BoundField
	DataField	Descript
	HeaderText	Description
4	Type	BoundField
	DataField	UnitCost
	HeaderText	Unit Cost

Figure 12-27 shows how the page will be displayed in the browser (IE6). When a new category is selected in the DropDownList, a postback occurs. During the postback, the value of the selected item is passed as the selection parameter to the odsProducts control. The odsProduct control calls the select method passing this parameter. The select method passes back a datatable, which is automatically bound to the dgvProducts control.

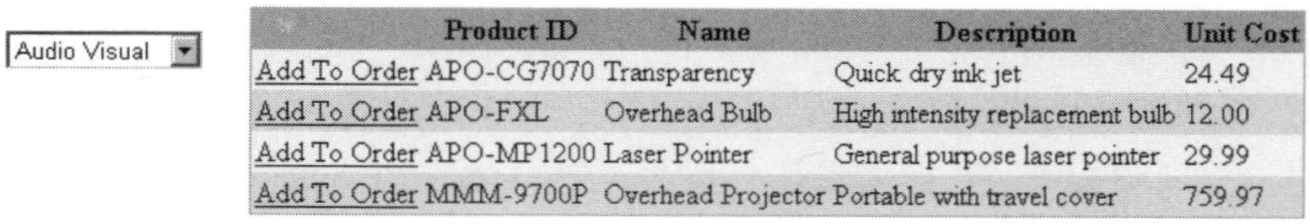

Figure 12-27. *Displaying products in IE6*

Initiating an Order

When a user clicks the Add to Order link, a postback occurs and a server-side SelectedIndexChanged event handler executes. It checks to see whether the value of Session("EmployeeID") has been set; if not, it redirects the user to a login page.

```
If IsNothing(Session("EmployeeID")) Then
    Response.Redirect("Login.aspx")
...
```

■**Note** This functionality could also be implemented using the Forms Authentication service of ASP.NET.

Validating Employees

To implement the employee login functionality, the user is presented with a login.aspx page, shown in Figure 12-28.

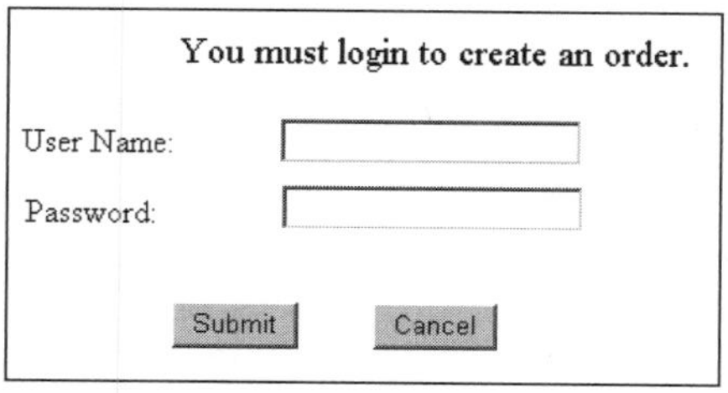

Figure 12-28. *The login page*

The properties of the Web Form controls have been set to the values shown in Table 12-8.

Table 12-8. *Control Property Values*

Control	Property	Value
Label	id	lblMessage
	Text	You must login to create an order.
Label	id	Label1
	Text	User Name:
Label	id	Label2
	Text	Password:
TextBox	id	txtUserName
	Text	[Blank]
TextBox	id	txtPassword
	Text	[Blank]
	TextMode	Password
Button	id	btnSubmit
	Text	Submit
Button	id	btnCancel
	Text	Cancel

In the btnSubmit_Click event handler, the Login method of the Employee object is called for verification. If the employee is validated, the Session("EmployeeID") value is set, and the user is redirected back to the OrderForm.aspx:

```
Private Sub btnSubmit_Click(ByVal sender As System.Object, _
    ByVal e As System.EventArgs) Handles btnSubmit.Click
        Dim oEmployee As New Employee()
        Dim strUserName As String
        Dim strPassword As String
        Dim EmployeeID As Integer

        strUserName = txtUserName.Text
        strPassword = txtPassword.Text
        EmployeeID = oEmployee.Login(strUserName, strPassword)
        If EmployeeID > 0 Then
            Session("EmployeeID") = EmployeeID
            Response.Redirect("OrderForm.aspx")
        Else
            lblMessage.Text = "You could not be verified. Please try again."
        End If
End Sub
```

Adding Order Items

A Button, Label, and DataGrid ASP.NET control are added to the OrderForm.aspx page. The properties of the server controls are set as shown in Table 12-9.

Table 12-9. *Server Control Property Values*

Control	Property	Value
Button	id	btnPlaceOrder
	Text	Place Order
	Enabled	False
Label	id	lblMessage
	Text	[Blank]
DataGrid	id	dgvOrderItems
	runat	server
	AutoGenerateColumns	False

The properties of DataGrid columns are set as shown in Table 12-10.

Table 12-10. *DataGrid Column Property Values*

Column	Property	Value
0	Type	BoundField
	DataField	ProductID
	HeaderText	Product ID
1	Type	BoundField
	DataField	UnitPrice
	HeaderText	Unit Price
2	Type	BoundField
	DataField	Quantity
	HeaderText	Quantity
3	Type	CommandField
	SelectText	Remove
	ShowSelectButton	True

When a user clicks the Add to Order button after logging in, an Order object is created. The item selected is added to the OrderItem collection of the Order object. Instead of binding the DataGridView to an ObjectDataSource control, the dgvOrderItem grid is bound to the OrderItem collection, as shown in here:

```
Protected Sub dgvProducts_SelectedIndexChanged _
    (ByVal sender As Object, ByVal e As System.EventArgs) _
    Handles dgvProducts.SelectedIndexChanged
    If IsNothing(Session("EmployeeID")) Then
        Response.Redirect("Login.aspx")
    End If

    If Not IsNothing(Session("Order")) Then
        oOrder = CType(Session("Order"), Order)
    Else
        oOrder = New Order()
    End If
    ' Get the currently selected row using the SelectedRow property.
    Dim gvProducts As GridView = CType(sender, GridView)
    Dim row As GridViewRow = gvProducts.SelectedRow

    Dim ProductID As String = row.Cells(1).Text
    Dim UnitPrice As String = row.Cells(4).Text

    oOrder.AddItem(New OrderItem(ProductID, CDbl(UnitPrice), 1))

    BindOrderGrid()
    gvProducts.SelectedIndex = -1
End Sub
```

```
Private Sub BindOrderGrid()
        dgvOrderItems.DataSource = oOrder.OrderItems
        dgvOrderItems.DataBind()
        Session("Order") = oOrder
        If oOrder.OrderItems.Count > 0 Then
            btnPlaceOrder.Enabled = True
        Else
            btnPlaceOrder.Enabled = False
        End If
        dgvOrderItems.SelectedIndex = -1
End Sub
```

Figure 12-29 shows the Web order form with order items in the grid.

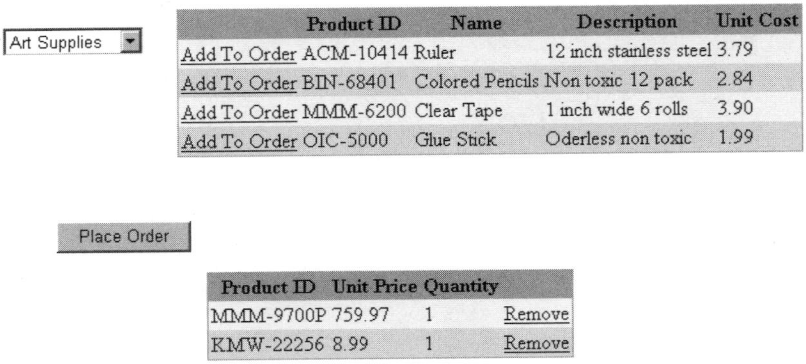

	Product ID	Name	Description	Unit Cost
Art Supplies				
Add To Order	ACM-10414	Ruler	12 inch stainless steel	3.79
Add To Order	BIN-68401	Colored Pencils	Non toxic 12 pack	2.84
Add To Order	MMM-6200	Clear Tape	1 inch wide 6 rolls	3.90
Add To Order	OIC-5000	Glue Stick	Oderless non toxic	1.99

Place Order

Product ID	Unit Price	Quantity	
MMM-9700P	759.97	1	Remove
KMW-22256	8.99	1	Remove

Figure 12-29. *Adding order items*

■**Note** When the Add to Order button is clicked again for the same product, the quantity is incremented by one.

Removing Items

When a user clicks the Remove link in the dgOrder DataGrid, the following event handler passes the Product ID of the item to the RemoveItem method of the Order object. This method removes the OrderItem from the OrderItem array and rebinds the dgOrder DataGrid.

```
Protected Sub dgvOrderItems_SelectedIndexChanged _
    (ByVal sender As Object, ByVal e As System.EventArgs) _
    Handles dgvOrderItems.SelectedIndexChanged
        oOrder = CType(Session("Order"), Order)
        'Get the currently selected row using the SelectedRow property.
        Dim gvOrderItems As GridView = CType(sender, GridView)
        Dim row As GridViewRow = gvOrderItems.SelectedRow
        Dim ProductID As String = row.Cells(0).Text
```

```
        oOrder.RemoveItem(ProductID)
        BindOrderGrid()
End Sub
```

Placing an Order

When a user is ready to place an order, the btnPlaceOrder_click event handler runs. This method calls the PlaceOrder method of the Order object and displays the OrderNumber returned to the user:

```
Private Sub btnPlaceOrder_Click(ByVal sender As System.Object, _
  ByVal e As System.EventArgs) Handles btnPlaceOrder.Click
    oOrder = CType(Session("Order"), Order)
    If oOrder.OrderItems.Count > 0 Then
        lblMessage.Text = "Your order has been submitted as order #" & _
        oOrder.PlaceOrder(CType(Session("EmployeeID"), Integer)).ToString
    Else
        lblMessage.Text = "There are no items in the order."
    End If
End Sub
```

Activity 12-3. Testing the OSO Web GUI

In this activity, you will become familiar with the following:

- Testing the OSO Web GUI

To test the OSO Web GUI, follow these steps:

1. Start VS. Select File ➤ New Web Site.

2. Choose an ASP.NET Web Site. Change the name of the web site at the end of the location path to Act12_3. By default, web sites are stored in a folder under the path My Documents\ Visual Studio 2005\WebSites.

3. Right-click the Default.aspx node in the Solution Explorer and choose Delete.

4. Right-click the Act12_3 project node in the Solution Explorer and choose Add Folder ➤ App_Code Folder.

5. Right-click the App_Code folder node in the Solution Explorer and choose Add ➤ Add Existing Item. In the Add Existing Item dialog box, navigate to the Act12_3Starter folder.

6. From this folder, which contains the OSO business logic classes developed in Chapter 9, select the dbOrder.vb, Order.vb, Employee.vb, and ProductCatalog.vb files and click Add.

7. Right-click the Act12_3 project node in the Solution Explorer and choose Add ➤ Add Existing Item. In the Add Existing Item dialog box, navigate to the Act12_3Starter folder. Select All Files on the File Type drop-down list.

8. The folder contains the Web Forms and code-behind classes for the OSO Web UI. Select the Login.aspx, Login.aspx.vb, OrderForm.aspx, and OrderForm.aspx.vb files and click Add.

9. Right-click the `OrderForm.aspx` node in the Solution Explorer and choose Set as Start Page. Press the F5 key to launch the debugger. Verify that the product information is updated in the grid when the category is changed in the drop-down list.

10. Click the Add to Order link. You should be redirected to the `Login.aspx` page. Enter a user name of `jsmith` and a password of `js`. You should be validated as an employee and redirected back to the `OrderForm.aspx` page.

11. Test adding and deleting items in the order.

12. Place an order and verify that the order number is returned.

13. After testing the OSO Web GUI, stop the debugger and exit VS.

■**Note** The authentication used in this sample is for demonstration only. Production application should use Forms-based or Windows-based authentication. For more information, consult ASP.Net Security in the VS help files.

Summary

In this chapter, you looked at implementing the interface tier of an application using a Web Form-based frontend. Along the way you took a closer look at the classes and namespaces of the .NET Framework that are used to implement Web Forms-based user interfaces. You were also exposed to data binding Web server controls, in particular, the GridView control. In the next chapter, we will look at web services. Web services enable developers to expose the services implemented by their applications using open standards. Using web services, heterogeneous applications can communicate through XML-based messaging via open protocols such as HTML.

CHAPTER 13

■■■

Developing and Consuming Web Services

In the previous two chapters, you looked at developing the graphical user interface of an application. Graphical user interfaces such as Windows Forms and web pages provide human users a way to interact with your applications and use the services the application provides. This chapter covers building another type of interface for your application in the form of a web service. A *web service* provides a programmatic interface into your application. This allows other programs the ability to use the services exposed by your application without the need for human interaction.

After reading this chapter, you should be familiar with the following:

- What a web service is

- Web service processing

- How to create a web service

- How to consume a web service

What Are Web Services?

A web service provides a way for calling an application, requesting a service, and receiving a reply. This is essentially the same as a client object requesting a service (method) from a server object within the boundaries of your application. The difference is where the client objects and server objects reside. If they are in the same application, then they issue binary messages and inherently understand each other because they are speaking the same "language." As the applications you build start to grow more complex, it is common to split the application up into distinct components. Segmenting the application into components designed to perform distinct specialized services greatly enhances code maintenance, reusability, and reliability. Additionally, separate servers can host the client components and server components for increased performance, better maintenance, and security. Prior to web services, the client and server applications relied on distributed technologies such as DCOM and CORBA, which are based on proprietary standards. This is fine if the client and server applications utilize the same technologies, but when the client and server utilize disparate technologies, this becomes very problematic. The power of web services lies in the fact that they use a set of open XML-based messaging and HTTP-based transport protocols. This means that client and server components utilizing different technologies can communicate in a standard way. For example, a Java-based application running on an Apache web server can request a service from a .NET-based application running on an IIS server. In addition, because they communicate via HTTP, they can be located virtually anywhere in the world that has an Internet connection.

Understanding Web Service Processing

Web services facilitate remote communication between a client and a server application. In order to facilitate the communication, web services must define standards for discovery, description, message format, encoding, and transport. *Discovery* is the process by which a client resolves the location of the remote service. A web service provides discovery information through a UDDI file. Once a client resolves the location of a web service, it needs a description of how to interact with the service. The *description* consists of metadata describing the interface, including how to call the service, what parameters it expects, and the response returned. A Web service provides this description information using a WSDL file. In order to exchange data the client and server applications must agree upon how messages are *encoded* and *formatted*. Web services use SOAP to pass messages. SOAP is a universally agreed upon protocol defined and governed by the World Wide Web Consortium (W3C). Once the message is encoded, it needs to be *transported* between the client and server applications. The most common transport utilized by web services is through HTTP.

Figure 13-1 shows the request/response process that occurs when a client invokes a service. The SOAP engine handles the packaging, encoding, and decoding of the messages sent between the client and server applications. There is a lot of plumbing code that needs to occur just to facilitate the communication between the client and server. Fortunately, when you create and consume ASP.NET web services, the .NET Framework takes care of most the plumbing code for you.

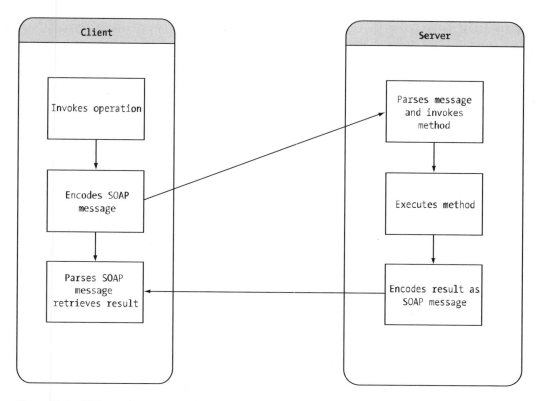

Figure 13-1. *Web service request processing*

Creating a Web Service

In order to create a web service using ASP.NET, you need to create an .asmx file and place it in a web site hosted on an ASP.NET web server. The .asmx file contains the following code:

```
<%@ WebService Language="vb" CodeBehind="~/App_Code/Service.vb"
Class="Service" %>
```

This code tells the ASP.NET runtime to process this page as a web service, including setting up any plumbing code required to process requests from the clients. It also defines the location of the code-behind class that contains the methods you want to expose to clients of the service. The following code shows the corresponding web service code-behind class:

```
Imports System.Web
Imports System.Web.Services
Imports System.Web.Services.Protocols

<WebService(Namespace := "http://tempuri.org/")> _
<WebServiceBinding(ConformsTo:=WsiProfiles.BasicProfile1_1)> _
```

```
Public Class Service
    Inherits System.Web.Services.WebService

    Public Sub Service

    End Sub

    <WebMethod()> _
    Public Function GetSalesTax(ByVal Location As String) As Double
        If Location.ToUpper = "PA" Then
            Return 0.06
        Else
            Return 0.05
        End If
    End Function

End Class
```

This class inherits from the WebService base class. The WebService base class provides direct access to common ASP.NET objects, including the Session, Application, and Context objects. For example, the following code demonstrates retrieving the name of the user making the request and the time of the request. This information is passed to a logging function for further processing.

```
<WebMethod()> _
    Public Function GetSalesTax(ByVal Location As String) As Double
        Logger.LogRequest(User.Identity.Name, Context.Timestamp)
        If Location.ToUpper = "PA" Then
            Return 0.06
        Else
            Return 0.05
        End If
    End Function
```

If you examine the class file, you should notice several class attributes and a method attribute, which are contained between the < > tags. The WebService attribute is used to add additional information about the service. The following attribute defines the default namespace and a description of the service:

```
<WebService(Namespace:="http://tempuri.org/", _
    Description:="My Demo Web Service")>
```

The WebMethod attribute exposes the method to clients calling the web service. It can also add additional information about the method such as a description or whether session state is enabled. The following WebMethod adds a description of the method and indicates session state is not enabled:

```
<WebMethod(Description := _
    "Returns sales tax when passed a location.", _
    EnableSession := False)>
```

After compiling the web service, you can request the page using Internet Explorer. Figure 13-2 shows the .asmx page in the web browser.

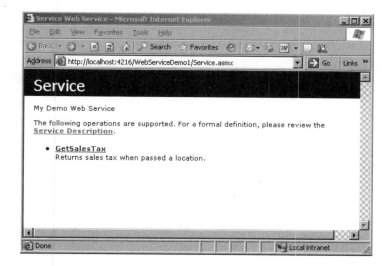

Figure 13-2. *Browsing the .asmx file*

Clicking the Service Description link shows the formal WSDL file that provides a complete description of the service, as you see in Figure 13-3.

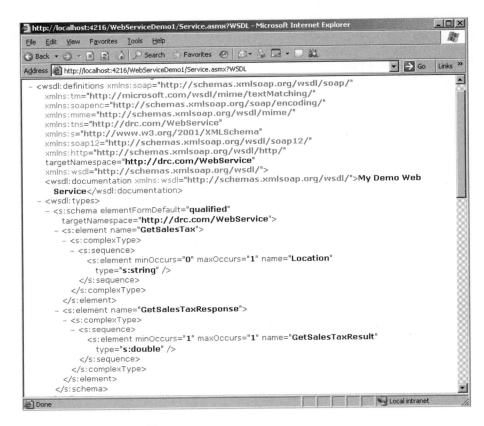

Figure 13-3. *The WSDL file*

Clicking the GetSalesTax link displays the page shown in Figure 13-4. This page allows you to test the web method and provides the SOAP encoding for the request and response messages. Figure 13-5 shows the response returned when the method is invoked using an input parameter of PA.

Figure 13-4. *Testing the web method*

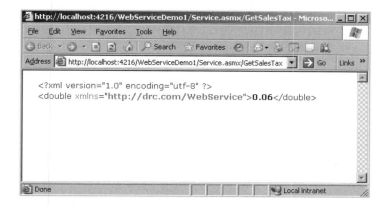

Figure 13-5. *The XML response*

Activity 13-1. Creating a Web Service

In this activity, you will become familiar with creating and testing a web service.

Creating the Web Service

To create the web service, follow these steps:

1. Start VS. Select File ➤ New Web Site.

2. Choose an ASP.NET Web Service template. Change the name of the web site at the end of the location path to `Act13_1`, and click OK.

3. Open the `Service` class in the code editor window as shown in Figure 13-6.

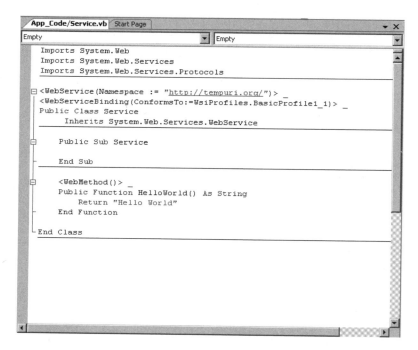

Figure 13-6. *The Service class code*

4. Replace the default `HelloWorld` method with the following method, which simulates looking up items in stock:

```
<WebMethod(Description:="Checks for products in stock.")> _
    Public Function CheckStock(ByVal productCode As String) _
    As Integer
        'simulate retrieving from Data Base
        Select Case productCode
            Case "ACM-10414"
```

```
                    Return 20
            Case "IMN-44766"
                    Return 15
            Case "KMW-12164"
                    Return 10
            Case Else
                    Return 0
        End Select
    End Function
```

5. Change the namespace in the `WebService` attribute to the following:

   ```
   <WebService(Namespace := "http://OfficeSupply.org/")>
   ```

6. Save the project and right-click the `Service.asmx` node in the Solution Explorer window. In the pop-up menu, choose View in Browser. If you get a warning dialog box asking whether you want to enable debugging, enable debugging and click OK.

7. Click the Service Description link and review the WSDL file. When finished viewing the file, click the browser's back button.

8. Click the CheckStock link and review the SOAP request and response encoding. Enter a `productCode` parameter of `IMN-44766` and confirm that a reponse of 15 is returned. Close the browser and exit VS.

Consuming a Web Service

In order to consume a web service, you need to create a proxy class. The *proxy class* encapsulates the process of encoding the request into a SOAP message and passing it to the web service. When the response returns from the web service, the proxy decodes the SOAP message and exposes the response. By using a proxy class, calling a web service is no different from calling a method of a class in your application. When you add a web reference to your project in VS, the proxy class is autogenerated for you. Figure 13-7 shows the Add Web Reference Dialog box in VS.

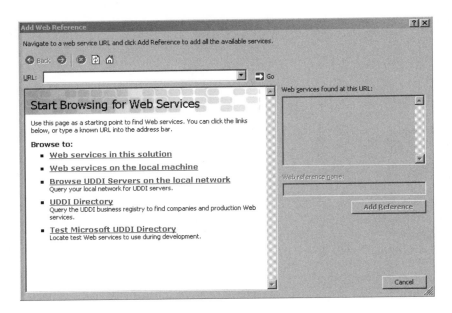

Figure 13-7. *Adding a web reference*

After browsing to the service, you can change the name of the web reference and add it to your project, as shown in Figure 13-8.

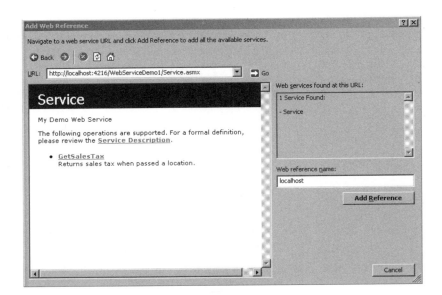

Figure 13-8. *Browsing for a web service*

Figure 13-9 shows the proxy class generated to communicate with the web service.

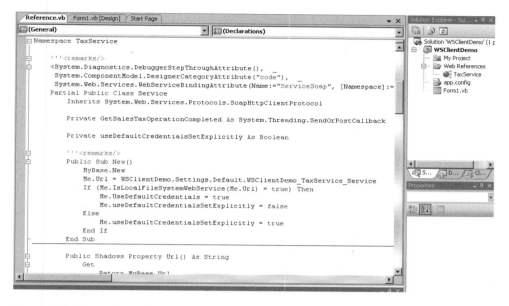

Figure 13-9. *The web service proxy*

To call a method of the web service, all you need to do is create an instance of the proxy class and invoke the method. The following code calls the GetSalesTax method and shows the results in a message box as in Figure 13-10.

```
Dim oTaxService As New TaxService.Service
MessageBox.Show(oTaxService.GetSalesTax(TextBox1.Text))
```

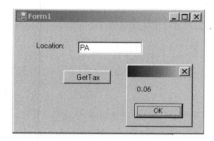

Figure 13-10. *Executing the web method*

Activity 13-2. Consuming a Web Service

In this activity, you will consume a web service in a Windows application.

Note This activity requires an Internet connection.

Consuming a Web Service

To consume the web service in a Windows application, follow these steps:

1. Start VS. Select File ➤ New Project.

2. Choose a Windows Application template. Change the name of the application to Act13_2 and click OK.

3. Add the controls to Form1 and set the properties as listed in Table 13-1.

Table 13-1. *Form1 Form and Control Properties*

Control	Property	Value
TextBox1	Name	txtAirportCode
	Text	[Empty]
Button1	Name	btnCheckWindSpeed
	Text	Check Wind Speed

4. In the Solution Explorer window, right-click the Act13-2 project node. In the pop-up menu, select Add Web Reference.

5. Enter a URL of http://live.capescience.com/wsdl/GlobalWeather.wsdl and click the Go button. The methods of the web service are displayed in the Add Web Reference dialog box as shown in Figure 13-11. Change the web reference name to wsWeather and click the Add Reference button.

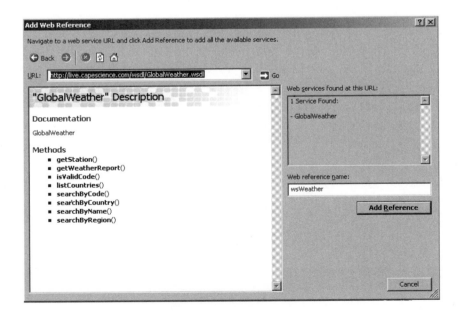

Figure 13-11. *Adding a web reference*

6. Add the following code to the btnCheckWindSpeed_Click event procedure. This code calls the getWeatherReport method of the web service. This method takes an input string parameter that represents the airport code. It returns a WeatherReport object that contains a wind object. The string property of the wind object holds the wind speed information. A MessageBox displays the information to the user.

```
Dim oWeather As New wsWeather.GlobalWeather
Dim oWeatherReport As wsWeather.WeatherReport
oWeatherReport = oWeather.getWeatherReport(txtAirportCode.Text)
Dim result As String
If oWeatherReport IsNot Nothing Then
    result = oWeatherReport.wind.string
Else
    result = "Invalid Code"
End If
MessageBox.Show(result)
```

7. Launch the form in debug mode. Enter an airport code of LAX and click the Check Wind Speed button. You should see a message box displaying the wind speed information as in Figure 13-12.

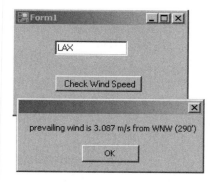

Figure 13-12. *Displaying the wind speed information*

8. Try experimenting with some other airport codes. After testing, stop the debugger and exit VS.

Summary

In this chapter, you looked at creating and consuming web services. Web services provide a programmatic interface to your application. Using web services, applications based on disparate technologies can easily exchange data using a standard set of messaging and transport protocols. Web services also allow businesses to easily exchange data and provide services for partners. Although you did not add a web service to the case study, you can easily see how an office supply retailer could offer valuable services to business customers. For example, they could build an ordering service that allows the placement of orders. They could also provide a web service that tracks the processing of an order. Web services are becoming an integral technology for enterprise-level application development and business-to-business data exchange. For the latest information on web services, visit the World Wide Web Consortium (W3C) web site at www.w3c.org.

CHAPTER 14

■■■

Wrapping Up and Reviewing

If you have made it this far, take a moment and pat yourself on the back. You have come a long way from the day you first cracked open the cover of this book, gaining valuable skills needed to successfully program using the .NET Framework and Visual Basic .NET. These include an understanding of the following:

- The importance of the application design cycle

- The Unified Modeling Language and how it can help facilitate the analysis and design of object-oriented programs

- The Common Language Runtime

- The structure of the .NET Framework

- How to create and use class structures and hierarchies

- How to implement inheritance, polymorphism, and interfaces

- Object interaction and collaboration

- Event-driven programming

- Structured error handling

- How to work with data structures and data sources using ADO.NET

- How to use the features of the VS integrated development environment to increase productivity and facilitate debugging

- How to implement a Windows Form-based graphical user interface

- How to implement a Web Form-based graphical user interface

- How to create and consume a web service

Congratulations! You can now call yourself a Visual Basic programmer (albeit a neophyte). However, do not get too high on yourself. If your goal is to become a professional Visual Basic programmer, your journey has just begun. The next stage of your development is to gain experience. In other words, design and code, and then design and code some more. If you are designing and coding Visual Basic at work, this will be easy. (Although it will be stressful if you are expected to be the expert after two weeks and that three-day course they sent you to!) If you are learning on your own, you will have to find time and projects on which to work. This is easier than you might think. Commit to an hour a day, and come up with an idea for a program. For example, you could design a program that converts recipes into Extensible Markup Language (XML) data. The XML data could then generate a shopping list. Heck, if you really want to go all out, incorporate it with an inventory tracking system that tracks ingredients you have in stock. However you go about gaining experience, remember the important adage: use it or lose it!

The following sections highlight some other important things to consider as you develop your programming skills.

Improving Your Object-Oriented Design Skills

Object-oriented analysis and design is one of the hardest tasks you will perform as a programmer. This is not a skill that comes easily for most programmers. It is, however, one of the most important skills you should strive to master. It is what separates what I call a *programmer* from a *coder*. If you talk to most Chief Information Officers and programming managers, finding coders is easy; it is the programmer they are after.

Remember that there is not one "true" methodology, rather several that are equally valid.

Investigating the .NET Framework Namespaces

The .NET Framework contains a vast number of classes, interfaces, and other types aimed at optimizing and expediting your development efforts. The various namespaces that make up the .NET Framework Class Library are organized by functionality. It is important you take the time to become familiar with the capabilities provided by these namespaces. Start out with the namespaces that incorporate functionality you will use most often; for example, the root namespace System and the System.Windows.Forms namespace, which provide the functionality required to create Windows-based graphical user interfaces (GUIs). After you become familiar with the more common namespaces, start exploring some of the more obscure ones. For example, System.Security.Cryptography provides cryptographic services such as data encoding, hashing, and message authentication. You will be amazed at the extent of the support provided by the framework. You can find a wealth of information on the members of the various namespaces in the VS integrated documentation.

Becoming Familiar with ADO.NET

Data is fundamental to programming. You store, retrieve, and manipulate data in every program you write. The data structure a program works with during execution is *nondurable* data—it is held in RAM. When the application terminates, this data is lost and has to be re-created the next time the application is started. *Durable data* is data that is maintained in a permanent data structure such as a file system or a database. Most programs need to be able to retrieve data from and persist data to some sort of durable data storage. This is where ADO.NET steps in. ADO.NET refers to the namespaces that contain the functionality for working with durable data. (It also contains functionality for organizing and working with nondurable data in a familiar relational database or XML-type structure.) Although I have introduced you to ADO.NET, this is such an important topic that it deserves a book devoted solely to working in the ADO.NET. (Do not worry—there are many!) This is definitely an area where you need to devote further study.

Moving Toward Component-Based Development

After you have mastered object-oriented development and the encapsulation of your programming logic in a class system, you are ready to move toward component-based development. *Components* are assemblies that further encapsulate the functionality of your programming logic. Although the OSO application's business logic tier is logically isolated from the user interface tier, physically they reside in the same assembly. You can increase code maintenance and reuse by compiling the business logic into its own assembly. You should start moving to a Lego approach of application development. This is where your application is comprised of a set of independent pieces (assemblies) that can be snapped together and work in conjunction to perform the necessary services.

Finding Help

An enormous amount of information is available on the .NET Framework and Visual Basic. The help system provided with VS is an excellent resource for programmers. Get in the habit of using this resource religiously. Another extremely important resource is www.msdn.microsoft.com. This web site provided by Microsoft for developers contains a wealth of information, including white papers, tutorials, and webcast seminars, and, quite honestly, it is one of the most informative sites in the industry. If you are developing using Microsoft technologies, visiting this site should be as routine as reading the daily paper. There are also a number of independent web sites dedicated to the various .NET programming languages. You can use your favorite search engine to discover the best sites on the Web.

Joining a User Group

Microsoft is investing a lot of support for the development of local .NET user groups. The user groups consist of members with an interest in .NET programming. The user groups provide a great avenue for learning, mentoring, and networking. There is a listing of .NET user groups available at www.msdn.microsoft.com. The International .NET Association (INETA) also provides support for .NET user groups. You can find a listing of INETA affiliated user groups at www.ineta.org. If you cannot find a .NET user group in your area, heck, why not start one?

Getting Certified

Microsoft has an extensive certification program, with two certifications available for application developers. The Microsoft Certified Application Developer (MCAD) is aimed at programmers who develop, test, and deploy Web and Windows applications. The Microsoft Certified Solution Developer incorporates the MCAD certification and extends it to include analysis and design of enterprise-level applications.

Obtaining these certifications is beneficial for two reasons. First, it verifies that you have the skills needed to successfully develop and architect applications using the .NET Framework. Employers are increasingly using these certifications as a verifiable method of measuring abilities. Second, it provides you with a well-focused path for learning the .NET Framework, Visual Basic .NET, and application analysis and design. Be forewarned, however: the certification process is not to be taken lightly. Microsoft is committed to maintaining high standards for the certifications. You can find more information on these certifications at www.msdn.microsoft.com.

Please Provide Feedback

Although every effort has been made to provide you with an error-free text, it is inevitable that some mistakes will make it through the editing process. I am committed to providing updated errata at the Apress web site (www.apress.com). I cannot do this without your help. If you have come across any mistakes while reading this text, please report them to me through the Apress site.

Thank You and Good Luck

I sincerely hope you found working your way through this text an enjoyable and worthwhile experience. I want to thank you for allowing me to be your guide on this journey. Just as your skills as a developer increased as a result of reading this book, my skills as a developer have increased immensely as a result of writing it. My experience of teaching and training for the past two decades (in a previous life I was a physics teacher) has been that you really do not fully comprehend a subject until you can teach it to someone else. So, again, thank you and good luck!

PART 4

■ ■ ■

Appendixes

APPENDIX A

■ ■ ■

Fundamental Programming Concepts

The following information is for readers who are new to programming and need a primer on some fundamental programming concepts. If you have programmed in another language, chances are the concepts presented in this appendix are not new to you. You should, however, review the material briefly to become familiar with the Visual Basic syntax.

Working with Variables and Data Types

Variables in programming languages store values that can change while the program executes. For example, if you wanted to count the number of times a user tries to log in to an application, you can use a variable to track the number of attempts. The variable is a memory location where the value is stored. Using the variable, your program can read or alter the value stored in memory. Before you use a variable in your program, however, you must declare it. When you declare a variable, you use the keyword Dim to reserve memory space for the variable:

```
Dim Counter
```

The compiler also needs to know what kind of data will be stored at the memory location. For example, will it be numbers or letters? If the variable will store numbers, how large can a number be? Will the variable store decimals or only whole numbers? You answer these questions by assigning a *data type* to the variable. A login counter, for example, only needs to hold positive whole numbers. The following code demonstrates how you declare a counter in Visual Basic with an Integer data type:

```
Dim Counter as Integer
```

Specifying the data type is referred to as *strong typing*. Strong typing results in more efficient memory management, faster execution, and compiler type checking, which reduces runtime errors.

Once you declare the variable, you can assign an initial value to the variable. You can also do this at the same time as the declaration statement. For instance, the following code:

```
Dim Counter as Integer = 1
```

is equivalent to this:

```
Dim Counter as Integer
Counter = 1
```

If you do not explicitly assign a variable an initial value when it is declared, the compiler will implicitly assign numeric data types to 0, Boolean data types to `false`, character data types to empty (`""`), date data types to 1/1/0001, and object data types to null (which is an empty reference pointer). The following sections further describe these various data types.

Understanding Elementary Data Types

Visual Basic supports elementary data types such as numeric, character, and date.

Integral Data Types

Integral data types represent whole numbers only. Table A-1 summarizes the integral data types used in Visual Basic.

Table A-1. *Integral Data Types*

Data Type	Storage Size	Value Range
Byte	8-bit	0 through 255
Short	16-bit	–32,768 through 32,767
Integer	32-bit	–2,147,483,648 through 2,147,483,647
Long	64-bit	–9,223,372,036,854,775,808 through 9,223,372,036,854,775,807

Obviously, memory size is important when choosing a data type for a variable. A less obvious consideration is how easily the compiler works with the data type. The compiler performs arithmetic operations with integers more efficiently than the other types. Often it is better to use integers as counter variables even though a Byte or Short type could easily manage the maximum value reached.

Nonintegral Data Types

If a variable must store numbers that include decimal parts, then the nonintegral data types are used. Visual Basic supports the nonintegral data types listed in Table A-2.

Table A-2. *Nonintegral Data Types*

Data Type	Storage Size	Value Range
Single	32-bit	−3.4028235E+38 through −1.401298E−45 for negative values; 1.401298E−45 through 3.4028235E+38 for positive values
Double	64-bit	1.79769313486231570E+308 through −4.94065645841246544E−324 for negative values; 4.94065645841246544E−324 through 1.79769313486231570E+308 for positive values
Decimal	128-bit	0 through +/−79,228,162,514,264,337,593,543,950,335 with no decimal point; 0 through +/−7.9228162514264337593543950335 with 28 places to the right of the decimal

The Decimal data type holds a larger number of significant digits than the Single and the Double and is not subject to rounding errors. It is usually reserved for financial or scientific calculations that require a higher degree of precision.

Character Data Types

Character data types are for variables that hold characters used in the human language. For example, a character data type holds letters such as *a* or numbers used for display and printing such as *2* apples. The character data types in Visual Basic are based on Unicode, which defines a character set that can represent characters found in all the various human languages. Visual Basic supports two character data types: Char and String. The Char data type holds single (16-bit) Unicode character values such as *a* or *B*. The String data type holds a sequence of Unicode characters. It can range from zero up to about two billion characters.

Boolean Data Type

The Boolean data type holds a 16-bit value that is interpreted as True or False. It is used for variables that can be one of only two values—for example, yes or no, or on or off.

Date Data Type

Dates are held as 64-bit integers where each increment represents a period of elapsed time from the start of the Gregorian calendar (1/1/0001 at 12:00 A.M.).

Object Data Type

An Object data type is a 32-bit address that points to the memory location of another data type. It is commonly used to declare variables where the actual data type they refer to cannot be determined until runtime. Although the Object data type can be a catch-all to refer to the other data types, it is the most inefficient data type when it comes to performance and should be avoided unless absolutely necessary.

Introducing Composite Data Types

Combining elementary data types creates Composite data types, examples of which are structures, arrays, and classes.

Structures

Structures are useful when you want to organize and work with related information. A single variable works with the information. For example, the following code demonstrates creating an Employee structure used to organize employee information:

```
Structure Employee
    Dim LastName As String
    Dim EmpID As Integer
    Dim HireDate As Date
End Structure
```

Once you define the structure, you can declare a variable of the structure type.

```
Dim aEmployee As Employee
```

Arrays

Although structures organize data of different data types together as a unit, *arrays* are often used to organize and work with groups of the same data type. You declare an array by placing parentheses after the variable name:

```
Dim Names() As String
```

To limit the number of elements of the array, you indicate the size of the array between the parentheses. Because the elements of the array are referenced by a zero-based index, the following array holds five elements:

```
Dim Names(4) As String
```

Visual Basic supports multidimensional arrays. When you declare the array, you separate the size of the dimensions by commas. The following declaration creates a two-dimensional array of integers with five rows and four columns:

```
Dim Names(4,3) As String
```

You access elements of the array using the variable name of the array followed by the index of the element in parentheses. For example, Name(2) references the third element of the Names array declared previously.

Classes

Classes are used extensively in object-oriented programming languages. Classes define a complex data type definition for an object. They contain information about how an object should behave, including its name, methods, properties, and events. The .NET Framework contains many predefined classes with which you can work. You can also create your own class type definitions. A variable defined as a class type contains a 32-bit address pointer to the memory location of the object. The following code declares an object instance of a `Clipboard` class defined in the .NET Framework:

```
Dim oClipboard As Clipboard
```

Looking at Literals, Constants, and Enumerations

Although the value of variables change during program execution, literals and constants contain items of data that do not change.

Literals

Literals are fixed values implicitly assigned a data type and are often used to initialize variables. The following code uses a literal to add the value of 2 to an integer value:

```
Count = Count + 2
```

By inspecting the literal, the compiler assigns a data type to the literal. Numeric literals without decimal values are assigned the `Integer` data type. Numeric literals with a decimal value are assigned as `Double`. The keywords `True` and `False` are assigned the Boolean data type. If the literal is contained in quotes, it is assigned as a `String` data type. In the following line of code, the two string literals are combined and assigned to a string variable:

```
FullName = "Bob" & "Smith"
```

Enclosing the literal in between pound symbols creates a `Date` literal:

```
#12/25/02#
```

It is possible to override the default data type assignment of the literal by appending a type character to the literal. For example, a value of `12.25` would be assigned the `Double` data type, but a value of `12.25S` would assign it the `Single` data type.

Constants

Many times you have to use the same *constant* value repeatedly in your code. For example, a series of geometric calculations may need to use the value of pi. Instead of repeating the literal 3.14 in your code, you can make your code more readable and maintainable by using a declared constant. You declare a constant using the `Const` keyword followed by the constant name and the data type:

```
Const pi As Single = 3.14159265358979323846
```

The constant is assigned a value when it is declared, and this value cannot be altered or reassigned.

Enumerations

You often need to assign the value of a variable to one of several related predefined constants. In these instances, you can create an *enumeration* type to group together the values. Enumerations associate a set of integer constants to names that can be used in code. For example, the following code creates an Enum type of Manager used to define three related manager constants with names of DeptManager, GeneralManager, and AssistantManager with values of 0, 1, and 2, respectively:

```
Enum Manager
    DeptManager
    GeneralManager
    AssistantManager
End Enum
```

A variable of the Enum type can be declared and set to one of the Enum constants:

```
Dim MgrLevel As Manager = Manager.AssistantManager
```

Note The .NET Framework provides a variety of intrinsic constants and enumerations designed to make your coding more intuitive and readable. For example, the StringAlignment enumeration specifies the alignment of a text string relative to its layout rectangle.

Exploring Variable Scope

Two important aspects of a variable are its scope and lifetime. The *scope* of a variable refers to how the variable can be accessed from other code. The *lifetime* of a variable is the period of time when the variable is valid and available for use. A variable's scope and lifetime are determined by where it is declared and the access modifier used to declare it.

Block-Level Scope

A code block is a set of grouped code statements. Examples of code blocks include code organized in If-Else, Do-Loop, or For-Next statements. Block-level scope is the narrowest scope a variable can have. A variable declared within a block of code is available only within the block it is declared. In the following code, the BlockCount variable can only be accessed from inside the If block. Any attempt to access the variable outside the block will generate a compiler error:

```
If iCount > 10 Then
    Dim BlockCount As Integer
    BlockCount = iCount
End If
```

Although the scope of the variable is limited to the block, the lifetime of the variable is for the entire procedure where the block exists. You will probably find block-level scope to be too restrictive in most cases and instead use procedure scope.

Procedure Scope

Procedures are blocks of code that can be called and executed from other code. Three types of procedures are supported in Visual Basic: Sub, Function, and Property. Variables declared outside of a code block but within a procedure have procedure-level scope. Variables with procedure scope can be accessed by code within the same procedure. In the following code, the counter is declared with procedure scope and can be referenced from anywhere within the procedure block:

```
Sub counter()
    Dim iCount As Integer

    Do While iCount < 10
        iCount = iCount + 2
    Loop
    MessageBox.Show(iCount.ToString)
End Sub
```

The lifetime of a procedure scope variable is limited to the duration of the execution of the procedure.

Module Scope

Variables with *module scope* are available to any code within the module, class, or structure. To have module scope, the variable is declared in the general declaration section (outside of any procedure blocks) of the module, class, or structure. To limit the accessibility to the module where it is declared, you use the Private access modifier keyword. In the following code, the iCount variable can be accessed by both procedures defined in the class:

```
Public Class Class1
    Private iCount As Integer
    Sub IncrementCount()
        Do While iCount < 10
            iCount = iCount + 2
        Loop
    End Sub
    Sub ReadCount()
        MessageBox.Show(iCount.ToString)
    End Sub
End Class
```

The lifetime of the variable declared with module scope is the same as the lifetime of the object instance of the class or structure in which it is declared. The lifetime of module scope variables declared within a module is for the lifetime of the application.

▉**Note** There are several additional variations of scope addressed in Chapter 7 and Chapter 11.

Understanding Data Type Conversion

During program execution, there are many times when a value must be converted from one data type to another. The process of converting between data types is referred to as *casting* or *conversion*.

Implicit Conversion

The Visual Basic compiler will perform some data type conversions for you automatically. For example, if a value of a numeric variable is assigned to a string variable for display, the compiler will perform an implicit conversion. In the following code, an `Integer` data type is implicitly converted to a `String` data type:

```
Dim iCount As Integer
Dim strCount As String
Do While iCount < 10
    iCount = iCount + 2
Loop
strCount = iCount
MessageBox.Show(strCount)
```

Although allowing the compiler to perform implicit conversion can make coding easier, it can cause inefficient code execution and introduce unintended results such as data truncation and runtime errors. In the following code, the value of the text contained in a text box, which is a `String` data type, is converted into an `Integer` data type:

```
Dim Count As Integer
Count = txtCount.Text
Count = Count + 1
```

This code executes fine as long as the user enters an integer into the text box. However, if a character text is entered into the text box, a runtime exception will occur.

Explicit Conversion

Explicit conversion is when you use a type conversion keyword. The following code is the same as the preceding example except that explicit conversion converts the `String` type to an `Integer` type. This results in faster code execution.

```
Dim Count As Integer
Count = CInt(txtCount.Text)
Count = Count + 1
```

■**Note** To convert between various composite data types, use the `CType` conversion keyword.

Widening and Narrowing Conversions

Widening conversions occur when the data type converted to can accommodate all the possible values contained in the original data type. For example, an Integer data type can be converted to a Double data type without any data loss or overflow. Data loss occurs when the number gets truncated. For example, 2.54 gets truncated to 2 if it is converted to an Integer data type. Over-flow occurs when a number is too large to fit in the new data type. For example, if the number 50000 is converted to a Short data type, the maximum capacity of the Short data type is exceeded, causing the overflow error. *Narrowing conversions*, on the other hand, occur when the data type being converted to cannot accommodate all the values that can be contained in the original data type. For example, when the value of a Double data type is converted to a Short data type, any decimal values contained in the original value will be lost. In addition, if the original value is more than the limit of the Short data type, a runtime exception will occur. You should be particularly careful to trap for these situations when implementing narrowing conversions in your code.

Working with Operators

An *operator* is a code symbol that tells the compiler to perform an operation on a value. The operation can be arithmetic, comparative, or logical.

Arithmetic Operators

Arithmetic operators perform mathematical manipulation to numeric types. Table A-3 lists the commonly used arithmetic operators available in Visual Basic.

Table A-3. *Arithmetic Operators*

Operator	Description
=	Assignment
*	Multiplication
/	Division
+	Addition
-	Subtraction
^	Exponential

The following code increments the value of an Integer data type by one:

```
Count = Count + 1
```

Visual Basic also supports shorthand assignment operators that combine the assignment with the operation. The following code is equivalent to the previous code:

```
Count += 1
```

Note String data type values are combined using the concatenation operator (&).

Comparison Operators

A comparison operator compares two values and returns a Boolean value of `True` or `False`. Table A-4 lists the common comparison operators used in Visual Basic.

Table A-4. *Comparison Operators*

Operator	Description
<	Less than
<=	Less than or equal to
>	Greater than
>=	Greater than or equal to
=	Equal to
<>	Not equal to

You use comparison operators in condition statements that determine whether a block of code executes. The following `If-Then` block checks to see whether the number of invalid login attempts is greater than three before ending the application:

```
If InvalidAttempts > 3 Then
    Application.Exit()
End If
```

■**Note** Two special case comparison operators are `Like` and `Is`. The `Like` comparison operator is for string pattern matching. The `Is` operator is to compare two object references.

Logical Operators

Logical operators combine the results of conditional operators. The three commonly used logical operators are `And`, `Or`, and `Not`. The `And` operator combines two expressions and returns `True` if both expressions are true. The `Or` operator combines two expressions and returns `True` if either one is true. The `Not` operator switches the result of the comparison. A value of `True` returns `False` and a value of `False` returns `True`. The following code checks to see whether the logged-in user is a manager or assistant manager before loading an instance of a form:

```
If CurrentUserLevel = UserLevel.Manager Or _
    CurrentUserLevel = UserLevel.AssistantManager Then
        oEmployeeInfoForm.Show()
End If
```

■**Note** The first line of the `If` block uses the line continuation character (_). This enables you to wrap long lines of code for easier viewing.

Introducing Decision Structures

Decision structures allow conditional execution of code blocks depending on the evaluation of a condition statement. The If-Then statement evaluates a Boolean expression and executes the code block if the result is True. The Select-Case statement checks the same expression for several different values and conditionally executes a code block depending on the results.

If-Then Statements

To execute a code block if a condition is true, use the following structure:

```
If condition Then
    Code statements
End If
```

To execute a code block if a condition is true and an alternate code block if it is false, add an Else block:

```
If condition Then
    Code statements
Else
    Code staments
End If
```

To test additional conditions if the first evaluates to False, add an ElseIf block:

```
If condition Then
    Code statements
ElseIf condition then
    Code staments
Else
    Code staments
End If
```

You can have multiple ElseIf blocks. If a condition evaluates to True, the corresponding code statements are executed, after which execution jumps to the End If statement. If a condition evaluates to False, the next ElseIf condition is checked. The Else block is optional but if included must be last. The Else block has no condition check and executes if all other condition checks have evaluated to False. The following code demonstrates using the If-Then statement to evaluate a series of conditions. It checks a performance rating to determine what bonus to use. It includes a check to see whether the employee is a manager to determine the minimum bonus:

```
If Performance = 1 Then
    Bonus = Salary * 0.1
ElseIf Performance = 2 Then
    Bonus = Salary * 0.08
ElseIf EmployeeLevel = "mgr" Then
    Bonus = Salary * 0.05
Else
    Bonus = Salary * 0.03
End If
```

Select-Case Statements

Although the `Select-Case` statement is similar to the `If-ElseIf` statement, it is used to test a single expression for a series of values. The structure of the `Select Case` statement is as follows:

```
Select Case [Test Expression]
    Case [expression list]
            Code statements
    Case [expression list]
            Code statements
    ...
    Case Else
            Code statements
End Select
```

You can have multiple `Case` blocks. If the test expression value matches the expression list, the code statements in the `Case` block executes. After the `Case` block executes, execution jumps to the `End Select` statement. If the test expression does not match the expression list, execution jumps to the next `Case` block. The `Case Else` block does not have an expression list. It executes if no other `Case` blocks are executed. The `Case Else` block is optional, but if used, it must be last. The following example uses a `Select Case` to evaluate a performance rating to set the appropriate bonus rate:

```
Select Performance
    Case 10
        BonusRate = 0.1
    Case 8,9
        BonusRate = 0.08
    Case 5 To 7
        BonusRate = 0.05
    Case Is < 5
        BonusRate = 0.02
    Case Else
        BonusRate = 0
End Select
```

Using Loop Structures

Looping structures repeat a block of code until a condition is met. Visual Basic supports the following looping structures.

While Statements

The `While` statement repeats the execution of code while a Boolean expression remains `True`. The following code executes until the counter is greater than 10:

```
Dim Counter As Integer
 While Counter > 10
```

```
        'code statements
        Counter = Counter + 1
 End While
```

Do-Loop Statements

Do-Loop statements repeat the execution of code until a Boolean expression evaluates to either True or False depending on the Do statement. The condition can also be evaluated before or after the loop executes. The following Do While-Loop is similar to the previous While statement. It executes until the counter is greater than 10:

```
Dim Counter As Integer
 Do While Counter > 10
        'code statements
        Counter = Counter + 1
 Loop
```

The Do While-Loop repeats until the test expression returns False. A Do Until-Loop will repeat until the test expression returns True:

```
Dim Counter As Integer = 20
 Do Until Counter < 10
        'code statements
        Counter = Counter - 1
 Loop
```

Both of the previous Do-Loop statements evaluate the test expression at the beginning of the code block. If the evaluation needs to occur at the end of the code block, a Do-Loop Until or Do-Loop While statement can be used. The following Do-Loop Until statement repeats until the test expression evaluates to True:

```
Dim Counter As Integer = 20
 Do
        'code statements
        Counter = Counter - 1
 Loop Until Counter < 10
```

For-Next Statements

For-Next statements loop through a code block a specific number of times based on a built-in counter. They are a better choice when you know the number of times the loop needs to execute at design time. You use Do-Loop statements when the number of iterations can vary depending on the condition. The following code block will repeat five times:

```
Dim Count as integer
For Count = 1 to 5
     'code statements
Next
```

The counter is automatically incremented as the loop iterates. By default the increment is one, but it can be changed using the Step keyword. The counter can also be decremented by using a negative Step value. The following code will start with a counter value of 100 and loop until the counter has a value of 20. After each iteration, the counter is decreased by a value of 10.

```
Dim Count as integer
For Count = 100 to 20 Step -10
    'code statements
Next
```

For Each-Next Statements

The For Each-Next statement loops through code for each item in a collection. A *collection* is a group of ordered items; for example, the controls placed on a Windows Form are organized into a Controls collection. To use the For Each-Next statement, you first declare a variable of the type of items contained in the collection. This variable is set to the current item in the collection. The following For Each-Next statement loops through the controls in the form's control collection and resets the text property to the default value:

```
Dim oControl As Control
For Each oControl In Me.Controls
    oControl.ResetText()
Next
```

Introducing Procedures

Procedures are blocks of code that can be called and executed from other code. Breaking an application up into discrete logical blocks of code greatly enhances code maintenance and reuse. Visual Basic supports Sub procedures and Function procedures. The main difference between the two is Functions return a value to the calling code but Sub procedures do not. When you declare a procedure, you specify an access modifier, the procedure type, and the name of the procedure. The End keyword followed by the procedure type designates the end of the procedure block. The following code declares a Sub procedure used to encapsulate and reuse the previous For Each-Next loop:

```
Private Sub ResetControls()
    Dim oControl As Control
    For Each oControl In Me.Controls
        oControl.ResetText()
    Next
End Sub
```

You can declare procedures with a parameter list that defines arguments that must be passed to the procedure when it is called. The following code defines a Function procedure that encapsulates the calculation of a bonus rate. The calling code passes an Integer type value to the function and receives a Single type value back:

```
Private Function GetBonusRate(ByVal Performance As Integer) As Single
    Dim BonusRate As Single
    Select Case Performance
        Case 10
            BonusRate = 0.1
        Case 8, 9
            BonusRate = 0.08
        Case 5 To 7
            BonusRate = 0.05
        Case Is < 5
            BonusRate = 0.02
        Case Else
            BonusRate = 0
    End Select
    Return BonusRate
End Function
```

The following code demonstrates how the function is called:

```
Dim Salary As Double
Dim QuarterPerformance As Integer
Dim Bonus As Double
'Retrieve salary and performance from database
' ...
Bonus = GetBonusRate(QuarterPerformance) * Salary
```

If the access modifier of the procedure is private, it is only accessible from code within the same class or module. If the procedure needs to be accessed by code in other classes or modules, then either the Public or Friend access modifier is used.

APPENDIX B

■ ■ ■

Exception Handling in VB

The topics discussed in this appendix are an extension of the exception handling topics covered in Chapter 8. It is assumed you have thoroughly reviewed Chapter 8 prior to reading this appendix. The focus of this appendix is to review Microsoft's recommendations for exception management and the exception classes provided by the .NET Framework.

Managing Exceptions

Exceptions are generated when the implicit assumptions made in your programming logic are violated. For example, when a connection is made to a database, it is assumed that the database server is up and running on the network. If the server cannot be located, then an exception is generated. It is important that your application gracefully handles any exceptions that may occur. If an exception is not handled, your application will terminate.

You should incorporate a systematic exception handling process in your methods. To facilitate this process, the .NET Framework makes use of structured exception handling through the Try, Catch, and Finally code blocks. The first step is to detect any exceptions that may be thrown as your code executes. To detect any exceptions thrown, place the code within the Try block. When an exception is thrown in the Try block, execution transfers to the Catch block. You can use more than one Catch block to filter for specific types of exceptions that may be thrown. The Finally block performs any cleanup code. The code in the Finally block executes regardless of whether an exception is thrown. The following code demonstrates reading a list of names from a file using the appropriate exception handling structure:

```
Function GetNames(ByVal FileName As String) As ArrayList
    Dim Names As New ArrayList()
    Dim Stream As System.IO.StreamReader

    Try
        Stream = System.IO.File.OpenText(FileName)
        While Stream.Peek > -1
            Names.Add(Stream.ReadLine())
        End While
    Catch fnfExcep As System.IO.FileNotFoundException
        'Could not find the file
    Catch flExcep As System.IO.FileLoadException
```

```
            'Could not open file
        Catch IOExcep As System.IO.IOException
            ' Some kind of error occurred. Report error.
        Finally
            If Not IsNothing(Stream) Then
                Stream.Close()
            End If.
        End Try


            Return Names
    End Function
```

After an exception is caught, the next step in the process is to determine how to respond to the exception. You basically have two options: either recover from the exception or pass the exception to the calling procedure. The following code demonstrates recovering from a DivideByZeroException by setting the result to zero:

```
  ...
Try
    Z = x / y
Catch dbzEx As DivideByZeroException
    Z = 0
End Try
  ...
```

An exception is passed to the calling procedure using the Throw statement. The following code demonstrates throwing an exception to the calling procedure where it can be caught and handled:

```
Catch fnfExcep As System.IO.FileNotFoundException
    Throw fnfExcep
```

As exceptions are thrown up the calling chain, the relevance of the original exception can become less obvious. To maintain relevance, you can wrap the exception in a new exception containing additional information that adds relevancy to the exception. The following code demonstrates wrapping a caught exception in a new exception and then passing it up the calling chain:

```
Catch flExcep As System.IO.FileLoadException
    Throw New Exception("GetNames function could not open file", flExcep)
```

You preserve the original exception by using the InnerException property of the Exception class.

Implementing this exception management policy consistently throughout the various methods in your application will greatly enhance your ability to build successful, flexible, and highly maintainable applications.

Looking at the .NET Framework Exception Classes

The Common Language Runtime has a set of built-in exception classes. The CLR will throw an object instance of the appropriate exception type if an error occurs while executing code instructions. All .NET Framework exception classes derive from the SystemException class, which in turn derives from the Exception class. These base classes provide functionality needed by all exception classes.

Each namespace in the framework contains a set of exception classes that derive from the SystemException class. These exception classes handle common exceptions that may occur while implementing the functionality contained in the namespace. To implement robust exception handling, it is important that you are familiar with the exception classes provided by the various namespaces. Table B-1 summarizes the exception classes in the System.IO namespace.

Table B-1. *Exception Classes in the System.IO Namespace*

Exception	Description
IOException	The base class for exceptions thrown while accessing information using streams, files, and directories
DirectoryNotFoundException	Thrown when part of a file or directory cannot be found
EndOfStreamException	Thrown when reading is attempted past the end of a stream
FileLoadException	Thrown when a file is found but cannot be loaded
FileNotFoundException	Thrown when an attempt to access a file that does not exist on disk fails
PathTooLongException	Thrown when a path or filename is longer than the system-defined maximum length

All exception classes contain the properties listed in Table B-2. These properties help identify information about where the exception occurred and the cause of the exception.

Table B-2. *Exception Class Properties*

Property	Description
Message	Gets a message that describes the current exception
Source	Gets or sets the name of the application or the object that causes the error
StackTrace	Gets a string representation of the frames on the call stack at the time the current exception was thrown
InnerException	Gets the Exception instance that caused the current exception
HelpLink	Gets or sets a link to the help file associated with this exception

In addition, the ToString method of the exception classes provides summary information about the current exception. It combines the name of the class that threw the current exception, the message, the result of calling the ToString method of the inner exception, and the stack trace information of the current exception.

You will find that the exception classes in the .NET Framework provide you with the capabilities to handle most exceptions that may occur in your applications. In cases where you may need to implement custom error handling, you can create your own exception classes. These classes need to inherit from `System.ApplicationException`, which in turn inherits from `System.Exception`. Creating custom exception classes is an advanced topic beyond the scope of this text. For more information on this topic, consult the .NET Framework documentation.

■ ■ ■

Installing the Sample Databases

In order to complete the exercises throughout this book, you need to have SQL Server 2000, SQL Server 2005, or SQL Server 2005 Express installed. For information on downloading and installing a trial version of SQL Server 2000/2005 or the free 2005 Express version, visit the SQL Server Developer Center at www.msdn.microsoft.com/sql/.

Once you have installed SQL Server, download the sample database scripts from the Apress web site, www.apress.com. You should have three files: instOSODB.sql, instnwnd.sql, and instpubs.sql. Follow one of the following procedures, depending on the version of SQL Server installed.

Running the Scripts on SQL Server 2000

To run the scripts using osql:

1. Open a command prompt window.

2. From the command prompt, use the cd command to navigate to the folder containing the Sample Database Scripts:

   cd c:\SampleDatabases

3. Run osql specifying either instOSODB.sql, instpubs.sql, or instnwnd.sql as the input file. Here are some examples:

   To install the **Northwind** database on a default instance:

   osql -E -i instnwnd.sql

   To install the **Northwind** database on a named instance:

   osql -E -S ComputerName/InstanceName -i instnwnd.sql

Running the Scripts on SQL Server 2005/2005 Express

To run the scripts using SQLCmd:

1. Open a command prompt window.

2. From the command prompt, use the cd command to navigate to the folder containing the Sample Database Scripts:

   ```
   cd c:\SampleDatabases
   ```

3. Run SQLCmd.exe, specifying either instOSODB.sql, instpubs.sql, or instnwnd.sql as the input file. Here are some examples:

   To install the **Northwind** database on a default instance:

   ```
   SQLCmd.exe -E -i instnwnd.sql
   ```

   To install the **Northwind** database on a named instance:

   ```
   SQLCmd.exe -E -S ComputerName/InstanceName -i instnwnd.sql
   ```

Verifying the Database Installs with Visual Studio

To verify the database installs:

1. Start VS. If you do not see the Database Explorer window, shown in Figure C-1, open it by choosing Server Explore on the View menu.

Figure C-1. *The Database Explorer window*

2. In the Database Explorer window, right-click the Data Connections node and select Add Connection. In the Add Connection dialog box, shown in Figure C-2, fill in the name of your server, select the Northwind database, and click OK.

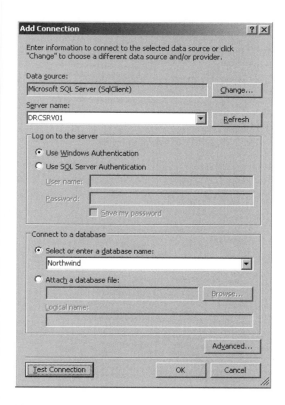

Figure C-2. *The Add Connection dialog box*

3. Expand the Northwind database node and the Tables node in the Database Explorer window, shown in Figure C-3. Right-click the Supplies table node and select Show Table Data. The suppliers table data should display as shown in Figure C-4.

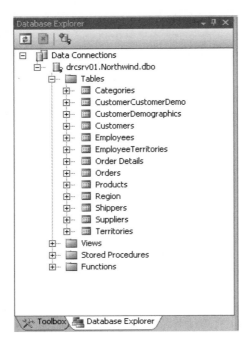

Figure C-3. *Expanding the Tables node*

	SupplierID	CompanyName	ContactName	ContactTitle	Address	City
▶	1	Exotic Liquids	Charlotte Cooper	Purchasing Mana...	49 Gilbert St.	London
	2	New Orleans Caj...	Shelley Burke	Order Administrator	P.O. Box 78934	New Orleans
	3	Grandma Kelly's ...	Regina Murphy	Sales Represent...	707 Oxford Rd.	Ann Arbor
	4	Tokyo Traders	Yoshi Nagase	Marketing Manager	9-8 Sekimai Mus...	Tokyo
	5	Cooperativa de ...	Antonio del Valle...	Export Administr...	Calle del Rosal 4	Oviedo
	6	Mayumi's	Mayumi Ohno	Marketing Repre...	92 Setsuko Chuo...	Osaka
	7	Pavlova, Ltd.	Ian Devling	Marketing Manager	74 Rose St. Moo...	Melbourne
	8	Specialty Biscuits...	Peter Wilson	Sales Represent...	29 King's Way	Manchester
	9	PB Knäckebröd AB	Lars Peterson	Sales Agent	Kaloadagatan 13	Göteborg
	10	Refrescos Ameri...	Carlos Diaz	Marketing Manager	Av. das America...	Sao Paulo
	11	Heli Süßwaren G...	Petra Winkler	Sales Manager	Tiergartenstraße 5	Berlin
	12	Plutzer Lebensmi...	Martin Bein	International Ma...	Bogenallee 51	Frankfurt
	13	Nord-Ost-Fisch ...	Sven Petersen	Coordinator For...	Frahmredder 112a	Cuxhaven
	14	Formaggi Fortini ...	Elio Rossi	Sales Represent...	Viale Dante, 75	Ravenna
	15	Norske Meierier	Beate Vileid	Marketing Manager	Hatlevegen 5	Sandvika
	16	Bigfoot Breweries	Cheryl Saylor	Regional Accoun...	3400 - 8th Aven...	Bend

Figure C-4. *Viewing the table data*

4. Repeat steps 2 and 3 to test the pubs and the OfficeSupply databases. After testing, exit VS.

Index